Particulars of My Life

DATE DUE			
			PRINTED IN U.S.A.

Particulars

OF

My Life

Part One of an Autobiography

B. F. SKINNER

New York University Press
Washington Square, New York
1984

Copyright © 1976 by B. F. Skinner

Library of Congress Cataloging in Publication Data
Skinner, Burrhus Frederic, [date]
Particulars of my life.
1. Skinner, Burrhus Frederic, 1904–   2. Psychologists—Correspondence,
reminiscences, etc.   I. Title.
BF109.S55A33   150'.19'4340924   [B]   75-34927
ISBN 0-8147-7843-7
ISBN 0-8147-7846-1 set

Manufactured in the United States of America

Remembering
Raphael Miller

1904–1929

Do thou stand for my father and examine me upon the particulars of my life.

—*Henry IV, Part I*

PART I

THE SUSQUEHANNA RIVER, named for an Iroquois tribe, rises in Otsego Lake in New York State. It flows southwest and south and crosses into Pennsylvania a few miles below the town of Windsor. Almost at once it meets a foothill of the Alleghenies, which proves unbreachable, and it abandons its southern course, swings west and north, and returns to the hospitable plains of New York State. It flows west past Binghamton and Owego and tackles Pennsylvania again at a more vulnerable point. This time it succeeds and, picking up the support of a large western branch, continues south past the state capital of Harrisburg and into Maryland and Chesapeake Bay, and so at last into the Atlantic Ocean.

In that first attack on Pennsylvania the river has cut a deep sickle-shaped valley about fifteen miles long. The left bank, the outside of the curve, presses tightly against that foothill of the Alleghenies, and the right bank has little land flat enough to be worth farming, but it was once all part of a great hardwood forest, and lumbermen and trappers came, and five towns sprang up within that fifteen-mile stretch—Lanesboro and Hallstead on the left, named for early settlers, and Oakland, Hickory Grove, and Great Bend on the right, named for two of the most valuable hardwoods and the arc of the river itself. In that narrow sweep of a river valley I spent the first eighteen years of my life.

Toward the end of the eighteenth century an area south and east of the river was cleared, and much of it proved to be good farmland. In the perfectionist spirit of the time it was named Harmony, and its settlers had appropriate visions of progress. A north-south road, coming down from Binghamton, crossed the river at Great Bend and Hallstead, and someone dreamed of a branch to the east that would form part of a trade route from the Atlantic seaboard to the Great Lakes.

3

That dream perished, but something like it came true in what was eventually called the Erie Railroad. It started at Pierpont on the Hudson (and was only later extended to Jersey City), ran west to the Delaware River, which it followed northwest as far as possible, and then crossed into the Susquehanna valley.

The route was not without its problems, the biggest of which was the hill separating the two river valleys. There was no convenient pass, and grades almost too steep for the engines of the time were needed. Once over the top, the roadway had to be cut into the precipitous left bank of the Susquehanna until it reached river level, and in that descent there were two large tributary valleys to be crossed.

In the first of these, the valley of the Cascade Creek, a great rock-and-earth fill solved the problem, with a tunnel drilled in solid rock at one side to take care of the creek. Except during spring floods, water simply collected in a pond above the fill and seeped into the ground. My friends and I often played in the dry tunnel, hallooing from one end to the other, but we never swam in the pond because it had slippery clay banks, and we were afraid of it because it was called the Devil's Punchbowl.

The second valley, cut by the Starrucca Creek, was wider, and since there were people living in it, a bridge was needed. Two attempts to build one failed, but a Scottish engineer succeeded, using stone quarried in the neighborhood. The bridge looked like a Roman aqueduct and was officially named the Starrucca Viaduct, but we always called it the Stone Bridge. It is said that there were doubts about its safety and that the first engine to cross it (the "Orange") did so under a small head of steam without benefit of engineer.

The roadbed finally reached the level of the river at a particularly narrow part of the valley—at the mouth of still another creek small enough to be diverted through a culvert—and there, on a strip of land only a few hundred yards wide, the Erie Railroad Company built a storehouse for supplies and shops where equipment could be repaired, and called the place Susquehanna Depot. A long one-story stone building (the Long House) was finished during the Civil War. It contained a carpenter shop, a machine shop, a boiler factory (responsible for a few "boilermaker's ears" among the older people I knew), and a roundhouse with a locomotive turntable. Beyond it

4

were a freight terminal and a station, the latter equipped for the passenger traffic of a day when there were no diners or sleeping cars and many people preferred to break a long journey. Susquehanna was about a day's run from New York City, and the station included a hotel with a large neo-gothic dining room and seventy-five bedrooms.

It was inevitable that a town would grow up around all this, but the Railroad had used almost all the available flat land. It would have been better to locate Susquehanna Depot a mile or two farther west, but that would have conflicted with one of its purposes—to service the powerful engines called "pushers" which got behind heavy trains and helped them up the hill and across the Stone Bridge and the Cascade fill until they could start down into the Delaware valley. There was no point in pushing before the grade began, and hence the town of Susquehanna (the "Depot" was soon dropped) was left to find space for itself where it could. Main Street ran parallel with the Shops and was almost level, but all the other streets were graded. Flagstones in the sidewalks were kept from sliding by driving iron spikes between them, and some roads proved too steep to be used. Stairs were built for pedestrians at many points, and Susquehanna was sometimes called the City of Stairs.

In spite of these difficulties, hotels, churches, business blocks, banks, a livery stable, a post office, and hundreds of houses went up in the decade following the Civil War. Work was available, and people flocked to the area, and among them were my grandparents.

MY GRANDMOTHER SKINNER, born Josephine Penn, was one of ten or twelve children of a dirt farmer who lived near Starrucca, a small town on the creek that flowed under the Stone Bridge. She claimed a connection with William Penn, and my father once investigated but found nothing. Farther south in the Appalachians her family would have been called poor white, and I saw something of their way of life because my father often took us to Penn reunions. A different family would take the reunion each year, and I was struck by the unpainted houses with their bare floors and "backhouses" in place of indoor toilets.

A sister of my grandmother's moved out of that culture and had a son who became a banker in Hallstead, and another sister, my father's Aunt Althea, whom we all called Aunt Alt, I knew when she lived with her husband in a pleasant house on the banks of the Delaware River in Walton, New York. Two or three brothers escaped, too, and so did my grandmother, though it is hard to say why. She was not intelligent and must have had very little schooling; she could read, write, and do simple sums, and she went to church on Sundays and pretended to read a bit of the Bible every day, putting on her glasses and looking at a few verses in the belief that they improved her spiritual health, but that was the extent of her intellectual attainments.

She was small and thin and walked with a slight limp because she had "water on the knee," the result of an accident while chopping wood as a child. There was something cat-like about her face: she had globular cheeks, sharply undercut, and a short nose, and the long cleft above her lips seemed to demand two sprays of whiskers. She used too much powder, rouge, and lipstick. Her hair was frizzly, and as she grew older it thinned, and my father bought her a "transformation," which she wore as if it were a kind of fur hat.

She moved hesitantly, never seeming to know whether she was properly dressed or about to do the right thing, but she was an obsessive talker and never in want of anything to say because she had no hesitation in repeating herself. She had a small repertoire of stories, mostly about her numerous relatives, and a small stock of "sayings." If I coughed while eating ice cream, she would say, "If you cough, you've had enough," and she could not pick up a pin without saying, "Find a pin, pick it up, and all the day you'll have good luck." She was hesitant even in her speech, and laughed nervously after every remark, as if it might have been a mistake. I never played any kind of game with her, though she insisted that when I was very young I called her "Kinnykins" and followed her about the house, not crawling but hitching across the floor.

She cooked, as she would have said, by guess and by gosh. Her specialty was sugar cookies, and my brother and I liked them because they were sprinkled with sugar and had large raisins pressed into their centers, but the texture varied from chewy to crumbly to powdery, depending upon how big a scoopful of flour or how many spoonfuls

6

of butter she happened to put into the dough. She could sew on a button, but she had trouble with knitting and crocheting, and tatting was quite beyond her. Her plants never flourished, and the fruits and vegetables she put up in glass jars often exploded.

Her taste in humor was curiously scatological. She loved to tell about the time I was left with her when a baby and mussed my pants. (The nearest thing to this sense of "muss" in the *Oxford English Dictionary* is "to make untidy," but it had a specific local meaning. When I was in fifth grade, a girl reading from *Rip Van Winkle* threw our class into hilarious merriment and our teacher into consternation when she mispronounced "musing" and told us that "for some time Rip sat mussing over this scene.") My grandmother would go into minute detail about how she cleaned me and my clothing after the accident, wrapping me in a blanket while my clothes dried over the stove.

She loved to tell the story, years before James Joyce used it, of a woman who when praised because she made strong tea said, "When I make tea I make tea, when I make water I make water." She had a clipboard and often told us how she came by it. At one time she and my grandfather were said to have "kept hotel," and a traveling salesman who had stayed with them found during the night that the chamber pot had no cover. He used his clipboard as a substitute and went off and left it. My grandmother would tell us how thoroughly she had cleaned the board before putting it to its proper use.

She was not by nature generous, and my grandfather never earned much money, and when upon occasion it fell to her to pay for the ice cream when we were out for a drive, she would recall the event for days, describing "her treat" and the kinds of ice cream each of us had chosen for our cones. Whenever we complimented her on the food she served, she would say, "It was the best I could get."

Her closest friend was her canary, whose cage hung in the bay window of the dining room, surrounded by potted plants in brass jardinieres. She talked to it as she gave it its bath in a saucer of water on newspapers spread on the kitchen table, where it splashed recklessly, and it would stand on her finger, and by putting a seed between her lips she could induce it to kiss her, as she called it.

Only one thing makes any sense of the fact that she escaped

from her family background. For some curious reason she had aspirations: she would be a lady. And when my father was born, he was included: he would be a great man. She never made it, and neither did he, but where her aspirations cost her nothing, for she was quite satisfied with her life, the aspirations she gave her son cost him dearly. She once told me that when he was a baby she pinched his nose to make it sharp and more distinguished-looking, but she pinched him in other ways, not so easily identified or described, and in the long run the other pinches were more painful and possibly not much more successful.

My GRANDFATHER, James Skinner, was born in Devonshire, England, and came to America with two half-brothers, Edward and William Dumble, in the early seventies. The half-brothers stayed in New York, where one of them eventually ran a successful decorator's store on Broadway. Somehow my grandfather found his way to Starrucca, where he met and married my grandmother.

He must have cut an attractive figure in that farming community. An early full-faced photograph shows a dapper young man with a handlebar mustache reaching well beyond his cheeks. His light hair is parted on the left and brushed up and away from his right temple. He is wearing a wing collar and a cravat. His eyes are clear, trusting, friendly.

If he attracted my grandmother because he was English, she could not complain of misrepresentation, because he maintained that distinction all his life by dropping an occasional *h* and adding one where it was not needed. He trimmed that great mustache and could dispense with his mustache cup, but he kept a lock of hair swept across his forehead in pub-keeper's style. He grew rather heavy, and his most characteristic gesture was the way he hoisted himself out of the large, black-leather platform rocker in which he spent much of his life. He had a strawberry nose and the florid face of a drunkard, but in fact drank very little.

He grew deaf at an early age, though perhaps not as early as most people supposed. He would respond to most of the things my grand-

8

mother said with a quizzical but rather amused grunt, but if what she had to say was important, she adopted a special manner, and he knew the sign and would then listen and had no trouble in hearing her. He could never manage the hearing aids my father bought for him and accepted his deafness without complaint. He never went to church and I should have supposed him entirely indifferent to religion if he had not once picked up a copy of Tom Paine's *Age of Reason* that I had left about and, after reading a page or two, thrown it down in disgust exclaiming, "Why, that man doesn't believe in the crucifixion of Jesus Christ!"

He was always looking for work but never found any that suited him. Shortly after their marriage he and my grandmother went to Massachusetts and sampled life in the shoe industry in Amesbury, but they soon returned to Starrucca and then settled in Susquehanna. The only evidence I have that they "kept hotel" is the story of the chamber pot and a number of small gadgets in their attic which were said to have survived from hotel days, when they may have functioned a little like pinball machines. In one of them you put a penny in a slot and it fell downward, bouncing against pins and ending in compartments some one of which may have meant at least a free play.

If my grandfather had any trade at all, it was that of a house painter. He painted the more accessible parts of our house and all of his own. He used paint lavishly, and the lower edges of window frames and eaves developed a series of droplets—true *guttae*—which grew larger with each new coat. In his later years this profession became official: my father got him a job tending the Erie paint shop, where his duty, never onerous, was to mix pails of paint of various colors for other workmen.

He was involved in a business venture that had to do with a patented stove polisher. I never saw one in its finished form, but an advertising circular shows a rectangular strip of felt with serrated edges glued to the underside of a wooden block with a handle. On the top of the block is a small tin cup with a sponge stuffed into the open end. A piece of rubber tubing runs through the handle and into the cup. I am not sure how it was to be used. It sold for only thirty-five cents, but no one seems to have bought any, and for years the hayloft in my grandfather's barn contained a barrel of felt pads, a barrel of wooden blocks with handles, a barrel of tin cups, a barrel of small sponges, and great coils of white rubber tubing. The sponges proved useful in the kitchen and in polishing the brass on our Ford.

My grandfather had absolutely no ambition. He could scarcely be said to have waited for something to turn up. He read the newspapers closely and loved politics and baseball, though he never, I suppose, saw a game properly played. My grandmother cared for him and fed him, and somehow expenses were met. If he lived any life at all, it was my father's. Every Sunday morning for many years my father would walk over to his parents' house and spend an hour or two telling my grandfather about the law business he had transacted during the week. In warm weather they sat on the side porch, and as my grandfather grew deafer, some question arose about the confidentiality of Lawyer Skinner's business.

My grandfather seemed proud of my grandmother, though he laughed with the rest of us at her foibles. Their domestic life seemed perfectly tranquil. I never saw either one angry with the other. They owned their house on Jackson Avenue, and it was reasonably convenient. The front door led directly into a small living room dominated by a black parlor stove with fancy nickel trim, parts of which, when the weather was cold, were red hot and had to be carefully avoided. A large parlor, well lighted but not heated, contained an overstuffed sofa with chair to match in orange-and-gold velour and a large glass case enclosing a model of an ocean-going steamer set in a glassy sea. There was some sail rigging, but it was indubitably a steamer because cotton wool poured from a large stack. It may have been the boat on which my grandparents went back to the "old country" for a brief visit before I was born. The parlor was never used except when I played the organ, and I seldom did so because the only music was a book of transcriptions from oratorios or operas, with an ancient fingering system in which x stood for the thumb.

A bedroom on the first floor saved my grandfather the trouble of climbing stairs. He could wash in the kitchen sink and use the backhouse at the far end of the lot. When, presumably at my father's urging and no doubt at his expense, a bathroom was installed on the second floor, my grandfather was obliged to climb the narrow stairway, but he accepted this chore cheerfully as the price of progress.

A driveway which once ran to the barn at the rear was as green as the rest of the lawn, but a steppingstone bearing a heavy iron ring for tethering a horse survived from another era. The floor of the barn also showed a long history of carriage tires and shod hooves, but there was no horse there in my grandparents' day. The stall had been converted into a chicken coop opening into a screened run behind the barn. Some of the tools of my grandfather's trade were to be found on a heavy bench near a window—dried brushes, putty knives, and cans of long-solidified paint.

MY FATHER, William Arthur Skinner, the rather surprising fruit of the union of Josephine Penn and James Skinner, was born on June 22, 1875, in Starrucca, before his parents moved to Susquehanna. Early photographs show a well-dressed child with nicely combed hair and a sensitive, inquiring face, and in pictures taken in high school he appears again immaculately groomed. Later he sported a mustache for a few years but abandoned it, and when it became necessary to wear glasses, he chose pince-nez and continued to wear them all his life, deep red indentations on the bridge of his nose seeming a standard part of his anatomy when he shaved or bathed.

As an only child, pushed forward by his mother, he never learned to get along easily with other people. He often appeared conceited and was called "bumpy," and I once heard another boy, borrowing the phrase from his parents, refer to my father as "Big I and little u." That reputation haunted him all his life, but he never stopped trying to live it down and to be hail-fellow-well-met.

He was of medium height and became rather stocky. He walked a good deal and continued to do so long after the advent of automobiles and convenient public transportation. As a young man he played indoor baseball and later golf. He was a competent performer on the cornet, and he was second in a graduating class of eleven.

When he finished high school, he followed the local custom and went into the Railroad Shops, but since he lacked mechanical skills and had little taste for the life of a carpenter or machinist, he apprenticed himself as a blueprint boy and draftsman in the Mechanical Engineering Department. In a photograph of the employees of the division my father is surrounded by older people with whom it is hard to imagine him being comfortable, nor was the future which presumably lay ahead likely to meet his or his mother's aspirations. He therefore turned to "reading law" in the office of a local lawyer and then went on to New York Law School, supporting himself by keeping books in his half-uncle's decorator's shop and playing cornet in a church. It was a two-year law course, but because he had read law, he was allowed to take the second-year courses (he said that Woodrow Wilson lectured in one of them), and he passed the second-year examinations. But he had been there only one year and therefore got a handwritten certificate rather than a diploma:

The University of the State of New York

Be it known that William A. Skinner passed satisfactorily examinations for the degree of Bachelor of Laws to which he will be entitled on completion of all other requirements prescribed by law or by University ordinances. Countersigned for the School. George Chase. June 10, 1896.

It was not quite the kind of thing to frame and hang in an office.

He returned to Susquehanna and passed the bar examination two months after his twenty-first birthday. He set up an office in two dark, grimy rooms with two heating stoves, a desk, and a few chairs. A bookshelf held his law-school texts, a few volumes purchased with a loan from his father, and a number of large and impressive books borrowed from an older friend which had no connection whatsoever with the practice of law.

MY FIRST NAME, Burrhus, was my mother's maiden name, and it has always been troublesome: it must be spelled out and explained. The spelling may have been adopted at a time when it was fashionable to latinize North European names. My mother's father, Charles Burrhus, was born in Walton, New York, in 1848. When not quite sixteen, he lied about his age and enlisted in the Grand Army of the Republic. He saw duty with a regiment of the New York Voluntary Infantry, which by the time he joined it was in South Carolina. He was on duty until the end of the war, when he was honorably discharged. He would never tell me about his war experiences. Other old vets came to our school on Memorial Day, but if I started to repeat their stories, my grandfather would dismiss me gruffly.

He was a short, stocky, muscular man with a bushy mustache and a shock of brown hair that never turned gray. He favored bow ties and smoked a pipe with a straight stem. He came from New York State in August of 1875 to work for the Railroad in an emergency when the fill across the Cascade Creek washed out, and he met my grandmother in Thompson, a small town south of Lanesboro in the Harmony region. His early pictures show a rather dashing young man who must have had the manners of a reasonably genteel small-town family and who was perhaps then not unwilling to describe his war experiences. In any event, he wooed and won my grandmother, and they came to Susquehanna in 1879, where he found work in the Carpenter Shop, of which he eventually became foreman.

I am sure he was a good craftsman although I have only two pieces of evidence. He put marvelous points on my pencils—a series of thin isosceles triangles, all of the same size, done with a pocket knife kept razor sharp—and he could peel an apple in one long unbroken string of reversing *s*'s. If you threw the string over your shoulder, it would fall on the floor in the shape of the swash capital of the initial of the girl you were to marry—a different girl almost every time. Except for these modest achievements, I never saw any sign of the craftsman, for he never built anything or tinkered with anything about the house.

He enjoyed life and wanted me to do so too. When I was quite small, he would put a spoonful of coffee in my milk over my mother's protest that it would stunt my growth. When I was in high school he gave me extra spending money when I had a date, and he encouraged me to attend dances in the hall of the Odd Fellows, a lodge to which he belonged, and teased me a bit about the girls I danced with, but only to make sure that I danced with them again.

Though he never owned a house, he owned automobiles, beginning with a Ford in 1911 and moving on to a Maxwell. Once when he was taking my grandmother, my brother, and me for a ride, something distracted him and he drove into a fence. We were not going very fast and it was not a serious accident. He was able to drive us back to our summer place on the river, but while we were waiting for lunch, someone put a sentimental song on the phonograph, and he broke down and wept. He was not very well known and had few friends. He spent a good deal of time with another Civil War veteran, who would come over to talk about politics and the misbehavior of the townsfolk.

I sensed that he was rather a disciplinarian with his men in the Carpenter Shop, but his relations with them were good until near the end. A strike, called in 1922, was not going well, and pressure was put on the foremen to join it and walk off their jobs. In the past the foremen had been assumed to be part of the company and had kept their places. Now all of them left except my grandfather, who stubbornly stuck to tradition and was made to suffer. I drove his car to a garage to have it washed, and the manager asked, "Isn't that Charlie Burrhus's car?" and when I said it was, he refused to wash it. My grandfather did not dare walk to work, and one day when I drove him toward the Shops through the Italian section of the town, he was obviously frightened and urged me to drive as fast as possible. The strike came to an end, but I doubt whether he ever again enjoyed his work.

He served the Erie for nearly fifty years, and shortly before his death he was commended in a company magazine for his services, but the words were chosen for company purposes:

> One of the valuable features of this veteran's career with the Erie is his proverbial economic use of lumber. While he is not unnecessarily frugal in its use, he always takes care not to waste any, for he knows that lumber costs money nowadays. Also he has been active in reclaiming asbestos boiler lagging.

My grandmother Burrhus left a paper sealed in an envelope to be read after her death, and when she died my father assembled my grandfather, my mother, and my uncle and aunt and opened the envelope. He read a few sentences to himself and then got up and threw the paper in the parlor stove, saying, "I don't think this should be read." He told me later that my grandfather looked very sheepish, but he did not tell me what was in the letter or at what period in their marriage my grandfather had sinned.

*　　*　　*

MY GRANDMOTHER Burrhus was born on Washington's birthday, 1855, and we celebrated both anniversaries with cardboard hatchets filled with small candies called red-hots. An early photograph shows a rather countrified young lady, not at all sure of herself, with her hair done in tight curls for the occasion. She is wearing a patterned shirtwaist with choker, rings hang from her pierced ears, and steel-rimmed eyeglasses dangle from a long chain pinned to one shoulder. When I knew her, she wore her hair drawn back in a bun and dressed mostly in gray or black shirtwaists and long skirts which concealed all but the toes of her buttoned shoes. When she went out, she wore the kind of hat later to be made famous by Queen Mary.

Her family had been in America from the early eighteenth century. An ancestor had fought under Washington. Her mother had come from Vermont as a child when her family settled in Thompson, long before Susquehanna was founded, and there my grandmother was born and there she grew up. They were all quietly successful farmers or small businessmen who showed little or no inclination to be anything else, and the trait ran true in my grandmother. She completely lacked the aspirations of my grandmother Skinner. Her speech retained a provincial touch. She served "victuals" and the bread she did not bake herself was "boughten." She would say, "Don't plague your brother."

She belonged to the Women's Auxiliary of the Odd Fellows and would come and watch me dance in the Odd Fellows' Hall, and she enjoyed a drive in the country, wearing her big black hat and a black duster, especially when she visited her relatives near Thompson. Except for these occasional forays, she stayed home. When I was young she kept in touch with the world through a Mrs. Bronson, the wife of a jeweler, who also wore Queen Mary hats and was as outgoing as my grandmother was reticent. Mrs. Bronson stopped in almost every day to bring the news. She had a great sense of humor, and I loved to hear them talk. They both wore "creepers," small metal treads like miniature crampons attached to the heels of their gaiters, which could be folded into the instep when not in use but snapped back under the heel when necessary to prevent slipping. One day when the sidewalks were particularly icy, Mrs. Bronson reported to my grandmother that in spite of her creepers she went back two steps for every step she took forward. I was at just the right age: I thought it an excruciatingly funny remark.

My grandmother read a good deal of fiction and was the only one of my grandparents or parents to do so. She subscribed to pulp magazines and closely followed their continued stories. I read them too and discussed them with her. I saw her almost every day for years. I would drop in after school to play a few hands of rummy, or a card game called Pedro, or a game or two of dominoes. I don't think she deliberately allowed me to win, but she could act the bad loser consummately, so that whenever I won, it was a great occasion. When she had no domino that would play, she would go to "the boneyard" and draw dominoes slowly, showing a separate frustration for each piece that would not fit.

In a back pantry I could always get a piece of "Grampa's cake," brown and spongy and cut into squares, and there was usually a large block of maple sugar from which a lump could be broken off. Apples were always available, although by spring they would be russets— small apples with an unattractive brown, rather shriveled skin and rubbery flesh but with the merit of keeping well over the winter. When she served mackerel—salt mackerel soaked overnight before cooking— I stayed for dinner. I loved mackerel, and we never had it at home because my father disliked it and it made the house smell. The height of her art was apple pie—made of fresh or dried apples as the season dictated, with brown sugar slightly burned around the edges of the tin. There was always a pie in the pantry with a knife and a supply of cheese (the word meant Cheddar).

She knew the power she wielded. Once I had quarreled with her and was staying away, but as I came by on my way home from school, she called to me from behind a screen door, and I went near and saw that she was holding up a piece of maple sugar.

Her great skill was needlework. She crocheted and tatted doilies, borders for pillowcases, tablecloths, and even whole bedspreads. She was extremely quick, and I could not follow the movement of the small bobbin with which she tatted. When the war came and the women in town began to knit sweaters, helmets, socks, and mittens, she was a miracle of productivity.

She was a worrier. She never mentioned any future plan without adding, "—if I live and have my health." When my mother had a serious appendectomy with complications, however, it was my grandmother Burrhus who managed the family. She protested violently when I once said, "I wish Christmas were here." "*Never,*" she exclaimed, "wish away a single hour of your life!" She had a chronic dry cough, and she wore on her chest pieces of red flannel on which a man named Starkweather had placed his hands. Starkweather worked in the Machine Shop, and it was believed that his contact with metal gave him curative powers.

My grandmother and grandfather called each other Mr. and Mrs. B, and my father, my brother, and I followed that practice most of the time, but my mother called them Máma and Pápa. They lived out their lives in a series of rented houses, of which I remember three. The yard in front of the first was badly kept, the sour soil growing only moss and a wiry grass. In the earth-floored cellar a toad lived for many years, keeping it free of insects. A parlor, never used, was furnished with upholstered and tasseled chairs, and twice a year its lace curtains were washed and stretched to dry on a frame and its patterned carpet was beaten on a clothesline.

In the living room a center table bore my grandmother's work basket, in which, among darning eggs, crochet needles, tatting bobbins, spools of thread, and thimbles, there was a small slab of talc. It was like soft green jade, and when scraped with a knife, it yielded real talcum powder.

I knew their other houses better, because I stayed in them from time to time when my parents were away. Several clocks which ticked loudly were taken from one house to another like lares and penates, and as a vestige of an earlier culture my grandmother always kept an oil lamp burning dimly in the kitchen during the evening.

They had a few books, among them one called *Aunt Samantha Among the Brethren*, rather like the things being written at the time by Mark Twain, Artemus Ward, and Josh Billings, poking fun at the Shakers, Adventists, and other perfectionists. There was also a *Hill's Manual*, long out of date by the time I saw it, which advocated a different kind of perfectionism; I remember a picture of a dinner party at which each guest was demonstrating some social error: one was feeding a dog and another waving his arms and talking loudly.

They had four children, two of whom died when very young. They lived together in apparent tranquility. I saw no sign of the resentment which led my grandmother to plan that exposure of my grandfather's sins after her death.

MY MOTHER, Grace Madge Burrhus, was born on June 4, 1878. She graduated from the Susquehanna High School when she had just turned sixteen and, like my father, was second in her class. She had studied typing and shorthand and went to work immediately as secretary to E. R. W. Searle, a lawyer. Later, as the local paper reported it, she "began her duties as stenographer and typewriter in the office of A. E. Mitchell, mechanical superintendent of the Erie. The selection of Miss Burrhus for this position is a merited recognition of her superior attainments in her chosen profession and many friends will unite with the *Transcript* in extending congratulations."

She had long chestnut hair and was rated something of a beauty. She was popular, and according to the scrapbook which her mother kept she often visited friends in Binghamton, Scranton, and elsewhere, as well as relatives in Walton, New York. She was occasionally reported "on the sick list," but it seemed to be nothing serious. She played the piano in an orchestra and accompanied singers in recitals, and she herself had a lovely contralto voice which inspired the editor of the paper to write: "We, with others, have heard considerable foreign vocal talent, in this place of late, but all who have an idea of purity of tone and correct rendition of theme, acknowledge that as an alto-soloist, Miss Grace Burrhus, of this place, has no superiors. It is really a treat to hear her renditions." Her repertoire was limited, however. She sometimes sang the same song on different occasions with an appropriate change of text. J. C. Bartlett's "A Dream" begins, "Last night I was dreaming of thee, love, was dreaming." That would do for a recital, but my mother's copy contains a version for use at funerals with another text in her hand beginning: "Come Jesus Redeemer, abide thou with me-e." All her songs were sentimental— "Just for Today," "The Song That Reached My Heart," "The Day Is

Ended"—and many had a religious touch—"My God, My Father, While I Stray," "Thy Will Be Done," or "Savior, Comfort Me." She herself was no doubt sentimental, but she was not particularly devout, and her religious repertoire must have reflected the demands of her listeners.

BY THE EARLY 1890s Susquehanna had its first crop of young people who had grown up together. They had talent and made the most of it, and the town, with a population of only 2500, became known for its musical and theatrical performances. The principal of the high school left his stamp on many of these. He was a "reader and impersonator," and he had students in the same line. On a program for the benefit of the library in Hallstead, billed simply as "Susquehanna Talent!" he recited "The Light from Over the Range," and one of his pupils "The Yarn of the Nancy Belle." Miss Grace Burrhus sang "A Dream," and a penciled memorandum on the program indicated that she appeared as "Bachelor's Lady Love, bright colored dress, huge bonnet, holds fan in one hand, parasol in the other." On another program she played the piano for tableaux depicting "Mary Queen of Scots Confronting Elizabeth" and "Mary Queen of Scots Taking Leave of Her Attendants." On the same program someone sang "I Want to Pawn My Dolly," and Mamie Metzger, who years later would be my first-grade teacher, recited "How Uncle Henry Dyed His Hair."

Various "professors" moved about the countryside carrying scenery and costumes and organizing local talent. The operetta *Esmeralda* was an especially ambitious undertaking, in which W. A. Skinner appeared as Dave Hardy and Grace Burrhus as Kate Desmond.

The *Transcript* reported the premiere as follows:

> That Susquehanna is possessed of superior dramatic and histrionic talent, was fully demonstrated last evening, when the popular play of "Esmeralda" was presented at Hogan Opera House by the Susquehanna Dramatic Club. . . .
>
> The admirable impersonation of the different characters in the play by the members of the club, coupled with their apparent lack of

stage fright, was appreciated by the audience and contributed to the grand success of the entertainment.

WILL SKINNER and Grace Burrhus saw a good deal of each other while displaying their talents, and in a small community there were many other occasions when they were together. My father was on the committee of a social club which arranged one such occasion, though he was not, I am fairly sure, the correspondent who reported it in the *Transcript* with such a surfeit of quotation marks:

MOONLIGHT EXCURSION

The weather last evening for the "moonlight excursion" of that popular social organization, the Crescent Club, up the river on the steamer Erminie, to Forest House Park, could not well have been more propitious had it been "made to order" by the bureau having in charge the varied climatic changes. . . .

Married men and their better halves, young men and their best girls, marriageable young ladies, marriageable young men assembled on Drinker street "suspension bridge" at 7:30 o'clock, and under the active management of the "perishable freight" committee of the Crescent Club, were "sandwiched" into "fondly waiting" busses and transported by horse power in the twinkling of an eye to the Oakland dock of the placid river, where the steamer Erminie, puffing and wheezing, was in waiting to receive the multitude and proceed seven miles up the winding and watery course to that popular resort, Forest House Park. . . .

Shortly after nine o'clock "Erminie," the Pride of the Susquehanna, "tooted" for the Forest House dock, where the human cargo was discharged. . . . Crescents and their guests thronged the park, and were not slow in finding the pavilion, where terpsichorean exercises were set in motion to excellent music discoursed by Warner & Sperl's orchestra.

My father presumably had strong competition, for my mother was always described by the *Transcript* as popular, and years later I heard occasional references to early rivals. A second cousin, a student at Cornell College, visited the Burrhuses twice in the late 1890s, and my mother gave a musicale in his honor. My father would have lacked his sophistication and style. His mother must have been a problem, but he resorted to a rather clever strategy. In June of 1899 the *Transcript* reported that

Mr. and Mrs. James Skinner, Attorney William A. Skinner, Miss Grace Burrhus, Mr. and Mrs. W. H. Dumble, Mr. and Mrs. Ed Dumble, accompanied by fishing tackle and the necessary provender, are enjoying an outing at Page's pond today.

My father was covering the deficiencies of his father and mother by bringing in his two half-uncles and -aunts from New York. They were far more interesting and polished, and they knew how to silence my grandmother.

In August of the following year my father and mother were among a party of young people—including my Uncle Harry Burrhus and his fiancée, Leila Outwater—who spent ten days at Heart Lake. They were chaperoned by my grandmother Skinner and my father's Aunt Alt. Aunt Alt was a jolly, generous, thoroughly likable person, as down to earth as my grandmother was highfalutin, as simple and honest as my grandmother was pretentious, and as warm and natural as my grandmother was artificial. She would take care of the atmosphere in the cottage at Heart Lake.

The strategy was successful, and eventually my mother capitulated. The *Transcript* for May 1, 1902, contained the following item:

MARRIED LAST EVENING

At their own home, on Grand street, last evening, at 8 o'clock, were united in marriage, by Rev. E. E. Riley, Mr. Wm. Arthur Skinner and Miss Grace Madge Burrhus. . . . The bride and groom left the same evening for a trip to Philadelphia and Washington D.C. They will be at home after May 10.

The bridegroom is a popular and rising young lawyer, and the bride one of Susquehanna's fairest and most accomplished daughters. Many warm friends extend the best wishes possible for a happy and prosperous life.

My father and mother were married "in their own home" because my father had bought a house and they had worked together to furnish it for their marriage. No. 433 Grand Street was a fairly good location. Many of the older families lived on Grand Street, and the house was near the top of a hill, above much of the cinders and smoke of the Shops and trains. Still, it could not have cost my father very much. It was next to a cemetery, which was not to everyone's taste, and it was a box of a house, with a pyramidal roof, in no particular style. It had been lived in for a long time and needed updating. A few years later its wooden siding was covered with stucco and its roof with slate (I was old enough to watch and I was fascinated by the foot-operated device which punched holes in a slate without cracking it). Round pillars and a "steel ceiling" were added to the front porch, and a small wing in which for a while the former owner had continued to live was made into a library with a great red brick fireplace. And room by room the old planked flooring was replaced or, rather, covered by a hardwood floor.

There was running hot and cold water in kitchen and bathroom, but it was hot only so long as a good fire burned in the kitchen stove. The bathroom, added to the house to replace an outdoor privy, was awkwardly located, since it was necessary to pass through it to reach the main bedrooms, until a second stairway was added when the wing was taken over. Electricity replaced kerosene, but the wires were mounted on white ceramic blocks on the surface of the walls and ceilings. (Two delicately tinted Tiffany wall lamps, more recently installed alongside the brick fireplace in the library, had no visible electrical connections.)

My father's first move was to put in central heating. He selected an underfeed furnace which burned a small, inexpensive size of anthracite coal but was hard to operate. A hopperful of coal was forced up under the firebed by repeatedly lifting the end of a wooden arm seven or eight feet long and pulling it down with a great crunch. The furnace had to be damped at night, and in cold weather the water pipes under the kitchen sink often froze. In short, it was not a convenient house, and certainly not an attractive one, but there my father and mother lived for twenty years, and there my brother and I were born.

* * *

MY BIRTH was difficult and my mother nearly died—a fact of which I was occasionally to be reminded. There were two newspapers in Susquehanna at the time, and one reported my birth as follows:

NEW ARRIVAL

Born yesterday morning March 20, 1904 to Attorney William A. Skinner and his wife Grace a handsome boy. The many friends of the overjoyed parents are sending congratulations by the bushel. Long live the youngster, and his papa and mama.

The *Transcript* could not resist a lighter touch: "Susquehanna has a new law firm—Wm. A. Skinner & Son," a theme which I am sure had already occurred to my father. The paper in Montrose, the county seat, carried on the joke: "The Susquehanna *Transcript* says that town has a new firm—W. A. Skinner & Son. We don't suppose the recently added member can be termed a 'silent partner.'"
The supposition was apparently correct. When I was quite small my father and mother took me to Milford, a resort town on the Delaware River, and they were asked to leave the first hotel in which they registered because I cried all night.

I was nevertheless healthy, nursed by my mother, and later fed a kind of breakfast cereal or baby food called, ahead of its time, Force. When I was able to move around the house, it was discovered that I was eating dirt from the potted plants, and I once pushed a bean up my nose and it was not discovered until it had swelled enormously and had to be extracted by a doctor, but these were minor complaints.

My brother, Edward James Skinner, was born on November 6, 1906, and I have always thought that I remembered the event though I was only two and a half. I remember being taken into my mother's and father's bedroom on what was obviously a very solemn occasion and shown something just to the left of the bed, the side on which my mother slept and on which a bassinet would have been placed.

LIFE AT 433 Grand Street, as I began to be aware of it, followed a stable pattern. We all rose at seven, and in cold weather my father's first duty was to take care of the furnace. (When he was out of town on business it was my mother's first duty, until I was tall enough to reach the end of the arm and heavy enough to pull it down.) He returned to the bathroom, where he shaved, working up lather in a shaving mug and sharpening his razor on a leather strop. Back in his room, he retrieved his trousers from the back of a chair where he had carefully folded them the night before. (Years later my mother gave him an expensive gold watch, paid for with money she had filched, a coin or two at a time, from the trousers that hung over that chair.) He wore the same shirt for two or three days but with a fresh starched collar each day taken from a leather case in the top drawer of his chiffonier. He added a conservative four-in-hand tie and secured the knot with a garnet stickpin. He retrieved his coat from a clothes tree in the corner of the room, shined his shoes with polish and cloth kept in a small footlocker in the bathroom, and went down to breakfast.

In cold weather I pulled my underclothes into bed with me to warm them and put them on under the covers. Then I dressed quickly, washed, cleaned my teeth, brushed my hair, and went down to hover (with my brother and in very cold weather my mother) on the large grille between living room and dining room where the first warm air had begun to rise.

My mother would have shaken down the ashes in the kitchen stove and added kindling wood and coal carried from the shed at the rear of the house. One or two concentric cast-iron rings could be removed from a lid on the stove for direct access to any available flame. We breakfasted on bacon and eggs, or pancakes baked on a large round griddle, or boiled eggs mixed with broken toast in large cups. The toast was made on a fork over the coals of the stove, and if done too hastily was merely cold white bread sprinkled with black char. (My father once won an electric toaster at a fair. It was a small metal table with a few wires under a grid, and we pulled down the shades to darken the room to assure ourselves that the wires actually turned a dull red. It was too slow to be useful.) On a Sunday morning my mother might take the time to make "fried cakes," better known as doughnuts.

After breakfast my father walked to his office. He had moved to a suite in the Post Office Building on Main Street. It was just a step from the First National Bank, and his office on the corner of the second floor had two conspicuous windows in which glass panels hanging on brass chains read "W. A. Skinner" and "Attorney and Counselor at Law" in gold letters.

An outer office was furnished with a large safe, a paper-press used to put sharp creases in deeds and contracts, and a typewriter. The inner office contained my father's desk, an impressive chair, and a non-functional corner fireplace above which hung a picture of my mother, my brother, and me. On his desk were a tobacco jar, a pipe rack, and a device which stamped his signature—W. A. Skinner, with a flourish underlining the whole name—and returned the stamp to a concealed ink pad. There was also a kind of punch which in a single operation cut a tongue and slot in two or three sheets of paper and threaded one through the other to bind the sheets together.

He began his day by reading the Binghamton paper, which had come down on the morning train. Later his secretary brought the mail from the box in the post office downstairs, and a client or two might come in. For many years a daily visitor was Frank Zeller, the local brewer, who came to talk about business ventures, or the marital problems of his daughter, or politics, or things in general.

When the Shop whistle blew at noon, my father started home. In fair weather we waited for him on the front porch, and when my mother saw him coming up the street, walking jauntily along, slapping his thigh with the rolled-up morning paper, she went in and put things on the table. We had our big meal at noon and called it dinner, and it was almost always meat and mashed potatoes with a side vegetable. For dessert there was usually pumpkin, huckleberry, or custard pie, or strawberry shortcake in season.

After dinner my father walked back to his office, and my mother took her nap (and woe to anyone who made a noise and woke her up!). Home again in late afternoon, he did any necessary odd jobs around the house or went over his fishing tackle or polished the brass on our Ford. Supper was a lighter meal and in place of pie we had "sauce"—canned fruit or stewed rhubarb—or rice pudding with raisins, or maple syrup poured over hot baking-powder biscuits.

After supper, wearing a smoking jacket, my father took his place in his chair in the living room beside an oak table, the claw-and-ball feet of which I first knew at baby-eye level, and filled his pipe with

Prince Albert tobacco. The reading lamp had a green glass shade, and in addition he often wore a green celluloid eye shade. We subscribed to the *Philadelphia Inquirer* and the *Literary Digest*, and they, together with the *Transcript* and the Binghamton paper, kept him up to date.

He had given up the cornet. He had "lost his lip," and I never heard him play more than half a dozen notes at any one time. He turned to other forms of expression. He made an ashtray by pasting cigar bands on a shallow glass dish so that the patterns could be seen through the glass and then covering the outside with felt. He took up pyrography. He bought slabs of wood on which designs, pictures, and mottoes had been lightly printed, and he burned the lines away with the needle-like flame of an alcohol lamp produced by a jet of air from a rubber bulb covered with string netting. He made some of the picture frames on our walls and one ambitious plaque for my grandfather and grandmother Skinner showing a puppy wearing a big muzzle and alongside it the words: "All I did was growl a little bit."

MARRIAGE HAD MADE very little change in my father's day-to-day life, but it was not so with my mother. She was no longer serving as typist, secretary, and notary public in the busy office of the chief executive of the Railroad; instead she was keeping house in an inconvenient, ramshackle structure which needed much work to make it livable. Although we had a telephone, few people had, and my mother took advantage of the fact that a man would drop by from the grocery store to take orders. A little later in the morning Jackie Kane would arrive with his meat wagon, stopping in front of our house and putting a block of wood under a rear wheel to rest his horse. He would open the back of the wagon and bring out unrefrigerated slabs of meat from which he cut the pieces wanted by my mother, weighing them on a spring scale hanging from the ceiling of the wagon. He would give my brother and me half a frankfurter each to eat raw, and there was always plenty of free liver for the cat. The iceman would disturb no one because a small window had been cut into the outside wall of the pantry, through which a block of ice could be put directly into the icebox.

On Mondays Mrs. Barnes came to do the laundry. We had a washing machine, manufactured by a local company of which my father was a director. It consisted of a large wooden tub with a hinged cover on the underside of which was an agitator, looking rather like a milking stool, rotated forward and back by an electric motor mounted on the top of the cover. You filled the tub with water from a hose or pail, added the clothes and soap, lowered the cover, and turned on the current, allowing the agitator to run as long as the condition of the clothes seemed to require. All this was done in the kitchen or woodshed or, in good weather, on the back porch, but Mrs. Barnes always ironed in the kitchen because the sadirons were heated on the stove.

My mother practiced many economies. She cut buttons off garments before they were thrown away and stored them in a bag decorated with dancing figures whose heads were made of buttons. Somewhere she had read that soap lasted longer if thoroughly dried, and in the cramped space above the library which served as attic there were small pyramids of dusty bars, unwrapped and drying. The main result was that they lost all their perfume. It was only at my grandparents', where soap was bought a cake at a time, that it smelled good —Packer's Tar Soap at my grandmother Burrhus's and Colgate Cashmere Bouquet at my grandmother Skinner's.

Whenever eggs were cheap, my mother put them down in large butter crocks full of "waterglass." It was often my duty to go down cellar with a bowl and a long spoon and fish out a few eggs coated with a white gelatinous matter. My mother, like almost everyone else, also "canned." Food poisoning from badly canned vegetables was fairly common, but badly canned fruit seemed simply to ferment, and we often ate it for sauce even though it stung our tongues.

THE FIRST PERSONAL POSSESSION I remember was my Teddy Bear. Its imitation fur was light brown and it had a white knitted cap and jacket. The Teddy Bear was a fairly recent innovation: a newspaper cartoon had shown Theodore Roosevelt sparing a bear cub during one of his big-game exploits, and copies of the cub came on the market as toys for children. It was the kind of doll a boy might respectably play with. At about the same time I had a "rag book"—an alphabet book printed on cloth with a picture for each letter or figure.

My brother and I usually played on the pale blue-green carpet in the parlor, a room opening into both living and dining rooms and containing our upright piano and two mahogany chairs upholstered in green watered silk. One of our favorite toys was a set of stone blocks. Some were brick red, others slate blue, and others a warm honey color. There were arches, cornices, and a steeple, and they were heavy and would stay where you put them. A book showed a great variety of buildings that could be made with them, all very Germanic.

We had a jigsaw puzzle advertising the Delaware, Lackawanna, and Western Railroad, which used anthracite coal rather than bituminous and claimed that its passenger cars were therefore free of cinders. The puzzle showed a beautiful girl named Phoebe Snow, dressed all in white because she "rode the road of anthracite," standing on the back platform of the train, the polished brass railings of which made it easy to fit the pieces of the puzzle together.

Our toy trains were primitive. The sections of track were easily bent—especially when stepped on—and never fitted very snugly together. The engine was heavy and ran for some time when wound up with a key, but the cars were too light to stay on the uneven track, and they were hooked together insecurely.

Our set of dominoes, already "antique," was made of thin slabs of ivory and ebony held together with brass pins turning green in the crevices. We soon acquired a set of double nines, much more impressive than double sixes though simply of unpainted wood, and much more useful in setting up those long snake-like chains that fall down like burning fuses. We set up chains on a card table, being careful not to jiggle it, and leaving gaps every so often to be filled in at the last moment to minimize the risk of accident.

We played checkers on a board made years before by my father with his drafting instruments—the squares neatly ruled in India ink on red cardboard and numbered so that annotated games could be followed. My father occasionally played with us, but always a little didactically. When we played checkers he would stop to show us how to get a king out of a double corner and when we played dominoes, how to count the number of pieces already on the board to see whether we could block the game.

A favorite toy was a spelling board. Letters of the alphabet printed on disks could be moved in a large circular channel from which single letters could be selected and moved into a horizontal channel to spell a word, the meaningless jumble of letters in the great circle yielding a pattern that said something.

We made pinwheels and paper airplanes, and we knew how to bend the wings to make them loop the loop. We cut thin sheets of red gelatin into fish-shaped pieces which, placed on a warm, moist palm, slowly curled with a semblance of lethargic life. We made buzzers of large buttons and loops of string, spinning a button with great speed first one way and then the other as we tightened and relaxed the string in a lovely rhythmic pulsation.

My mother sang to us with that voice so much admired by her townsfolk. Her songs were consoling, yet not without a touch of sorrow. "The Slumber Boat" began:

> Baby's boat's the silver moon
> Sailing in the sky,
> Sailing o'er the sea of sleep
> While the clouds float by.
> Sail, baby, sail, out upon that sea,
> Only don't forget to sail back again to me.

The sobering note of that last line was echoed in the chorus of "Sing Me to Sleep"—

> Love, I am lonely, years are so long.
> I want you only, you and your song.
> Dark is life's shore, love, night is so deep.
> Leave me no more, love, sing me to sleep.

Both my father and mother read to us, but the stories were often the bloodthirsty kind of which the brothers Grimm were masters. I once went to bed terrified by "Hänsel and Gretel." Would parents deliberately leave their children in the woods to be rid of them? Was there a wicked witch who lured children with a house built of candy and then put them in cages and fed them until they were plump enough to eat? "Goldilocks and the Three Bears" had a happy ending, though by the merest luck, and a happy ending had not yet been invented for "Little Red Riding Hood." Even "Cinderella" seemed threatening in spite of her triumph (how often could one count on a fairy godmother?).

At eight o'clock we were sent off to bed after kissing our parents good night. There came a time when I kissed my mother and started upstairs and she protested, "You haven't kissed your father," and my father said quickly, "That's all right." He understood; I had reached the age at which boys did not kiss their fathers.

When my mother and father were going to a party, they would come into our bedroom so that we could see them all dressed up. On some occasions my father wore a "tux" and my mother a beautiful gray satin gown. When they entertained at home, our library came to life. A roaring fire was built of lengths of oil-soaked oak planks from a discarded floor of the Erie Shops. The Tiffany lights on the two sides of the fireplace were turned on, and they and the flames were reflected dozens of times in the glass covers of the sectional bookcases which lined two walls. Even the freshly waxed black-leather platform rocker (like my grandfather Skinner's) glistened with points of light. We were allowed to taste the marguerites (cookies made with egg white and nuts) and to see the place cards and table decorations, but we were sent upstairs before the guests arrived and were condemned to enjoy only what we could hear. My father and mother did not drink, nor, so far as I know, did any of their friends.

WE HAD most of the childhood diseases—chicken pox, mumps, measles, and whooping cough. Our doctor reported each case to the Board of Health, and an officer came and tacked a large sign on our door, the color of which told the nature of the infection. This put us in quarantine, and we were not allowed to leave the house until the sign was taken down, nor was anyone else allowed in. There was only one case of polio in the town in my day, but I myself had a brief bout of rheumatic fever. I awoke one morning with very sore knees and could scarcely get downstairs. The doctor ordered me confined to a chair. I had some very small toy cars at the time and the arms of the chair had channels of the right gauge and I spent many hours running the cars up and down. Starkweather was called in, and this time there were to be no flannel pads; he put his hands directly on my knees. (Starkweather's services were always gratis; it was a gift he freely shared.) The illness disappeared within a week.

When I was quite young, I came home late one afternoon to find both my grandmother Skinner and my mother in tears. My father was doing his best to smooth things over. My grandmother had come to insist that my brother and I be wormed. At the time children were given some kind of medication which produced a gray stool, apparently showing that intestinal worms had been killed and excreted, but my mother would have none of it, and she accused my grandmother of meddling.

When I was somewhat older, I was troubled with large, painful boils, mostly on my bottom. I fell on one of them once and got up with blood and pus streaming down my leg. My father treated them according to our doctor's instructions: I lay face down across my bed, and he touched the boil first with carbolic acid and then a few moments later with alcohol. Once he spilled something on my leg and was not sure whether it was the acid or the alcohol. Instead of taking no chances and wiping it off, he left it until it began to burn into the skin, and I limped around with a painful acid burn for weeks.

SHORTLY BEFORE CHRISTMAS we made fondant. My mother boiled sugar and water in a large kettle until a sample formed a ball when dropped into a glass of water. Around a marble-topped table, moved into the kitchen for the occasion, my father, my brother, and I sat waiting, armed with spatulas and pancake turners. The syrup, colored and flavored, was poured slowly onto the middle of the marble slab, and we kept it from running off the edges by using the spatulas as fast as possible. Slowly the mixture hardened and developed a fine grain, and we made it into small flattened balls, on some of which we impressed almonds or halves of walnuts. There were green ones flavored with almond, yellow with lemon, pink with a rosewater flavor I never liked, and white mixed with coconut shreds and vanilla. They were put on sheets of wax paper to season in the attic and then taken around to relatives and friends as presents.

The day before Christmas a tree was set up in the parlor, and candles were attached in little sockets clipped to branches in the safest places. On Christmas Eve we went to the Presbyterian church, where there was a tree, and under it the presents we had given our Sunday-school teachers and the very small presents they had given us. Jakey Brandt, the dentist, unsuccessfully disguised as Santa Claus, read the names on the packages and passed them out with great spirit. We sang a few carols and came home. Then, in spite of the danger, we lighted the candles on our own tree and allowed them to burn for fifteen or twenty minutes.

In bed we stayed awake listening to our parents as they put our presents around the tree. We knew there was no Santa Claus long before we were supposed to know it. On Christmas morning we were up before dawn, and we dashed downstairs in our pajamas to play with our presents. Later in the morning we walked to our grandparents', carrying baskets, bearing small gifts and returning with large ones.

Our two sets of grandparents had few tastes or interests in common and saw little of each other, although they lived no more than five or six blocks apart. They could not avoid being together on Thanksgiving, Christmas, and New Year's Day. My mother would "take" Christmas because it belonged to my brother and me. Both grandmothers preferred Thanksgiving, but my grandmother Skinner usually got it for one trumped-up reason or another, and that left New Year's for my grandmother Burrhus, when we had scarcely recovered from Christmas. There was an unspoken contest between them about the size of the turkey, number of side vegetables, and kinds of pie. My grandmother Burrhus was by far the better cook and won easily when it came to quality.

And so the years passed, and I became aware of their passing. I remember lying awake on New Year's Eve, 1910, regretting the passing of that year with its lovely round number.

*   *   *

Soon after passing the bar examination, my father plunged into politics. I do not know whether he began as the confirmed Republican he was to remain all his life or whether he convinced himself by his early successes as a speechmaker, but successful he was. A newspaper reported a meeting in the county seat:

> A rousing meeting was held at the rooms of the McKinley and Roosevelt Club on Saturday evening. . . . The speaker was William A. Skinner, Esq. . . . With no thought of flattery, but a simple desire to bestow praise where it is due and in such measure as merited, constrains your correspondent to say of Mr. Skinner's address that it was the most exhaustive, comprehensive and convincing argument in behalf of the Republican cause that has been heard in Montrose during the campaign, while in choice diction, eloquent periods and graceful delivery it is seldom equalled.

He was then twenty-four years old. Four years later he was on the hustings again and a paper published the following account:

> Mr. Skinner speaks in a tone clear and strong, using few gestures and depending largely for the effect which has made him popular as a public speaker by the mere inflection and modulation of the voice, eliminating haranguing entirely. He is not one who attempts charming his listeners with figurative language but on the opposite deals in clean-cut, convincing facts, presented in an intelligible manner.

He was speaking on behalf of Theodore Roosevelt, and his enthusiasm knew no bounds:

> Never before has there been a higher type of true manhood. Never before any better example to young and old. Never before has there been any officer who more conscientiously said what he knew was right. With him the first question is, "Is it right?" not, "Is it expedient alone?" If it is right then go ahead regardless of whom it hits or hurts. . . . He has courage, intelligence, and strict honesty. . . . He has no apologies to make and what he says he says straight from the shoulder. Such are a few Republican principles, and such is our candidate. Democrats may steal our principles but they cannot steal our—man.

By 1912 Roosevelt had founded his own Bull Moose Party, and my father sang a different tune. He taught me a little campaign verse:

Mary had a little lamb.
It soon would turn to mutton.
And every time it wagged its tail,
It dropped a Bull Moose button.

His lecture on "The Muckraker and Representative Democracy" was said by a Montrose paper to be an "eye-opener." "Muckraker" was Roosevelt's word, and I am sure my father did not believe that it was part of the vocabulary of representative democracy.

(When I was perhaps twelve, we were at a summer resort, and one of the guests was a distinguished man from Binghamton who was well liked by everyone but who, my father told me with mixed amusement and contempt, was a socialist.)

Not all my father's speeches were political. At a men's meeting at the Railroad YMCA he spoke on "The Arrest, Trial and Conviction of Jesus from a Legal Standpoint." The *Transcript* reported that the lecture showed a large amount of study, but it was not my father's study, for he had taken the whole thing from a book bearing a similar title that I had seen in our library. Other books, such as five small volumes of *Gems of Humor*, had no doubt also been acquired for their usefulness in speechmaking. He was always rather nervous before he spoke and read his speeches or at least followed notes closely, but he was nonetheless effective. He may have profited from his experience in *Esmeralda* and the other displays of Susquehanna talent. The *Transcript* reported that he held an audience "spellbound" by reading Dr. Conwell's "Acres of Diamonds," a lecture that Dr. Conwell himself was said to have given several thousand times.

WITH OR WITHOUT the help of his eloquence, my father's business was expanding. (He overcame the slight handicap of his name. An out-of-town paper reported that "Susquehanna actually has a lawyer named Skinner," and I occasionally heard the comment, "Skinner by name,

Skinner by nature.") His practice took him to the county courthouse in Montrose and to the Superior and Supreme Courts of Pennsylvania in Philadelphia. The clippings my mother cut from the *Transcript* describe only cases of local interest and are no doubt not a fair sample of his first ten or fifteen years as a lawyer, but they are illuminating. He defended a man charged with stealing part of a ninety-foot length of rope: he lost the case, but the plaintiff was awarded only eighty cents and required to pay costs of twenty dollars. He defended a man charged with stealing brass from the Railroad, and another charged with stealing two hundred pounds of hay. He defended two hoodlums charged with reckless and drunken driving and horsewhipping a number of people as they passed. He represented a company suing to recover payment for a cheese cutter, a man from whom a silver watch and nine dollars in coin had been stolen, the Commonwealth in a raid on a bawdy house, the Railroad in a suit against employees whose carelessness had caused a fatal collision, a bankrupt against a receiver who was said to be persecuting him, a group of creditors against a man who wanted to be declared a bankrupt, and a man who claimed to have been assaulted by the Chief of Police of Oakland.

In 1903 he became United States Commissioner, hearing and disposing of cases involving the Federal government—seldom anything more important than tearing down mailboxes on a rural postal route or stealing from the post office. In 1907 he went to New York to be interviewed for the position of local attorney for the Erie Railroad. He had won a case for the company involving a fairly large amount of money and had come to the attention of a Judge Willard who was then attorney for the Erie Company as a whole. He sent a cryptic wire to my mother: "Three hundred year ten fifteen thirty first annual for you home in morning Will."

In spite of his eloquence his own political career had not prospered. He lacked the gifts of a politician. His childhood had not prepared him to make friends quickly. He often seemed to glower, and some of my acquaintances were rather afraid of him. He was the Republican candidate for Mayor of Susquehanna in 1903 but lost to a Democrat. In 1904 he was a candidate for the Republican nomination for District Attorney but ran a poor third. And his first really big case was to put an end to all political aspirations.

*   *   *

On May 24, 1907, the Machinists' Union called a strike in the Erie Shops. Employees who were not members of the union stayed on the job, and the company brought in strikebreakers and housed them in a business block. Most of them did not speak English, and the Machinists' Union hired an "interpreter," whose main task seems to have been to persuade the strikebreakers to quit their jobs. Possibly through company maneuvering, the interpreter was arrested and found to be carrying a revolver, and he was held on bond and brought to trial. He was declared not guilty of carrying a weapon "with the intent to injure anyone," but just before Christmas a union member was arrested and a revolver found on him, and as if in retaliation the same thing soon happened to a strikebreaker.

Joseph Frank, an Italian who had lived in Susquehanna for some time, was one of those who remained at work in the roundhouse of the Shops. He was threatened by pickets, who called him a scab, and on one occasion they chased him home, and so he, too, bought a revolver at a local hardware store. On the day after Christmas the man whose job it was to blow the Shop whistle was a little befuddled and blew it fifteen minutes early. Frank heard it while he was eating his breakfast and jumped up, put on his coat, and hurried off to work. His wife had not had time to fill his dinner pail, and so at noon he came out of the Shops to get something to eat. He was stopped by two pickets named Hannigan and Sullivan. A scuffle ensued, and Frank pulled out his pistol and shot Sullivan dead.

Three lawyers were chosen to defend him. One was W. D. B. Ainey of Montrose, who, as the papers later reported, argued points of law. Another was an Italian from New York who never put in an appearance and, when the trial was finally called, was said to be in Italy. My father was the third, and it was up to him to prepare the case.

Frank was well known in Susquehanna, and my father was able to find many witnesses to speak in his defense. One said that he saw Sullivan pick up a large stone and throw it at Frank, and when Sullivan stooped to pick up something else, Frank backed up and put his hand out as if to make Sullivan go away, but Sullivan put his arms around Frank and "knocked him." The witness heard a shot fired and saw Frank stop a moment, and he took Frank's arm and led him into the roundhouse. These facts were known before the trial, and it was clear that it would be claimed that Frank had fired in self-defense. The prosecution would presumably accept a plea of second-degree murder. At the very least the verdict would be manslaughter. But to everyone's surprise Frank was declared not guilty.

After the verdict Frank held a reception in the Sheriff's office, and it must have been my father's finest hour. The expressions of gratitude of Frank and his friends, congratulations of the lawyers and officers of the court—could life be more wonderful? All the papers gave my father full credit. They carried a two-column photograph showing him with a rather stern expression, pince-nez, a bushy mustache, and a high starched collar with tie and stickpin. There was talk of his running for District Attorney.

The real impact of the trial was soon felt. It was an exceedingly unpopular verdict. According to the *Transcript*:

> Citizens of Susquehanna were thoroughly wrought up when the news was flashed here about 5:30 last evening that Joe Frank had been acquitted, that a verdict of not guilty had been rendered, in very quick time, and a murderer had been released.
>
> While there were very few persons who expected that a first degree verdict would be found, there was scarcely anyone who thought the Italian would escape with less than manslaughter. . . .
>
> How the jury could figure it out that the Italian was justified in shooting Sullivan was a difficult problem to solve, but there is no way of telling how a jury will decide anything, they are always an uncertainty and in many instances verdicts are in favor of or against the attorneys instead of the man on trial.
>
> This verdict is clearly one of the worst cases of the miscarriage of justice that has ever taken place in Susquehanna and will do much to promote lawlessness in the sections of the County where this foreign element are numerous. It has produced a bitter feeling against the Italians in Susquehanna and will probably result in many more fights and even murders in an effort on the part of the citizens to avenge the murder of John Sullivan.

His success in defending Frank meant that my father could no longer look forward to a political future. He had defended a strike-breaker against a picket, and organized labor would not forget. He had defended an Italian against an Irishman, and the Italians were a minority group, many of them speaking only Italian and not yet enfranchised, while the Irish dominated local politics. And since judges were elected, the natural culmination of a legal career toward which he might aspire was now wholly out of reach. Five years later a long interview with my father in a Montrose paper contained the following: "Not withstanding his many activities in the Republican interest, he has no political aspirations. He is quite satisfied to continue giving good service—appreciated service—at the legal bar."

FIFTEEN YEARS had passed since my father had escaped from the Mechanical Engineering Department of the Erie Railroad and had gone to New York for that one-year course in law, and he had come a long way. The newspapers were correct in referring to him repeatedly as a rising young lawyer, but he was not to rise much further. He was then about as effective, personally and professionally, as he was ever to be. At the start of his career he began to keep a fifty-cent piece in his pocket. So long as he had it, "he would never be broke," and perhaps it is a proof of his success that it was in his pocket when he died. But it was by then only a thin disk of silver, wholly unmarked, with sharp edges. For more than fifty years it had survived the perils of loss or theft, but it had been buffeted and abraded by other coins and pocket knives and had lost its character and its value.

After the Frank trial my father suffered a similar fate. He had become a successful lawyer, but the minting was complete. The things that were to happen to him later would add no new details. Life was to abrade him, to wear him down. He struggled to satisfy that craving for a sense of worth with which his mother had damned him, but forty years later he would throw himself on his bed, weeping, and cry, "I am no good, I am no good."

MY FATHER apparently never knew how he looked to other people. Every successful step in becoming a self-made man intensified his zeal in improving himself, and he saw no reason why everyone should not improve—why Susquehanna should not be a self-made town—but few of its citizens agreed with him.

He campaigned by writing letters to the *Transcript*. In one he pointed to the filthy condition of the gutters with their grass and tin cans. In another he complained of the noise made by muffler cutouts:

> Many drivers seem to think that they are making an impression on the public as to the wonderful power and quality of their cars when they are making the most noise. A good muffler at most only decreases the power of an engine 3% and when one has to run his car with cutout wide open all the time he proves that his engine is so dirty that it is about to stall. Many drivers never go up any hill without opening the cutout and as Susquehanna is all hills we have no rest. Running with the cutout open is a violation of the State Law and the borough ordinance.

In another letter he pointed out that the town could easily increase its tax revenue by $30,000 a year, which should be spent "with some business judgment and for improvements." The limit on the amount of money the town could borrow had also been increased, and a "filteration plant" was no longer out of the question. When streets began to be paved, he wrote that the electric-light company should be required to put its lines in cables under the streets to remove unsightly poles.

Few people cared about these things, and those who did took a different position. It was not good strategy to argue that to use a muffler cutout was to concede the weakness of one's engine, and not many people cared to have their taxes raised or the town debt increased. The officers of the electric-light company would not put its lines underground willingly, and if they did so, they would raise the rates. My father was ready to sacrifice for the sake of progress but others were not. His proposals merely bolstered his reputation as "Big I and little u."

He continued to go to Penn family reunions—in part, no doubt, to show his relatives how far he had moved up in the world, but he wanted them to move up too. On one occasion a young boy played a saxophone solo as he had evidently learned to do from an instruction booklet, paying no attention to sharps or flats. It was pretty dreadful, and my father was tactless enough to criticize him. Why could they not find someone to teach the boy to play properly? This was "bumpy Will Skinner" at his worst.

At one time a former resident returned to Susquehanna to promote a hardware-manufacturing company, and for some reason the local priest presided at a meeting to consider this chance to create new jobs. It would be necessary for the citizens to subscribe $50,000 as an initial investment, and they were urged to act quickly because another town was said to be on the point of snapping up the offer. Shares were sold and a company was organized, but it failed before a factory was completed. My father, with Frank Zeller and Sid Hersh, the son of one of the proprietors of the Eisman and Hersh Department Store, sought help in New York City and then organized the Blue Ridge Metal Manufacturing Company to take over what was left of the old company (for $3,010). An enterprising and creative man, Mott Jones, was brought in as general manager. (He served for years as a kind of scientist in residence to whom my father and his friends appealed for solutions to all kinds of mechanical problems. When I once pointed out that the extra-large tires my father had bought for our Ford would reduce both the speed and the mileage registered on the speedometer, he naturally checked with Mott Jones.)

The old company had some orders to be filled, including one for 5000 lamps for a South African mine, and my father and his associates also negotiated a contract to manufacture candlesticks in which the candles, held in celluloid sleeves, were moved upward by springs as they grew shorter. There was once a claim for damages when a candle jumped abruptly and spattered wax on a man's tuxedo. When the war started, the company began to manufacture "trench mirrors"—small sheets of silver-plated brass—but the supply of brass ran out, and the steel that replaced it rusted in the trenches. Eventually no metal was available, and the company stopped production. My father and his friends had failed again to do something for the town.

MY MOTHER was on my father's side in all this. She herself served the local hospital in many capacities and worked in the Women's Relief Corps (associated with the war in which her father had played his small part), and during the World War she served in Red Cross canteens. Service, she began to say, was the main thing in life.

There was an element of service in her friendships. The only friend of whom this was not true was Dora Scheuer. Her father had come to the Susquehanna area as a pack peddler, selling cloth, thread, and tinware along country roads. He had made enough money to open a feed store in Susquehanna and then to move to Buffalo and start a business there. Dora shared many of my mother's interests and skills. She went to France as a nurse in the World War, and her long and interesting letters to my mother were published in the *Transcript*. When she returned she brought me a small bronze stamp box decorated with a Dijon lion. She was bright and witty, and I remember her best for her unrestrained laughter.

My mother's relationship with a friend whom I called Aunt Harriet was very different. Harriet had moved away when they were both quite young, and they wrote to each other every week until they married and had children, and after that every other week for almost seventy years. A dependency quickly developed. Aunt Harriet married a shoe clerk and lived for a number of years in Flatbush, where her son was born. Her husband died, and she was forced to shift for herself. She and my mother were approximately the same size, and my mother sent on to her all her discarded clothing. Whenever I saw Aunt Harriet it was like last year's version of my mother. The dependency continued during a second marriage, and when her second husband died and she took over his modest business, my mother continued to help. The loyalty she received in return was important to her.

She was even proud of the attention she received from a cat. There was a boardinghouse across the street from us run by an older woman whom we all called Gran'ma Graham. She had a cat named Varley. In fair weather we spent a good deal of time on our front porch, and once a day Varley came to see my mother. "Here comes Varley," she would say, with the intonation of "Didn't I tell you?" Varley would work his way up along the gutter on the far side of the road, look carefully up and down the street, and then hurry across, even if no wagon or car was in sight. He would come up on the porch and go directly to my mother's lap, where she would smooth the hair on his head and back and talk to him affectionately. So far as I know, she never fed him or gave him anything except this attention. After spending the proper amount of time for a social call, Varley would get down, again cross the road with care, and go home.

The whole thing was a great satisfaction to my mother, and there was something of the same sort in her relationships with her friends. If she had not heard from Harriet near the end of a week in which a letter was due, she would say again and again, "I haven't heard from Harriet." She was no doubt concerned for Harriet's welfare, but she was perhaps also needing reassurance that the friendship was intact.

Her relationship with Mrs. Barnes, our washerwoman, who worked for us in Susquehanna for twenty years, and with her daughter, Bernice, who worked in the same capacity after we moved to Scranton, had something of the same character. They were extraordinarily loyal, but only, I think, because my mother skillfully played the role of Lady Bountiful.

She was proud of her appearance. She stood up for twenty minutes after every meal to preserve her figure, and did indeed keep a good figure and posture all her life. She loved to tell a story about the picture in my father's office that showed her with my brother and me. A stranger had asked my father if it was a picture of his family and had then said, "How nice, two boys and a girl!" When someone made a complimentary remark about a friend, she would treasure it, and when she saw the friend, she would announce that she had a T.L. —a "trade last"—meaning that she would pass on the compliment in return for one the friend might have heard about her.

She laughed a good deal and often had uncontrollable giggling spells, but she tended to laugh *at* people. She thought it was screamingly funny when Mrs. Barnes said that a friend had reached the mental pause, or when a neighbor referred to Ethelbert Nevin's song as "The Rosarary." The news items published in the *Transcript* from small towns were her delight. She often clipped them out and sent them to friends and even mounted some in her scrapbook:

Miss Bernice Burchell is assisting Mrs. Clayton Slocum with her work, on account of Mr. Slocum's illness. The neighbors have been very kind in assisting with the barn chores.

Clayton Slocum had the misfortune to injure his back last week but is able to draw the milk again.

On the right occasion one of these would set off a giggling spell.

What she found funny was very much like what she knew was not "right." She could sit in a railway station and be amused by the odd people she saw, but the same shortcomings in those who were close to her were treated as almost sinful. A shirt and tie which did not go well together were amusing on a stranger; on a son they brought a violent protest. A neighbor's noisy car was terribly funny, but a squeak or rattle in our own called for immediate treatment, and we would drive up and down the street standing on the running board leaning over at precarious angles to spot the offending member. When other people mispronounced a word she would store it away to tell her friends, but when I mispronounced one she would sternly correct me.

She did what was right in a spirit of martyrdom. She told me once of finding a hair in the ice cream served by a friend at a party. It would not have been "right" to hurt her friend by taking the hair out of her mouth and so she chewed and swallowed it bravely. Perhaps she was thinking of my own difficult birth when she told me once that a boy who lived down the street "had no right to be alive" because his mother had died when he was born. When our minister, the Reverend Mr. Pritchard, gorged himself at a church supper and had an attack of indigestion, she called him as intemperate as if he had been a drunkard.

She had strong and curious tastes. She loved the smell of the gasworks in Binghamton which we passed as we drove into the city, but she hated the smell of apples. It was a mortal sin, immediately pointed out, to have an apple or two in the fruit bowl on the dining-room table if she was invited to call. When my grandmother Skinner once boasted of frequently serving apple pie because we loved it so much, my mother was challenged, and she baked a pie, holding the apples under running water as she peeled them. By a brook near Hickory Grove we gathered sprigs of mint to be made into sauce but my mother could not *stand* the odor of spearmint gum.

She had presentiments, and took them seriously in spite of my father's skepticism. "I know you don't think I can tell," she would say, and it was clear that she felt injured, and when a presentiment came true, her triumph knew no bounds: "What did I tell you?"—and then with a special twist, "I know you don't believe. . . ."

She had one ability about which there was no doubt: she could find four-leaf clovers. If she saw a patch of clover on someone's lawn, she would bend down and almost immediately come up with a stem with four leaves. She would frequently find two or three while the rest of us searched in vain. Her satisfaction was intense, and she never overlooked an opportunity to demonstrate her skill.

MY MOTHER was in many ways the dominant member of the family. She had *consented* to marry my father, and there was an element of consent in her behavior with respect to him throughout his life. She had been the more prominent, the more successful, and the more sought-after person in their group, and my father barely made the grade in persuading her to marry him.

There were some things my father had done of which she always spoke with great condescension. A flood had washed out a small bridge near the center of the town several years before they were married, and my father had apparently rescued two young girls, holding on to them when the bridge collapsed. My mother used to tell this story in a derisive way, possibly to offset the no doubt laudatory fashion in which my father or his mother reported the event. She occasionally referred slightingly to a detective story he had written, the plot of which hinged on the invention of a gun that could shoot a bullet around a sharp corner. He sent it off to a magazine and got it back with a flat rejection. She always hoped that I would be tall, and during my adolescent years she would comment on my growth in a way which must have hurt my father, who was not a tall man. (As it turned out, I disappointed her there too.)

Within his family and among his friends my father readily admitted his mistakes and acknowledged his limitations, and perhaps the most important role my mother played was that of confessor. I doubt whether he ever made a mistake that he did not report to her.

It could be something as simple as a verbal slip. I once heard him tell her that when a woman came to inquire about her bill with the telephone company, of which he was treasurer, and suggested a different way of keeping the books, he had started to reply, "If we did that we would get our books all balled up," but had said instead, ". . . we would get our balls . . ." Much later I heard him confess the agony he suffered when, because he had grown hard of hearing, he was unable to hear what a judge said to him when he was trying a case and was afraid to ask him to repeat. My mother always had a word or two of consolation: he should remember that everyone had problems. My father hated to lose a case and would be unhappy for days when he had done so, and it was my mother who would reassure him: "You cannot win them all."

E. R. W. Searle, the uninhibited lawyer who knew both my father and mother well before their marriage, said many years later that "Grace made quite a man of Will Skinner." It was an achievement of which my mother was not entirely unaware.

She was apparently frigid. Her mother may have been similarly disinclined or at least determined that her daughter would never have occasion to leave a document to be read after her death. Something of the intensity of my mother's responses to sexual advances can be inferred from an episode in her early twenties. She had a date with a young man named Joe Boyden, the son of my grandfather Burrhus's close friend, and something happened that deeply offended her—possibly some sudden pawing. In any case she refused to speak to him again. Fortunately he left Susquehanna fairly soon, but he would come back occasionally, and in spite of the fact that his father and my grandfather continued to be close friends, my mother never spoke to him again—never.

She apparently gave my father very little sexual satisfaction. When my brother and I were young, we slept in a room next to my parents', and the connecting door was usually left open. One night I heard murmurs and muffled activity in the next room. Then I heard my mother say, "Do you hate to quit?" and my father muttered some reply. E. R. W. Searle also once said that "Will Skinner would be a better man if he went to see the chippies now and then," but I am sure he never did.

He showed a rather surprising independence in his relations with other women, however. He developed a close relationship with a Mrs. Church, a younger, good-looking woman, whose sister had an apartment on the floor above my father's office. He would often take Mrs. Church with him when he drove to Montrose, the county seat, on business. Her husband apparently had no objection, and occasionally the two couples went out together. My mother referred to Mrs. Church as my father's "affinity," always with amusement. She told me later that my grandmother was terribly concerned about my father's behavior, but evidently she herself was not.

My father was also interested in Elisabeth Lamb, a young divorcee living in Binghamton, whose mother, a distinguished piano teacher, was later to play a role in my musical development. Mrs. Taylor and her daughter would come to call on us with some relatives who lived in Susquehanna, and Elisabeth Lamb would sing. She had a pleasant voice, but the only repertoire we heard was composed of things like "The Land of the Sky Blue Waters." She studied singing seriously but never had a career. My father had glamorous ideas about singers, and he once rather petulantly complained to some friends in my mother's hearing that Elisabeth Lamb had refused to have dinner with him when he had happened to be in Binghamton.

If he flirted with anyone in their immediate circle, it would have been Nell Owens, the wife of the owner of the hardware store. She was the most openly flirtatious and could be counted on for the latest sexual gossip, reported with the least use of innuendo. A bit of flirtation would explain an early memory. My father and I were on the train to Binghamton, and a seat had been turned over to make space for four. Nell Owens was sitting opposite us and talking with my father. I was playing with the latch of the window, and Nell said something to me about punching her ticket, as if the latch were a conductor's punch. Inexplicably, I burst into tears. It was quite unlike me, and it is possible that I had been annoyed by a flirtatious conversation designed to be unintelligible to me.

My father was necessarily involved in discussing sexual matters in connection with divorces, and for that or some other reason he had purchased a set of Havelock Ellis's *Studies in the Psychology of Sex*, which he kept concealed in his office. (He once complained that Nell

46

Owens had never returned one volume and had broken his set.) Allusions to sex around our house were never very frank. A picture called "September Morn" was popular at the time and frequently reproduced. It showed a nude girl standing in shallow water covering herself very effectively with her arms and long hair. "September Morn" was almost a synonym for nudity in our family.

Annette Kellerman had swum nude in a movie we had all seen, though we had by no means seen all of Miss Kellerman, but the standard bathing costume for women was a dark blue or black dress with a skirt and stockings and slippers. One evening when my mother was getting supper, my father cut out the bare arms of one picture of a bathing girl and fastened them on the legs of another so that she appeared to be bare-legged. He told me to show it to my mother in the kitchen. She was not amused.

PART II

I GREW UP in a bountiful world, in which many wonderful things were to be had for the asking. Our backyard offered black cherries, red cherries (shared with the robins), purple plums, green plums, Concord grapes, currants, raspberries, rhubarb, horseradish, and mustard. None of them needed any care; they were simply there in season. Our neighbors had other kinds of slipskin grapes, plums, and apples.

In the fall we went nutting. The chestnuts had not yet been blighted, and we took flour sacks and filled them until they were almost too heavy to carry home. We kept a few in our pockets and put them on the hearth of the fireplace to pop open. We often drove into the country after supper to gather hickory nuts, and sometimes we found butternuts or black walnuts, the shells of which were harder to crack, and you had to dig out the delicious meat with a horseshoe nail. Once in a while we found beechnuts, small and hard to peel but with a delicate flavor.

In the spring, wintergreen leaves and berries were among the first things to push through the matted leaves after the snow had melted, and when we were out for a drive, we knew where to stop to harvest watercress and the young fiddleheads of ferns. We enjoyed the odor of an occasional stand of pine trees and believed that it was good for people with tuberculosis.

It was a beautiful world. Susquehanna was a dirty, unkempt town, but the great sweep of the river valley was magnificent. There were fields and pastures on the inner bank, reaching well up into the hills, and some of what remained uncultivated was part of the original hardwood forest, which blazed with color in the autumn. In spring we knew where to find the delicate trillium, arbutus, fringed gentian, and jack-in-the-pulpit; and we did not even have to look to find honeysuckle, columbine, and dogwood. To the despair of farmers, pastures would fill with red and yellow devil's paintbrushes and goldenrod, and here and there patches of violets or bluets. Masses of Queen Anne's lace flourished along the roadside. In our backyard there were roses on an arbor and a large bleeding-heart plant, the blossoms of which could be pulled apart to reveal a fascinating inner structure. Along the porch we planted petunias and salvias, and every now and then someone made the standard joke of calling them spittoonias and salivas.

In the cemetery next to our house there were snowballs—white berries the size of marbles which gave satisfying plops when thrown against tombstones. We collected stems of plants with galls of interesting shapes. And everywhere there were the beautiful but troublesome burdocks, each bur composed of scores of small, barbed hooks like crochet needles. We pelted each other with the burs and in more creative moods made them into chains and baskets.

It was a world we shared with animals. Thornton Burgess and Ernest Thompson Seton told stories about animals that were scarcely less anthropomorphic than Br'er Rabbit or the characters in Aesop's Fables, but we did not learn from books. I had a cage-like mousetrap that caught mice alive, and I used it to catch chipmunks. I could never tame them, and I let them go when red marks developed on the sides of their snouts as they tried to force their way between the wires of the trap. Not much could be done with frogs, toads, or lizards, but turtles were easy to catch, and I used to make ladders and teeter-totters for them to perform on. Later we killed snakes rather than capture them, and on that rare occasion when it was a rattlesnake, we counted the buttons in its rattle to evaluate our achievement. In early summer we caught fireflies and put them under an inverted drinking glass to see them glow in the dark—a steady glowing which, alas, meant death. In autumn we found cocoons and brought them into the house, and we might be rewarded months later when a butterfly emerged. I could catch a bee in a hollyhock blossom, folding the petals together to make a small bottle, the bee buzzing furiously until I tired of the game and released it. We knew and stayed away from hornets' nests, but I once watched a swarm of bees taken out of a tree in front of my grandmother Burrhus's by a man wearing a hat with a veil falling over his shoulders; he smoked the buzzing mass with a small smudge pot until it became quiet and then simply pried it free and took it away.

My friend Raphael Miller took care of his father's carriage horse, and I used to help him clean the stable. The horse frightened me not so much by its size as by the loud sound of its hooves on the plank floor. A runaway horse pulling terrified passengers in a careening carriage at breakneck speed was, like a house on fire, something to see and talk about. A few of the citizens of Susquehanna hunted, and one of them was Billy Main, whose blacksmith shop was at the rear of our property. One of his dogs once tangled with a porcupine, and back at the shop I heard it howling mournfully as the quills were pulled out of its mouth one by one.

It could have been true, as we believed, that rattlesnakes traveled in pairs and when killing one you should watch out for the other, or that a bunch of bananas arriving in a grocery store might conceal a deadly tarantula, or that somewhere in the vicinity there might be quicksand as treacherous as that which permitted Captain Marion, the Swamp Fox, to escape from the British, but we also believed that the sounds made by robins when a storm was brewing were a way of "calling for rain," that the rays of light streaming through the clouds under certain atmospheric conditions showed that "the sun was drawing water," that a horsehair soaked long enough in water would turn into the fine snake-like creatures we occasionally saw at the edge of a pond, that bats tried to get in one's hair and that if you saw one in the evening sky and threw up your cap you might trick it into going into the cap in search of hair, that darning needles or dragonflies would sew up your ears, eyelids, or lips, and that a cat sleeping in one's bed could "draw out" one's vital forces or even one's life.

THERE WERE PEOPLE in that world, too, and some of them were interesting. Among them, predictably, was a blacksmith. He worked in Billy Main's shop, and I used to watch him crank the rotary blower of his forge and thrust a horseshoe deep into the hot, sparkling coals with long iron pincers. As he tested the hot shoe for fit, the air filled with the pungent smell of scorched hoof, and there was a burst of steam as he plunged a shoe heated to a cherry red into a tub of water to temper it.

In the yard outside there was a bender through which straps of iron were cranked to form wagon tires, and I was amazed to see holes drilled through them with a hand-operated drill press. A tire was heated before being pressed over the wooden wheel, and as it cooled it contracted and drew the rim and spokes tightly together. Also in the yard were the remains of two early automobiles far beyond repair, though I nevertheless dreamed of putting them in working order.

A block from our house in the other direction was a carpenter shop, and we often heard the coughing of its one-cylinder engine and the occasional whine of a planer or saw. The carpenter did cabinet work, and I was surprised to see how often he simply glued pieces of wood together, but the glue was hot and hence presumably stronger than the kind I used.

Almost directly across the street was the boardinghouse run by Gran'ma Graham and her daughter Nellie. The house was full of jovial, outgoing boarders—among them the head nurse at the hospital, the chief clerk at Ned Owens's hardware store, and the rector of the Episcopal church. They all sat around a big table at mealtime, with Nellie carrying dishes to and from the kitchen.

I never saw Gran'ma Graham outside her house, but every Christmas Nellie or one of the boarders would bring over baskets for my brother and me with great red and green bows tied on the handles, filled with apples, oranges, dates, figs, bunches of raisins on stems, and candy—ribbon candy in bright colors and strong flavors that broke into dangerously sharp pieces when you bit it, or stubby cylinders with colored pictures—flags or bouquets—running straight through from one face to the other.

I had a small reciprocal duty to perform on New Year's Day. Gran'ma Graham believed that if the "first foot" to cross her threshold was a dark-complexioned man, the year would bring bad luck. I could solve the problem because I was fair, and I went over as early as possible on the first day of each new year to knock at the kitchen door. Gran'ma Graham would be up getting breakfast and would welcome me and give me a bit of silver as part of the ritual. It was always a dime.

Miss Nugent had a candy store, on the corner of Myrtle Street and Jackson Avenue, which I passed four times a day for twelve years on my way to and from school. It was a small, red, one-story building, the back half screened off for living space, and all business transacted in the right front corner, where there were two glass cabinets full of penny candy, with a box for short children to stand on, and beyond them some shelves of tablets, pencils, crayons, rubber balls, and notebooks.

The same staple candies were available year after year—Tootsie Rolls, red-hots, licorice sticks, spongy yellow bananas, jujubes, lemon drops, and paraffin chewing gum—but once in a while there were novelties, such as large blocks of brown, dry, frothy sugar, light as feathers and quickly reduced to small chewy bits in the mouth, or very small tin frying pans holding candy eggs, sunny side up, with a tin spoon to eat them with. It would take us several minutes to chose a nickel's worth, but Miss Nugent had all the time in the world. Once she put in some cheap golf balls and my mother evidently told someone that they were dangerous because they had compressed gas at the center. Miss Nugent had a boy cut one in half and she was very serious as she told me, one of her best customers, that my mother was wrong. I was surprised that she would let a boy risk doing it, and also embarrassed at being a member of an opposing faction.

Lizzy Smith lived in a badly run-down house on Jackson Avenue. The town may have forgiven her her taxes as a gesture of welfare, but she made her living by peddling drugs and cosmetics from door to door and baking bread, rolls, and cakes. I went to her house one cold evening at suppertime to pick up some Parker House rolls my mother had ordered for a dinner party and was astonished by all the things I saw spread out on great tables in her hot and steamy kitchen.

When I was four or five years old, a girl down the street played school, and I was one of her pupils. All I learned about school was that you sat with your hands folded on the table in front of you. It was not a bad preparation. Miss Metzger, who taught first and second grades, was a pleasant, well-disposed woman, but discipline was a part of life in Susquehanna and we did indeed sit some of the time with our hands folded on the desks in front of us. We held up one finger when we had to go to the toilet to urinate and two fingers for something more serious. Both grades were taught in the same room, Miss Metzger moving from one side to the other. To teach us to read she held up cards and we called out the names of letters and later pronounced words.

Miss Graves came to the room to teach art. We had sewing cards, with holes punched in patterns through which we drew colored yarns with safe, dull-pointed needles and we also colored printed figures. Miss Graves was once scandalized when she discovered that I was using an orange crayon to color a man's face, and she dug into a box of scraps until she found a small flesh-colored crayon. Mrs. Mooney, the Catholic-church organist, came to teach singing. She put up great charts showing notes on staves, and in a rough but accurately pitched voice led us through the *do, re, mi* of a primitive *solfège*. We all learned to read, draw, and sing.

When it came time to go home we were sent to the cloakroom to bring out our coats, hats, leggings, and overshoes. A girl named Annabelle Harding sat in front of me. She lived two doors down the street from us and was plump and pretty, and I was in love with her. Once when she was putting on her coat, she laid her bonnet on the seat, and a ribbon came through and I put my foot on it. I simply meant to keep her from picking up the bonnet but she pulled it sharply and the ribbon broke off and I was mortified.

One day I was playing on our porch with some rubber alphabet stamps, and I decided to print a letter to Annabelle. I told my mother what I was doing and a moment or two later asked her how to spell "kiss." I was aware of a certain reserve as she told me. She need not have worried, for my romance was short-lived. The Hardings left Susquehanna "between two days"—that is, during the night to escape the Sheriff.

Annabelle's place in my affections was taken by a little blonde girl from West Hill. She went to a different grade school, but I saw her at dancing class, which met in a small room with a hardwood floor over Henry Perrine's furniture store. We dressed up—though it was probably past the time when I wore a Little Lord Fauntleroy suit—and were on our best social behavior, the boys sitting on one side of the room and the girls on the other side. In one ceremony a girl stood on a chair and held out a burning candle. The boys marched around in a circle and jumped and blew at the candle as they passed, and the one who blew out the candle danced with the girl. My little blonde friend always lowered the candle so that I could blow it out easily. She was very pretty, and although she often had bad breath, I was in love. A song by Victor Herbert with the words "I'm falling in love with someone" was then popular, and I whistled the tune and sang the words around the house hoping that my brother would tease me about my pretty friend on West Hill. Alas, her family, too, soon left town.

WE GOT OUR FIRST CAR, a Ford, in 1910 from a dealer in Great Bend. It was painted black, but there was a great deal of brass on it. The radiator, with the word *Ford* in raised cursive letters on the front, was all brass, and so were the frame of the vertical windshield, the upper half of which could be folded down so that the driver could enjoy the breeze, and the long rods which braced it against the wind. We polished the brass almost daily, using a special white paste and sponges from my grandfather's barn. We usually rode with the top down but put it up when it rained, and if it rained hard we put on black side curtains which were held in place with twisting tabs. The curtains had small isinglass windows.

The unpaved roads were dusty, and you maneuvered to be ahead of or far behind other cars when the dust was bad. We wore linen coats called dusters, and caps and goggles, and my mother wore a scarf over her hat. Driving at night was a hazard because the gas lights were not very bright. The gas was generated in a tank on the running board. When it grew dark, you stopped the car and opened a cock on the tank which allowed water to drip onto calcium carbide. The resulting acetylene was piped to the headlamps, and you waited until you could smell gas and then touched a match to the little Y-shaped outlets, usually getting a small pop.

The horn had a large black rubber bulb. (A later invention, the

Klaxon, was operated by pushing on a plunger; it made a loud, raucous noise.) The tires had no tread, and since there were nails from carriages and wagons in the dirt roads, there were many punctures and it was necessary to know how to repair them. My father once paid two men to come to our garage and inject our tires with a fluid said to contain powdered rubber, which would flow into any hole and stop a leak. We still had punctures.

To start the car you inserted a crank in the front end until it engaged the crankshaft and gave it a turn or two. After the first few explosions you raced around to the steering wheel and moved the spark and throttle levers up and down to "catch" the motor. My father once failed to disengage the crank quickly enough when the motor started, and the crank spun around and broke his arm.

The spark was advanced or retarded depending on whether the engine was knocking, especially in going uphill. There was a long hill south of Hickory Grove that we called the Hog's Back, and it was my father's pride that he could take it without shifting into low gear. He would get a running start and then carefully work the throttle and spark as the car lost speed on the grade. The tension was great, and once, just as we were reaching the top still in high, he bit his pipestem in two.

A garage, approached by a driveway on the upper side of the house, was built near the rear of our lot. To avoid backing out or turning around, my father had a second door cut into the far side so that the car could be driven right on through and around the back of the lot and out another driveway. A car that had smooth tires and was hard to start in cold weather was worthless in winter, and it was left in the garage, jacked up on wooden blocks to save the tires.

We bought our gasoline at the coal yard, driving onto the platform on which wagonloads of coal were weighed. The gasoline was pumped from a drum in the office and brought out in a ten-gallon pail. The front seat of the Ford was removed and a large funnel put into the top of the gas tank. The funnel had a chamois stretched across it, and a few blobs of water remained on it when the gasoline had gone through. We liked to stand up in the back seat of the car and lean over to smell the gasoline as it was poured.

*   *   *

58

I saw my first airplane on Saturday morning, September 16, 1911. We got up rather late that day, and my father was later than usual in shaving. I was in the bathroom as he lathered his face and began to strop his razor. Suddenly we heard a strange clatter and, looking out the window, we saw the plane. It was over the river, almost on a level with our house. The pilot had written ahead to ask the postmaster to mark a white arrow with cloth or flour to indicate where he might land. The only possibility near Susquehanna was Beebe's Flats, and there indeed, he landed. We got in the Ford and drove over.

It was a biplane, mounted on three small bicycle wheels, with canvas wings and wooden struts and a web of wire braces. The engine turned a propeller at the rear, and the pilot sat in front and operated a wheel on a stick. A crowd had gathered, and the town constable was walking slowly around the plane with all the dignity he could muster, keeping people back out of reach of it, but I managed to touch a wing.

The pilot, Jimmy Ward, was in a coast-to-coast race for which William Randolph Hearst had offered a prize of $50,000. He was following the Erie Railroad. His wife arrived by train and their warm embrace when she joined him on Beebe's Flats was talked about by my mother and her friends for a week.

There was a good deal of discussion about taking off from the Flats and a good deal of pacing off of distances. Except for the part that was a baseball diamond, the ground was not very smooth, and to get the advantage of a slight wind Ward would have to take off toward the western end of the field, where there were tall trees and beyond them the superstructure of the bridge over the river. He ate some lunch and then had the plane pulled as close as possible to a cornfield at the eastern end of the Flats and got aboard. A few men pushed on the rear edge of the wings as the plane started and it bumped across the field, bounced into the air, and cleared the trees and bridge.

Later that year I went with my grandfather and grandmother Burrhus to watch a race between a motor car and an airplane at the fairgrounds in Binghamton. My grandfather pointed out that the plane was not keeping directly above the track at the turns.

*   *   *

59

A YEAR AFTER I WAS GRADUATED from college I wrote a "Historical-Religious" note recounting my religious education. It is probably more accurate than my present recollections, with which it does not always agree:

> The first religious teaching I can remember was at my grandmother Skinner's. It was her desire that I should never tell a lie, and she attempted to fortify me against it by vividly describing the punishment for it. I remember being shown the coal fire in the heating stove and told that little children who told lies were thrown in a place like that after they died. Not long after that—I could not have been more than five or six—a neighbor asked me whether a certain man was my uncle, and I said, "Yes." I found out later that he was a great-half-uncle and I was suddenly overwhelmed with the realization that I had told a lie. It may seem horribly absurd but I actually suffered torments over that incident. Some time later I went to a magician's show the final act of which concerned the appearance of a devil. I was terrified. I questioned my father as to whether a devil just like that threw little boys to Hell and he assured me it was so. I suppose I have never recovered from that spiritual torture. Not long afterwards I did tell a real lie to avoid punishment and that bothered me for years. I remember lying awake at night sobbing, refusing to tell my mother the trouble, refusing to kiss her goodnight. I can still feel the remorse, the terror, the despair of my young heart at that time. . . .
>
> Several years later I visited in Buffalo with my parents, and they took me to see a Passion Play. I went, fearing to go, fearing to refuse. There was terror in me as we approached the outdoor theatre.

My formal religious training, which covered many years, was much less frightening. When I was quite small I was sent off to Sunday school with five cents tucked into pocket or mitten. Mrs. Tisdell and her daughter held the primary school in the social quarters of the church. They passed out colored cards showing landscapes and costumes of the Holy Land. When I was older Miss Graves met a class of six or seven boys every Sunday for many years. The service began with songs by the whole school—"Rock of Ages" (cleft for me) or "Ship Ahoy" (hear the cry, oh, haste to the rescue today)—and the Lord's Prayer, and then our group would assemble in one corner of the church under a colored-glass window bearing the name of

Frazier, the donor. We had materials supplied by the Presbyterian church, and it took us years to get through the Pentateuch. I received a gold-and-enamel pin testifying to the fact that I had not missed one Sunday in five years, except for medical reasons.

Miss Graves was a liberal who told us that the miracles reported in the Bible could be taken as metaphors. This helped to relieve the sense of sin I had acquired from my grandmother, but I was not yet in the clear, and that rather turgid historical-religious note reported that "before I had satisfied myself in unbelief I was torn by the inbred tradition in me. I remember one incident in that period: ashamed of myself for being afraid of a God I did not believe in I went about saying to myself, 'God damn Jesus Christ, God damn Jesus Christ.' "

I was never physically punished by my father and only once by my mother who heard me use a bad word in talking with my brother. She took me to the bathroom, put soap and water on a washcloth, and washed my mouth out. It was a ritualistic gesture, and I wondered at the time how she knew when my mouth was clean. I must have been punished in other ways because my parents' disapproval was something I carefully avoided. I can easily recall the consternation when, in second grade, I brought home my report card on which under "Deportment" Miss Metzger had marked "Annoys others." My mother was always quick to take alarm if I showed any deviation from what she called "right," but she needed only to say "Tut tut," or to ask "What will people think?"

When I was perhaps no more than four or five I took a quarter from my grandmother Burrhus's open purse and spent it at Miss Nugent's candy store, and when Miss Nugent reported that I was spending beyond my accustomed means, I was questioned and readily confessed. There was a family conference about appropriate measures, but I was merely lectured and told the dangers of a criminal way of life. Years later I went with my family to Montrose, and my father took me through the county jail, which was connected with the courthouse. Three or four men were sitting around in a bare space behind bars, and I remember a little sign with a tin cup asking for contributions to buy tobacco. And once when we were on vacation, my brother and I were taken to see an illustrated lecture on life at Sing Sing showing prisoners in black and white stripes working on piles of rock with sledgehammers. I don't believe this was done to frighten us, and I never knew where the Susquehanna jail was located.

In whatever way it was accomplished my ethical and moral training was effective and long-lasting. When I was perhaps thirteen I saw some periscopes for sale in the five-and-ten in Binghamton. They consisted of tin tubes with holes near the ends on opposite sides. I picked one up and mistakenly pulled off the cap pressed on one end. A small mirror came out and I could not put it back properly. I was afraid to tell my parents, and I had no money of my own, so I put the mutilated periscope back in its bin and moved away. I felt guilty for days.

Once at a Halloween party at the Presbyterian church someone dumped a bowl of apples into a washtub full of water and walked away. I knew what was to be done and immediately dunked for one. I got it in my teeth and walked off eating it. Then I discovered that you were supposed to pay for the chance to dunk, and I thought I saw another child reporting my theft. I had no money and could not return a half-eaten apple, so I stayed guiltily away. Once I saw a chipmunk sitting on a fence post, and I threw a stone and quite unexpectedly hit it. I was unhappy for a week. My father once brought our Congressman home to supper. He asked me a few questions, and I replied as impressively as I thought the occasion demanded. Had I ever been in Washington? "No," I said, "I never were." I knew "were" was not right, but I made no effort to correct myself, and I suffered for a long time from the memory of that slip.

Another part of my early training could be summarized in "Waste not, want not." When I was perhaps twelve or thirteen I had a generator taken from an old-style telephone. I was cranking it rather aimlessly one day when my father warned me that it would wear out. I protested that it was built to last a long time, but he said, "It will only last a certain length of time, and every minute it is cranked will be subtracted from that time." I never wore it out, of course, but I no longer had much fun playing with it.

Unwilling to punish me, my parents showed some skill in finding alternative measures. I was round-shouldered. It was partly a matter of anatomy, for I was born with a long neck and sloping shoulders, but

I also drooped a little, and my family worried. My father would slouch across the room, his hands dangling in front of him like an ape's, to show me how I looked as I walked. There was talk of shoulder braces, but a different remedial step was taken: I was given an Irish Mail— a kind of car steered with the feet and driven by pushing and pulling a crossbar which stuck up in front of the seat and turned a wheel geared to the back axle. It moved forward or backward depending upon the position of the driving arm, and there was a dead center from which you escaped only by giving a little push with one foot. It could not be driven up a steep grade without getting stuck in dead center or suddenly and violently going into reverse. It no doubt meant excellent exercise for the back and shoulder muscles, but it was the only one in town and attracted a lot of attention, and I confined myself to Grand Street when I took it out.

My innocence about sex was extraordinary. In Binghamton I saw a vaudeville show featuring living statues, in which a curtain was lifted to reveal groups of people painted or powdered white and arranged in classical poses. In several of these it was quite clear that the women had no penises, and when I got home I experimented with myself to see how they could have tied their genitals out of sight.

I drew no conclusions from animals. I saw bulls and cows copulating and, like everyone else, was embarrassed by the occasional sight of two dogs stuck together. (Copulating cats were quite unsexual in their fighting and caterwauling.) I never saw horses copulate, although in a blacksmith's shop I saw a man stroke a stallion's penis to show a friend how big it became. Occasionally a carload of horses would be delivered at the station and driven through the streets on their way to a country market, and I once overheard my mother complain of the use of a lead horse to manage stallions en route; I was not sure what it meant but knew it had something to do with sex.

My brother and I once inadvertently discovered our parents' hypersensitivity about sex. One day when they were out we decided to play a trick on them. We stuffed stockings, knickers, and a shirt with dirty clothes and added shoes and some kind of improvised head, and put the "body" on one of our beds. We wanted to put a rather large nail file with a silver handle in it as a dagger, but the only place we could find where it would stay upright was just below the belt in the open fly.

We were out when our parents came home, and when we returned and asked my mother whether they had seen the dead body, she looked very black. We slowly realized that they had supposed that the nail file was meant to be a penis, and when we told her it was a dagger, she dashed off to explain to my father.

One day my mother was entertaining some of her friends on our front porch. A neighbor's property was held in place by a retaining wall, and below the wall, out of sight of their parents but in full view of our porch, their two children, a small boy and girl, were examining each other's private parts. Someone called my mother's attention to this, and she sucked in her breath and said, "If I caught my boys doing that, I would skin them alive!"

The nearest I came to being caught was when I was perhaps four or five and several boys and I were in the hayloft of a neighbor's barn, examining and talking about our penises. The mother of one of the boys heard us, and when she asked him about it later he confessed. She telephoned my parents, and I was called on the carpet. I lied my way out: I said I had not been doing anything myself, I was merely watching.

I must have been punished in some way for very early sex play, perhaps even as a baby, because I was once sent to bed without my supper and felt unjustly treated, and I clearly remember saying to myself, "If they do that, then I'll do this," and I began to play with myself.

I learned the technique of masturbation quite by accident, when I was perhaps eleven. Up to that point sexual play had consisted of undirected handling of genitalia. One day another boy and I had gone out of town on our bicycles and walked up a creek, beside which we were later to build a shack. We were sitting in the sun engaged in rather idle sex play when I made several rhythmic strokes which had a highly reinforcing effect. I immediately repeated them with even more reinforcing results. I began a steady movement, making an excited comment to my companion, and then, although I was too young to ejaculate, I had my first orgasm. The only effect was that my penis began to hurt badly. I was panic-stricken: I had broken it! I got up and walked down to the ledge of rocks alongside the creek in despair.

SINCE MY BROTHER was two and a half years younger than I, there was little competition between us. Following my mother's practice, I often called him "Honey" and was once ridiculed for doing so as we were pulling our sleds up Grand Street. "Is he made of honey?" said a boy contemptuously. Once when he was being kept indoors with a cold, I was working in the little shop back of the kitchen. We had received a new supply of kindling wood from the grocery store, and it included a number of orange crates, the ends of which were beautiful squares of clear white pine. With a brace and bit I could drill holes in the corners (the shavings rising in lovely helixes) and drive in sticks to make a stool. I brought one to my brother, and he was so delighted that I went right back and made a second one, and this pleased him so much that I went back and made a third. My mother eventually had to stop me, as the stools piled up.

Our sibling affection was memorialized by Delly Harding, Susquehanna's bachelor photographer, who posed us when I was perhaps six, in a series of pictures in which we wore: (1) stiff black oilcloth raincoats and hats, (2) Indian costumes with fringed sleeves and headdresses with turkey feathers, (3) primitive Boy Scout uniforms with stubby staffs, leggings, and wide-brimmed hats, (4) bathing suits in the current mode with tops and short skirts, (5) baggy overalls, one shot from in front, another from behind, and (6) our Sunday clothes—white coats, socks, and patent-leather slippers.

That a change in our relationship eventually took place is suggested by the inscription on the flyleaf of my copy of *Alice in Wonderland*. I had written:

> *From Grandma Skinner*
> *To Frederic Skinner*
> *Dec. 25 1913*

But below this, in my brother's hand, is to be seen:

> *Your a*
> BOOB

When my father and mother were away on business, we usually stayed with Mr. and Mrs. B. Here are two of my brother's letters on such an occasion:

Dear Mother,

How are you getting along? Frederic is feeling fine. We got your card but we didn't get any potatoes and frankforts [marzipan]. . . . If you could I wish you would bring me a bird book. Miss Graves says that we ought to have one because there are going to be a lot of birds over. Bring Fred something in place of that. Four kisses a day

Ebbe

Dear Mother,

We got your frankforts and potatoes. We had one session [section?] today. Did Papa win the case? We are anxious to know. How are you getting along? I am feeling fine. Miss O'Malley died this afternoon at 12 o'clock. Don't forget (if you will) get me a bird book and the others things.

Ebbe

P.S. Eight more than you had (kisses).

ooooooooooo

My grandmother Skinner was not to be left out and we occasionally stayed with her, sleeping in the isolation of a massive Victorian bedstead on the second floor. (At Mr. and Mrs. B's we enjoyed the security offered by a one-floor apartment.) She always gave us oyster stew for supper. The grocer kept oysters in a large, unrefrigerated crock, from which he would dip out enough to fill a small cardboard pail with a wire handle. My grandmother served the soup in shallow bowls with yellow lily pads of butter floating on the surface, and we sprinkled oyster crackers among them as we were not allowed to do at home.

There were no checkers, dominoes, or playing cards at my grandmother Skinner's, but there was always the barn to be explored with its hayloft converted into storage space. Not much could be done with those parts of stove polishers, but the white rubber tubing was useful until it grew brittle with age. I discovered the principle of the siphon. My grandmother had some large butter crocks, and on the back porch and cellar door I made elaborate hydraulic systems in which water flowed, miraculously it seemed, up out of one crock and down into a lower one and up out of that and down into one still lower.

My grandmother also had a bottle of camphor, used for moth-proofing, and I made camphor boats. I would cut a small piece of cardboard in the shape of a boat with a nick in the stern, and when it was floating in a tub of water, I would drop a crystal of camphor at the base of the nick, breaking the surface tension and sending the boat forward.

My grandmother could fold a piece of toilet paper over a comb and hum or sing through it with the dramatic result later exploited by the kazoo. She also collected jelly glasses, and by choosing different sizes and filling them with different amounts of water, I could get an octave or so of pleasant tones, to be played like a xylophone.

We had other ways of making noises. A blade of grass held taut between the knuckles and bases of the two thumbs could be blown to produce a powerful squawk, and a smooth leaf laid across the circle of thumb and forefinger would pop when struck with the other hand shaped like a cup. We made willow whistles, and we had small snare drums, and the sweet potato or ocarina was as much a mark of the life of Susquehanna as of any primitive culture.

Among our toys the stone blocks gave way to Erector and Meccano sets. I was given the Erector set, with which you could build large structures, but I much preferred my brother's Meccano set, because its strips of metal with equally spaced holes could be bolted together to create much more intricate devices.

I also had a small steam engine, perhaps ten inches high, with a piston and flywheel and a tiny whistle. It contained an alcohol lamp, and spilled alcohol was the first thing to burn when the lamp was lighted. When the pressure built up, you gave the flywheel a spin and it turned by itself, often running merrily for some time.

Mechanical engineering eventually gave way to chemistry and electricity. Solutions changed color when mixed, and bits of string, dipped in a solution and dried, burned like fuses, but there was not much else to be done. A friend, Otis Chidester, and I did try to design a system for getting oxygen out of sea water, because a submarine making a practice dive off Long Island had got its nose stuck in the mud and the crew had died before they could be rescued, and we took the idea to Professor Killian, then principal of the school, but it appeared that there would be no room in a submarine for the equipment needed. Electricity was more interesting. You rubbed a block of resin and then transferred the charge to metal disks held on insulating handles. A pith ball or a bit of charred match hanging on a thread would swing rapidly back and forth, transferring a charge from one object to another.

I had a simple electric motor that ran on a dry cell. Three equally spaced bosses on the rim of a flywheel passed between two coils, and a strip of copper served as a brush to energize the coils at just the right time to pull the bosses into their field and then release them. The brushes could be bent to get the best timing, and the whole operation was beautifully obvious.

I had a magic lantern with light supplied by a small kerosene lamp. The slides were strips of glass bound with *passe-partout*, each with perhaps six scenes. They were made in Germany and the stories they told were unintelligible, but the swift, effortless movement of the lantern image about the walls of a room never lost its magic.

There was nothing to be done with the magic lantern except show again and again those puzzling Teutonic scenes, but later I was given a stereopticon which had two electric bulbs and could project scenes from postcards, and I began to arrange travelogues, using cards collected in New York—the Flatiron Building, the Statue of Liberty— or on our automobile trips. When we got a Brownie camera I dreamed of telling a story with a series of still pictures (in the manner of penny-arcade machines) and photographed several sets and actions, but my mother thought the camera too expensive a hobby.

One Christmas I was given a miniature theatre with cut-out figures to be moved back and forth in grooves while a text was read, and later I made similar theatres out of spare boxes. I discovered how to fasten two curtains to a string passing over a pulley so that a single pull opened or closed both curtains. I cut out figures from magazines and pasted them on cardboard, and arranged to move them on sticks. I also made a shadow theatre, with colored transparencies that cast images on a screen from a candle.

I never learned to whip a top because tops had gone mechanical—spring-driven or, in a large metal version which hummed musically, spun by pumping a twisted metal strip through a slot. Our jackstraws were miniature rakes, spades, and hoes, all made of wood because plastic had not yet been invented. We played tiddlywinks, jacks, and marbles. We had some of the better marbles—migs and glassies—but the game we played most often was called "How Many Birds in a Nest?" One player held out his hand closed about a few marbles and the other guessed the number. He got them all if he was right but made up the difference if he was wrong.

We played mumblety-peg, hopscotch, and hide-and-seek. We roller-skated in groups, usually in the evening. We clamped our skates to our shoes with a key kept on a string around our neck. The first sidewalks in Susquehanna were flagstones from the quarries nearby, and we learned to hop over the uneven joints and take effective strokes on the bigger flags. Early concrete walks were not well constructed and rang hollow under our feet, though we could work up greater speed on them. We had to break our descent on the hills by running into the grass and stumbling to a stop or holding out our arms and swinging around a tree, and skating usually meant skinned knees and torn knickers.

Bob Perrine and I sometimes skated in the dance hall above his father's furniture store. The skates there had wooden wheels and we could take broad strokes and cut figures with a wild abandon.

I SPENT TWELVE YEARS of grade and high school in one small brick building on Laurel Street. In cold weather steam circulated through long horizontal pipes at the rear of each room, and there were a few minutes each day, as Mr. Shaughnessy stoked the furnace in the basement, when the pipes pounded as if pistols were being fired. Each room had rows of desks fixed in place, and the students stayed in their seats and were fairly quiet. We had our secret diversions. There were no screens and in warm weather we were bothered by flies. In third grade the boy who sat across from me and I began to shoot flies on the floor between our desks with long rubber bands. When we had killed a few, the carnage attracted others, and the floor was eventually red with gore.

There had been no sewer in the street when the school was built, and we continued to use large, smelly outdoor toilets in all kinds of weather. The play space in back of the school was divided between boys and girls by a solid fence, and there was no playground equipment. We might organize a game of pom-pom-pullaway, or someone might bring a ball and bat for a game of one-o'-cat, but that was all.

I was embarrassed on my first day in third grade when I turned in a perfect arithmetic paper and Miss Brosnam took me and the paper across the hall and Miss Metzger put her arm across my shoulder, held up the paper, and told the second grade how proud she was of the wonderful job I had done on my first day in third grade. We took our report cards home at the end of each month, and my father signed mine with that characteristic flourish, but I do not remember that he commended me for high marks. It was assumed that I would do well.

I was chosen as the subject of two educational experiments. Someone from the County School Board suggested a new way to do subtraction, and my teacher tried it on me. Instead of borrowing one from the minuend, I was to add one to the subtrahend. I don't remember that my performance improved, and I soon went back to the old way. I was also urged to try the Palmer method of handwriting. We had all learned Spencerian, and we perfected our hands by writing copybook maxims, each one a dozen times, but someone, possibly Miss Graves, showed me how to write r and final t in the Palmer style, together with a set of block capitals. The r was easily confused with v or some other carelessly written letter, and I eventually returned to Spencerian, though I kept the block capitals.

The school was being prodded to do something by way of manual training, and so in fifth grade we brought cigar boxes or other light wood to school and worked with scroll saws, staying after school and littering the floor near Miss Coyle's desk. There was no supervision, and I had much better supplies and equipment at home.

No one taught singing beyond the second grade, though we all sang in weekly assemblies, and there was no orchestra or band. Miss Graves did her best to find a little time for drawing and watercolors. A few students made personal appearances before the assembly, and the high-school students put on a play once a year, but the rest of my schooling was strictly curricular.

THERE WAS NEVER ANY DOUBT that Susquehanna was a railroad town. Its life was paced by the Shop whistle as the life of a religious community is paced by a bell. Stores opened and closed and meals were prepared and put on the table when the appropriate whistles blew. An early-morning blast warned the populace that the day was about to begin, and a second blast half an hour later got it fully under way. If you were near the Shops, you heard them grind into action. A single shaft running the length of the building was driven by a steam engine, and leather belts from wooden pulleys, slapping loosely and often smelling of ozone, drove lathes, saws, planers, and milling machines. When the whistle blew at noon the clatter ceased for an hour, and other blasts marked the beginning and end of the afternoon's work.

The whistle was also used as a fire alarm, sounding a two-digit number which identified the part of the town in which a fire had broken out. A card giving locations and coded numbers was posted in every home, usually near the telephone, and we all knew the most important numbers by heart and would listen and count when the whistle began to blow.

A Master Mechanic was assigned to the town as a bishop to a diocese, and his arrival and departure were appropriately honored. He lived in one of the better houses on Grand Street, owned by the Railroad. The children of the incumbent in my day were city-bred and more sophisticated than the rest of us.

Everyone knew the numbers of the passenger trains. A remark like "I came back last night on twenty-six" needed no further explanation. When the *Transcript* reported that "the happy couple, showered with rice and ancient shoes, departed on train seven for points in the West," everyone knew exactly when they left. My mother's salutatory address was called "The Block System"; she used the way in which signals were operated as a metaphor for life in general.

At grade crossings, like everyone else, we followed instructions painted on a great X and stopped, looked, and listened. In the distance we might hear an engine blowing its grade-crossing signal—a slow hoo-hoo-too-hoo—and at the crossing itself bells would start to ring and if there were gates, they would start to fall. Then the train would come in sight, its cowcatcher plowing through imaginary animals and debris, its cylinders leaking steam, its pistons and driving shafts oscillating, its smokestack breathing in short, asthmatic puffs, its engineer in goggles and a visored cap leaning out and looking clear of the side of his engine, the fireman shoveling coal into a glowing firebox of which we might catch a glimpse, and then a long string of cars, a hundred or more if they were empty freight cars, bearing names from all over the country—Baltimore and Ohio; Chicago and Rock Island; Missouri, Pacific; Milwaukee, St. Paul; Atchison, Topeka, and Santa Fe—and at long last the little red caboose, with the chimney of its own stove and a rear platform from which a brakeman might wave at us.

We who lived in a railroad town knew more about trains than that. We were familiar with the towers in the "yards" and the great levers that operated the switches that shifted trains from one track to another. We knew all the signals that blocked or cleared the tracks. We watched the water tower filling the tanks of engines, and we heard about a scheme on the New York Central in which water was scooped up from a mile-long trough as the train sped along without stopping. We knew the sound of the domino shock wave that ran the length of a train of a hundred empties when the engine started to pull or push, and we dreamed of riding on the handcars pumped by the track crews, which had to be lifted off the track quickly when a train was heard or spotted in the distance. We never hopped freights because we had been told about boys whose legs were cut off when they slipped and fell, but we put coins on the rails and crouched nearby to watch the wheels flatten them.

We saw the tramps and hoboes who dropped off the trains when they slowed down on entering the yards, harmless, dirty, poorly dressed, middle-aged men who called at kitchen doors for a handout and were said to leave a secret mark on fence or gate to indicate a sympathetic housewife. They congregated in a glen west of Susquehanna and they heated beans or soup in tin cans just as they were pictured as doing in the funny papers.

Susquehanna had its great day as a railroad town when the **Matt Shay** arrived. It was the most powerful steam locomotive ever built. There were three of them and we called them all Matt Shays although only the first—#5014—was so named in honor of the oldest living Erie engineer. They were over a hundred feet long, weighed nearly a million pounds, and carried sixteen tons of coal and more than eleven thousand gallons of water. Three cylinders on each side drove sets of four great wheels. The boiler was never able to make enough steam to fill all those cylinders at high speeds, but the engine had the power needed to push a train of any length up that grade to Gulf Summit.

THE UPWELLING OF LOCAL TALENT in the '90s had subsided by my day, though I once heard the daughter of our washerwoman (my mother "had hysterics" when she heard that she was said to be known in New York as "Sunshine" Barnes) recite a number of dramatic poems in a performance at the Methodist church. But movies were coming in, and every Saturday afternoon in my grade-school and early high-school years I went to the Hogan Opera House. It was a barn-like structure below the Main Street level reached by going down some stairs next to a saloon and walking along a dark alley. I paid ten cents to the cashier, the wife of the projectionist, and took my customary seat on the left side about five rows back. I was almost always early, and I read and reread the advertisements for local stores painted around the proscenium arch, while eating shredded coconut or a chocolate bar.

Eventually Miss Dooley came down the aisle and took her place at the piano, and she would join us in looking toward the balcony in the rear where the projectionist was busy with his reels. (He operated the machine by turning a crank, and it was said that at the second evening show he often ran it fast in order to get home to his wife.) At a signal from the projectionist Miss Dooley would start playing, the lights would go down, and the show would begin.

A program was composed of several movies, each of them one

or two reels in length. One was always a cliff-hanger. Pearl White was, of course, left in mortal peril at the end of each week's episode, and in another serial called *The Clutching Hand* the hero was once left enclosed in a metal cylinder, diving and twisting about to avoid being run through by steel knives which were being thrust through holes. Later there was a more sophisticated story called *The Trial of Mary Page,* in which the retina of a murdered man was developed like a photographic plate to reveal the person at whom he was looking when he died. There were comedies, of course, and I remember a very funny three-reeler called *Goodness Gracious.*

When I went on Saturday evening, I saw Mr. McManus, the Irish tenor, who edged out in front of the screen smiling brightly as Miss Dooley "vamped till ready," his gold teeth flashing in the spotlight. He sang popular songs with a touch of innuendo. Something special was happening in the shade of the old apple tree or down by the old mill stream, but I was never quite sure what it was.

Once a year we saw the movies of Lyman H. Howe—the Cinerama of the day. A sound-effects crew back of the screen imitated marching feet, the clatter of wheels on rails, the roar of the wind, thunder, bird calls, and the like. Once I saw and heard an early "talkie." A wire belt ran from the projector on the balcony over our heads and through two small holes in the screen to a phonograph behind it. A demonstrator dropped a plate, and we heard it strike the floor, and we heard a man play the cornet and a soprano sing.

We went to Binghamton in 1916 to see *The Birth of a Nation* with an orchestra that played "The Ride of the Valkyries" when the Ku Klux Klan galloped across the screen. We took my grandmother and grandfather Burrhus because he had been in the Civil War, and he was disgusted—not at the treatment of the blacks, which was not then an issue, but because the Confederate soldiers were always well dressed and smart while the Union soldiers were bedraggled and slovenly.

For many years a stock company made an annual visit to Susquehanna and put on a different play each night for a week. The leading characters stayed at the house of a friend of mine whose mother was stagestruck. I never saw more than one or two plays each year, and I remember only some kind of drawing-room comedy, but a second

74

company turned up one year with more dramatic material. In one play the heroine was tied to a log and was on the point of being split down the middle by a very real buzz saw when the hero arrived and opened the switch.

Another company staged *Uncle Tom's Cabin*. Eliza, the escaping slave, crossed a river, represented by three or four watery and icy cutouts pulled back and forth from the wings, by leaping from soapbox to soapbox between them, with bloodhounds baying but never appearing on stage. In a scene near the end little Eva was glimpsed safely in heaven. In a minstrel show everyone but the interlocutor was in black face, and the two end men played their standard roles.

Chautauqua was a vast improvement on all this. It was an experiment in public education, eventually superseded by radio and then by television but influential in its day. It began as a summer institute at Lake Chautauqua in New York State, but in the traveling version week-long meetings were held in selected towns throughout the East. It was necessary for a local group to guarantee the sale of 700 season tickets at two dollars each, and my father was one of the guarantors. He was also president of the local committee and at the first meeting always introduced the man or woman who would serve all week as a director or master of ceremonies.

The chief logistical problem was the speedy transportation of equipment, crew, staff, and talent, and Susquehanna could have a Chautauqua because it was on a railroad. The crew arrived on a Sunday and put up the tent on a vacant lot at the corner of Broad and Grand streets, only a block from our house. Performances were held every afternoon and evening, and there were children's meetings in the morning at which we sang a song confirming our allegiance:

> Chautauqua, Chautauqua, the name we love,
> The season that's best of the year.
> For its joys, girls and boys,
> Ga-ther here.

At one meeting we were asked to promise to clean our teeth twice each day, and I refused. When the director asked why, I said, "Because I might forget." (I had had too much trouble with Divine Sanctions.) "If you forget, you will be forgiven," he said, as if he were sure of it, and I reluctantly promised. "I respect you for that," he added, to my embarrassment.

Musical programs reported in the *Transcript* included the "Soirée Singers," a Florentine band with a soprano, a tenor who, I remember, sang "Oh, no, John, no, John, no," the Brooklyn Boys Choir with a famous boy soprano, a pianist, and the Tyrolean Alp Yodelers, who also rang bells. Each year there was a light opera. I remember *The Chimes of Normandy, The Bohemian Girl, Pinafore,* and *The Mikado.*

There was a chalk talk, and I remember one picture of a gloomy forest with a river and a house all very dead and lifeless until, with a single vertical stroke of a block of yellow chalk, the artist put lights in the window and reflections in the river, and was roundly applauded.

There were lectures: one on the north woods by a descendant of Daniel Boone, one on the conquest of the Arctic at which Whiskers, a dog hero, made a personal appearance, one on "Life in the Trenches" by Captain Vicker, "who has in his head a German bullet and a strong lecture," and one by Judge Kavanaugh, introduced by my father.

I remember best of all a lecture on science. In one demonstration two large nails were put together in a crucible and some powdered material was added, thermite perhaps, together with something that could be ignited by a few drops of water. The lecturer carefully wiped a piece of ice and held it above the crucible until a drop fell and the powder flared. He put on dark glasses, peered inside, and reported that, yes, the two nails were fused, as we should see a little later when they had cooled. He also demonstrated sympathetic resonance with two large tuning forks, one of which was connected with a tower of light wooden boxes. When he struck the other fork on the other side of the stage, the boxes tumbled down. He also had a powerful gyroscope, riding on wheels on a tight-wire, and when a weight was added to the end of a long arm, the arm *rose.*

There was a magician, and in one of his tricks he used two parallel rods about a yard long as a channel in which three balls rolled. He held the channel out at arm's length, the balls at rest near his hand, and then, as he turned slowly around, he commanded the balls to roll out one by one and to return one by one, and they obeyed. I saw that it was done by using balls of different weights and altering the speed of revolution or inclination of the channel, and I made a similar gadget the next day and reproduced the trick. My father was impressed and checked it out with Mott Jones.

FAIRS OR PICNICS were staged for various benefits. One began with a parade in which Jack Palmer as marshal rode one of the more spirited horses from his livery stable. It ended at the Hogan Opera House, where the seats had been removed and booths installed. The most popular booth was called the Wheel of Fortune—the only legitimate gambling enterprise in town.

Bigger fairs were held on Beebe's Flats and the most exciting thing for me was the merry-go-round. It belonged to Billy Main and was stored disassembled in a wing of the blacksmith shop behind our house. On the day before a fair the parts were carted over to the Flats and bolted together. A round platform supported by a number of wheels turned in a circular track, and each wheel drove a crankshaft that rocked a colorful wooden horse above it. The edge of the platform was grooved like a giant pulley, and a steel cable went around it and passed over the capstan of a wood-burning steam engine which had two great brass balls spinning on its governor—a magnified version of my toy engine. A barrel organ was operated by the movement of the platform.

We bought as many tickets as we could afford and took the most attractive horses we could find. As the platform began to turn, the horses came to life, the barrel organ came slowly up to tempo, and a man came around collecting tickets. There was a device alongside which held metal rings, one of which could be pulled free with a crooked finger as one passed, and an occasional ring was made of brass and was worth a free ride, but it was easy to fall off a horse while reaching for a ring and I was forbidden to try. If the engineer was busy stoking the fire or talking to a friend, we had a long ride, but sometimes it seemed terribly short. We could feel the horse begin to slow its stride, and the barrel organ would go into a slow rallentando. If we had another ticket, we would scramble for a better horse and stay aboard.

At a Labor Day picnic for the benefit of the hospital, a balloon ascension and parachute drop were announced, and I was one of several boys who were asked to help. The balloon was made of dirty gray cloth, and it was filled with hot air and smoke from an oil burner. We held on to ropes fastened to the side to steady it and keep it over the fire. Attached to the bottom and stretched out on the ground at one side was the parachute, like a great folded umbrella, its ropes extending still farther to a trapeze bar lying on the ground.

The balloonist was dressed in the tights of an aerial artist, and he seemed nervous as he helped his partner fill the balloon, for it was not lifting well and it was getting late in the day. Eventually he took his place on the bar, holding it under him like a seat, and we were told to let go. The balloon went up, and the balloonist, shaking the ropes and parachute clear of the ground, ran forward and put his weight on the bar and went up too. But not very fast. The wind began to carry the balloon toward a hill. It was not gaining much altitude, and the partner on the ground saw the danger to the guaranteed fee and yelled, "Jump!" and we all took up the cry. The balloonist was evidently supposed to do some acrobatics before jumping, but he merely waved his hand in the standard gesture of an artist who has just finished a difficult feat and pulled a rope which cut the parachute loose. He dropped, the parachute opened, none too soon, and he hit the ground. The balloon turned over, black smoke pouring out of its neck, and shriveled and fell on the top of the hill.

We had a balloon ascension of our own every Fourth of July. During the day we did the usual things—slung torpedoes against the sidewalk, ground sons-o'-guns under our heels, ignited small white snakes, lighted strings of tiny firecrackers in the Chinese manner with our sticks of punk, held somewhat larger firecrackers tightly by the bases at arm's length until they exploded, and blew tin cans into the air with three-inch salutes. In the evening we had sparklers, of course, with the wire stems bent so that we could whirl them in circles, Roman candles that lofted half a dozen glowing balls in a succession of soft plosions, small skyrockets launched from a wooden trough, and at last the fire balloon—made of tissue paper in red and white sections with a small alcohol lamp at the base—held until it was buoyant with hot air and then released. My father always launched it from the top of a stepladder, as if to give it a slight head start. It went up gracefully and glowed in the distant sky until the alcohol burned out, an incendiary threat throughout its voyage.

Small circuses came to Susquehanna and set up their tents on Beebe's Flats, and special trains bearing flamboyant labels stood on a siding while they were in town. Once my parents took us to Binghamton to Barnum and Bailey's, the main feature of which was a small automobile that ran down a steep track, flipped over in a loop-the-loop, and landed on a ramp at the bottom, its passenger unhurt.

A day or two before the thirtieth of May, when three or four veterans of the Grand Army of the Republic, seedy and unkempt, would come to school to tell us about their wartime experiences, we sang Civil War songs. There were many of these in the little green books supplied to the school by the Cable Piano Company (with an advertisement for the pianos on the back cover)—"Marching Through Georgia," "Just Before the Battle, Mother," "Tenting on the Old Camp Ground," and "There Will Be One Vacant Chair"—but we also sang from a hard-cover songbook with less commonplace selections. There was a particularly moving song about the brave men who lay sleeping—"under the laurel the blue, under the willow the gray."

Our most famous veteran, the highest-ranking officer in the area, was Colonel Telford, who lived on Broad Street just back of the school building. He had once run a furniture store but was now bedridden, and a few students would go to his house, stand on the front lawn, and serenade him. Once he was wheeled out onto a small balcony over the porch to acknowledge our salute.

The cemeteries were decorated on Memorial Day and since we lived next to one, we saw a great deal of that. Flags were put in the little metal standards bearing the letters GAR at the bases of the graves of veterans, and fresh flowers were put in glass jars on the graves.

MY FATHER BEGAN TO FEEL the lack of a summer cottage. C. Fred Wright, by all odds the most prestigious member of the community, had one, of course—the biggest and best. It was on the site of the old Forest House Hotel, which had burned—a mound-like hill once an island in an earlier course of the river and now covered with pines.

The large, attractive house at the top was called Pinecrest. Clarence Wright, a nephew, had a cottage nearby, and there was a row of houses in Columbian Grove, one of which, owned by E. R. W. Searle, was said to be the site of poker parties and a good deal of drinking. Elsewhere along the river there were small, rather ancient cottages bearing proper names, such as Dun Rovin, Dew Drop Inn, or Linger Longer. A few former residents of Susquehanna brought their families back to spend the summer in newly built cottages.

My father dealt with the problem in an unfortunate way: he bought a newfangled portable canvas house and set it up three miles from town in a pasture near the river. My grandfather Skinner helped him bolt panels together to form a floor and set up a prefabricated frame of two-by-two's which was covered with a dark brown creosoted canvas. The interior was divided by canvas walls into four very small square rooms, two at each end (one used as a kitchen, the other three as bedrooms), and a central living space containing camp chairs, a round table, and a small phonograph. Our Ford could not be left outdoors overnight in bad weather without putting on the side curtains, and so a small portable garage of the same brown canvas was also set up.

Housekeeping was difficult. My mother cooked on an oil stove, and water was brought from a farmer's well. There was no plumbing; we used a chemical toilet and buried its contents along with garbage a little distance from the house. When the *Transcript* reported that Attorney Skinner's cottage was attracting a good deal of attention, it was not exaggerating. Anyone who could claim any acquaintance with us managed to find an excuse to come and look us over and often stayed for a meal, in spite of the awkward kitchen facilities.

Thunderstorms were a more serious problem. We saw lightning strike on the opposite side of the narrow valley, and we could spot trees that had been hit. We were probably not in any great danger because two great shagbark hickory trees within a few yards of our cottage must have served as lightning rods, but the storms were nonetheless terrifying. A flash could be seen through the canvas, revealing the very ribs of the house, and there was nothing to deaden the thunder. The curved wall of the valley on the other side of the river focused the sound on us like a parabolic reflector. During a storm my mother would sit biting her lips, struggling not to show fear for the sake of my brother and me, and my father would try to reduce the tension by playing the Victrola. We often played a piece called "Glow Worm," but I doubt whether we ever noticed the irony of the singer's appeal to "shine, little glow worm, glimmer, glimmer."

One storm was a "cloudburst," and the river rose to the floor of our cottage. Albert Hillborn, the son of the man who owned the land, put on hip boots and waded to our door to make sure that we were all right. No one knew how near we were to floating off in a modern version of Noah's Ark. The next morning the river was back in its channel and there was only one casualty. Our cat, frightened by the lightning, had gone under the house and had been trapped as the water rose. We missed him for a week before we began to detect his fate and had to probe for his body under the floor.

John Hillborn, who owned the land, was a descendant of one of the first families in the Harmony region, from whom the Erie Railroad bought part of its right-of-way. He was pious, punctiliously dressed, rather crotchety and litigious. When the railroad broadened its roadbed and in doing so built up the bank on the other side of the river, Hillborn went to court, claiming that the channel would be changed and his land eroded. It was said that he had been offered $100 for a single tree—a bird's-eye maple—in the woods back of his farm and that he had loftily refused. Albert, his son, who kept house for him and ran the dairy farm, wore work clothes, was overweight, and wheezed softly as he moved about. His brothers had gone to Kansas, to "real farms," and he envied them. He was a lonely man and grew fond of my brother and me. We watched him as he sat on a little three-legged stool milking his cows. He would wipe the udders clean with a wet cloth and rapidly fill a pail with foamy milk as he worked his two hands in alternation, once in a while directing a stream at our bare feet. Later we watched him pour milk into the great steel bowl of a separator, and as he turned a crank, a trickle of cream came out one spigot and skim milk poured from another to be taken to the pigs. Sometimes we watched him operate a churn and salt and pack the butter in earthenware crocks. He gave us some of the buttermilk to drink before it, too, went to the pigs.

We worked the grindstone in his yard, sitting on the small metal seat and pedaling it like a bicycle, and we followed him into his ice-house, thrusting our bare feet down through the wet brown sawdust until we struck ice. The piles of sawdust near lumber mills were also wet below the surface, but they were hot—sometimes scalding hot—from the "slow, smokeless burning of decay."

My brother and I fished near our cottage with bamboo poles, baiting our hooks with nightwalkers and angleworms, and watching the bobbers on our lines. When a bobber sent out little waves, we knew we had a nibble, and when it dipped smartly we had a bite and pulled quickly. We ate the sunfish and perch we caught, but the sucker, a bottom fish with an ugly mouth, we believed to be a scavenger and never ate. Once in a while we caught an eel, three or four feet long, and we killed it with a baseball bat and skinned and cut it up into sections, but even in the frying pan the sections wove back and forth with what we thought was a trace of life.

My father fished for pickerel and bass, and his favorite spot was the Big Rock across from our cottage. It was a huge boulder which was said to have rolled down the side of the mountain in the memory of people still alive, leaving a trail of broken trees before plopping into the river. It was a natural dock, and around it grew a great deal of what we called eel grass. It was a favorite haunt of long, sleek pickerel. For bait my father caught minnows with a net in the shallow water near our cottage. He would put a hook through the back of a live minnow (I never watched him) and throw the struggling creature overboard. The minnow sometimes took revenge by weaving in and out among the eel grass so that the line could not be pulled in without breaking it, but once in a while a pickerel would take the bait and my father would make his catch.

Our boat was especially designed to take account of the fact that my father could not swim. Swimming was one of those things he had never had a chance to learn in his restricted childhood, and he tried hard to catch up. He would take off his glasses, two crimson patches glowing on the bridge of his nose, and wade out into the river up to his waist. He would stoop and take a few strokes and come up coughing. He even submitted to using our waterwings. But it was no use. Fortunately, my mother did not swim either and had no interest in learning.

The carpenter who built our boat had given it a very broad flat bottom, but as it turned out safety was not even then assured. One evening my father was rowing my brother and me back from the Big Rock when a motorboat bore down upon us, driven by three or four men who had been at a drinking party in a glen upstream. My father stood up and waved frantically to catch their attention, and they saw us just in time and swerved to one side. We clung to the sides of the boat and held on as we rocked with the waves.

A second year of this was enough, and a slightly used portable summer cottage with garage came on the market. I daresay it was sold at a loss (it was never seen in the area again), but the whole enterprise was a good investment, for it led my parents to think twice about a summer place, and no other effort was ever made to find one.

MY FRIENDS AND I enjoyed a peaceful co-existence. We were not physically aggressive toward each other, or toward more distant acquaintances. We had wrestling matches which sometimes led to a bit of meanness, but I do not remember ever striking anyone or being struck. It was unthinkable that Raphael Miller or Bob Perrine and I should ever come to blows.

Our culture permitted certain conventional forms of aggression, however. The archetypal pattern of an April Fool joke was the pocketbook or wallet placed on the street and pulled away by a concealed string when someone reached for it, but I never saw it done. Putting salt in the sugar bowl was a household version, and I came down before breakfast one morning to try it on my father, but my mother was not going to have cream wasted in salty coffee and archly told my father that he could not have much cream in his first cup. He pretended not to draw any conclusion, but I knew that I was the one being fooled.

Our evil spirit was more active on Halloween. We were not familiar with the convention of "trick or treat." We simply played tricks, and there was no way to buy us off. We moved porch furniture from one house to another, or hoisted a chair or two into a tree with a length of clothesline someone was thoughtless enough to leave outdoors. We jammed toothpicks into doorbells so that they rang continuously, and ran away before anyone could reach the door. We also used a spool nailed loosely to the end of a stick, with a string wound around it. The outer flange had been notched, and when we held it against a windowpane and pulled the string, the windowpane vibrated raucously. We also tied tin cans in groups of three or four and concealed them on opposite sides of the sidewalk with a string running between them high enough to catch the ankle of an unsuspecting pedestrian.

I REMEMBER THE WINTERS in Susquehanna as long and cold, with shoulder-deep snow continuously on the ground. We wore knitted caps and gloves and heavy belted coats called mackinaws, with leggings rather like those of the soldiers in the World War. They were laced, and ice would form on the lacings and under the instep band which held the legging to the shoe.

The unpolluted river froze to a safe depth and was excellent for skating when free of snow, but a small pond south of the town was safer and more often clear. Ice skates, like roller skates, were clamped to our shoes and tightened with a key. My first skates had double runners, each skate consisting of two miniature bobsleds, and I never learned to skate well on single runners. We had skis but with nothing more than a single leather strap over the toe as a binding, and great knobs of snow and ice would build up under our heels so that the skis twisted to the side. There were plenty of hills to ski down as long as we were willing to climb back up, using the prescribed but taxing herringbone pattern, and we were more inclined to ski across country.

In a town built on hills the major winter sport was coasting, and we all had sleds. There were still many heavy wooden bobsleds about, with steel runners, many of them no doubt made on company time in the Erie Shops, but younger people had Flexible Flyers, on which you could sit up and steer with your feet, or ride "belly-floppers" and use your hands. On a bobsled you leaned forward on both hands, sitting on one hip, trailing a leg like a rudder.

The street in front of our house had a long, steady grade and was particularly favored by coasters. The standard call for road clearance was "Yi-yi," and when the coasting was good we heard it all day long. Just in front of our house was a "thank-you-ma'am"—a small depression across the road intended to divert rainwater into the ditches—and in going over it a Flexible Flyer or bobsled would lift and sometimes leave the ground and land with a thud.

The most sophisticated coasting was done in the evening by young employees of the Shops and their girl friends. They used a great sled called the Dutchman, composed of two long planks separated by vertical blocks of wood, the top plank well padded. A bobsled was fixed at the back, and another in front could be steered with a wheel borrowed from a freight car. A large bell, also probably borrowed from the Railroad, was fastened under the seat and was operated by pulling a rope. As many as ten or twelve people could sit astride the Dutchman, and lying in bed my brother and I would hear them talking and laughing as they pulled it up the hill. At the top it was turned around and mounted, someone gave it a long push and hopped aboard, and we heard it coming down, the bell ringing and the riders yelling "Yi!" It would go over the thank-you-ma'am with a great clatter and screams of terror and delight.

My grandmother Skinner once rented a horse-drawn cutter from Jack Palmer for an hour or two and took us for a ride. We sat under lap robes smelling of the stable, and we smelled the horse itself. Bells on the harness jangled, hooves clopped on packed snow, and a whip jiggled sinuously in its socket. The hooves of the horse threw snow dust in our faces, and we breathed it in and allowed it to melt on our lips and eyebrows. The smooth glide of runners over snow was very different from the crunching, slipping, and jolting of wheels, and the sleigh was so light and so tightly linked to the horse that we felt each forward thrust.

We made "angels" by falling against snowbanks and leaving multiple imprints of our outstretched arms, and quite elaborate snowmen. We built igloos, either by hollowing out great piles of snow or using bricks made by packing snow into a bread tin as a mold. We also made forts: ringed walls in which snowballs were stacked in piles like the cannon-balls near the Civil War guns on village greens—though there was no land flat enough for a village green in Susquehanna.

In the spring the ice melted first in the shallow water near the banks of the river, and the great sheets in the middle, still quite thick, began to move downstream. Word would run through the town—"The ice is out!"—and we went to watch it come over the Lanesboro dam, huge sheets reaching out many feet before breaking off and falling into the water below with great splashes, or we stood on the bridge and watched the sheets strike the stone supports, which were shaped like the prows of ships pointing upstream, to turn the blocks aside or split them in two.

WHEN I WAS NINE, someone organized the Junior Boy Scouts in Susquehanna and I joined. I got a khaki coat and knee-length britches, with cloth leggings, and a red scarf to be tied around the neck. My hat had a flat brim and a crown dented in four places, like the hats of soldiers. It was all vaguely military, and when the war broke out in Europe, the military aspects were not overlooked. We drilled with long staffs, we had a special salute, and we recited an oath. We marched in numerous parades. (Once while crossing the bridge from Oakland to Susquehanna in formation with the Erie Band, we all began to stagger; we had forgotten to break step, and our right-left rhythm had set the heavy iron structure in oscillation.) Eventually, as America became involved in the war, we began to participate in Red Cross and Liberty Loan campaigns.

The ostensible function of Scouting was much more peaceful: we were to prepare ourselves for an attack on the wilderness. We carried big jackknives containing corkscrews, bottle openers, and curved blades with which we could ream holes in leather. We carried hatchets in special holsters fastened to our belts, and, observing a standard set forth in the Boy Scout Handbook, we kept them sharp enough to put a point on a pencil. We were also supposed to do one good turn each day—or presumably oftener if the occasion arose; that was "service," a red-letter word in our house.

I passed the Third Class or tenderfoot examination and joined the Beaver Patrol, but I was unable to earn any merit badges and never moved up to First Class. I once tried to get a merit badge for campfire cooking. I took some bread dough along on a hike, and I put it on a stick and held it over a fire, turning it until it developed a brown crust, but the inside was still doughy, and I failed the test.

We had trouble finding Scoutmasters, and no one held the job for much more than a year. Usually the summer camp was his undoing. When the Reverend Mr. Hinks, rector of the Episcopal church, who boarded at Gran'ma Graham's, was Scoutmaster, we camped beside the river below Great Bend. After we had been there a day or two, it rained, and the river rose during the night. We prepared for evacuation, but the rain stopped and the water receded, and we discovered that the only damage was the loss of some supplies which had been cached in a grove and had washed away. Several large beefsteaks were found still in place, however, and when Mr. Hinks smelled them to see if they were still good, he vomited.

Mr. Hinks once took us on an early spring walk in the woods to gather flowers to be put in the cemeteries on Memorial Day. We despoiled the countryside and returned with huge masses of mountain laurel, dogwood, honeysuckle, columbine, and small, quickly wilting bouquets of trilliums, jacks-in-the-pulpit, and arbutus. A photograph showing us with our loot, taken in Delly Harding's studio, was published in the *Transcript*.

My mother saved some of the letters my brother and I wrote from camp, and they show reasonably well what the Boy Scout movement meant to me. I was eleven when the first one was written and my brother two and a half years younger. My father and mother were taking advantage of our absence to spend some time in Atlantic City:

Boy Scout Camp   East Lake RFD New Milford, Pa

July something

Dear Mother and Papa,

We are certainly having some time—great eats 'n everything. Just finished a supper of hash, crackers and cheese, bread and butter and peaches—some feed!

Everything runs like clockwork. This afternoon we had water races and tomorrow a quoit tournament. Thursday we have a game of "lost battalion" and Friday we are going to give a show and invite the people around the lake. Not an idle moment.

We have sentry duty and Ebbe is on to-night. He's getting along fine. All I've done so far is K.P. (kitchen police).

Armstrong is strict and this morning we nearly stryped naked out in the dew and had calisthenics. Then later he inspected us and our tents. It's great and nobody kicks.

There is so much going on outside I'll have to close, wishing you are having as good a time as we. Us at $8 per wk. and you, 10 bucks per day.

Lovingly,
Fred

My brother reported the beginning of another fairly successful week three years later:

July 15 1918 Susquehanna, Pa

Dear Mother,

We arrived here safely about nine. When we got here we put up the tents and then built and fireplace. Then we went in swimming. While we were there James Smith was drowned but was safed by George Larson and John Springsteen done the artifical respiration on and he is now living. My address is Boy Scout Camp, RFD No 2, Thomposon, Pa. I will write you again.

With love,
Ebbe

Don't forget to write and tell me the news. xxxxxxxxxxxx *etc*

Trouble was brewing, however:

Boy Scout Camp RFD No. 2 Tomposon, Pa.

Dear Papa,

How are you? I am awfully sunburned and do not feel good. Are you going away anyplace? This is a nice place to camp. I wish you would come up and see me and Fred. It is awful hot here. I am in the largest tent, No. 1. . . . I've been fishing 3 times and have not caught much. The kids made so much noise I could sleep good last night, but John Springsteen says that they won't make so much noise to-night so I think I can sleep. It is nearly dinner time so I will have to close. Give my love to mothers. Don't forget to write soon and come up to see me.

With love,
Ebbe

Tell Mother I will write her again. WRITE SOON

I added further details:

July 9, 3 o/clock
Dear Mother,
We aren't having a very good time after all. All day today the wind has blown very hard and one of the tents fell in. The eats are not appetizing and I can't eat. If I don't get something good pretty soon I'll starve. All I have had to eat in five meals is one dish of cereal, two small potatoes and six crackers. My stomach is all out of order and yesterday I vomited twice and last night we had a circus. I woke up in the night and heard Raphael Miller vomiting outside the tent. That started Bob Perrine's and he had to throw up suddenly. He could not reach the door in time so he vomited all over me, in my eyes, and mouth. Then I started in again.

Ebbe has a canker sore and if things don't improve I think I'll come home.

Don't tell anybody about this for I don't want them to think I am always raising a fuss.

They haven't given us a full meal since we've been here. Today they had half boiled potatoes, weak coffee and bread. I didn't eat any dinner or breakfast so I feel pretty weak.

If I had a good excuse I'd come home but I don't want them to think I'm homesick or anything like that.

I've only had about eight hours sleep in the last too nights.
Lovingly,
B. F. Skinner

MY MOTHER OCCASIONALLY PLAYED and sang for her own pleasure or rehearsed for an exceptional recital and, of course, I heard her. Like our lullabies, her songs were sentimental and often rather morbid. Bartlett's "A Dream" ended:

> I dream'd thou wert living, my darling, my darling,
> I dream'd that I held thee once more to my breast,
> While thy soft perfumed tresses and gentle caresses
> Thrilled me and stilled me and lulled me to rest.

Another of her favorites, "The Mission of a Rose," was the story of a rosebud that longed to brighten the day of a sick child, but, alas, when "the bud was a rose at the dawn of day . . . the soul of the child had passed away." Eugene Field's Little Boy Blue puts his toy dog and soldier away for the night, saying, "Now, don't you go till I come." He dies in his sleep, but his "little toy friends" are true!

> Ay, faithful to Little Boy Blue they stand,
>   Each in the same old place,
> Awaiting the touch of a little hand,
>   The smile of a little face.

Fortunately, life seemed to grow brighter as the years passed, and I heard things like Carrie Jacobs Bond's "A Perfect Day" or even "The Sunshine of Your Smile."

The phonograph brought a different kind of music into our life. A neighbor had an early wax-cylinder model with one or two pieces I liked—one of them from *William Tell*. Our Victrola brought waltzes —"Millicent," "Hesitation," and "The Missouri Waltz"—and songs, one of them, "Mississippi," sung with a coy lisp:

> It yutht to be tho hard to thpell
> It yutht to make me cwy
> M, I, eth—eth, I, eth—eth, I, P, P, I.

Later we went classical. My father was fascinated by coloratura sopranos, and we had Galli-Curci's records of the Mad Scene from *Lucia di Lammermoor* and the Bell Song from *Lakmé*. The Victrola was faithful to flutes and sopranos imitating flutes, but the great musical thrill of my life was our Red Seal record of Nellie Melba singing Tosti's "Goodbye." I must have listened to it a hundred times. Possibly no greater nonsense has ever been set to music:

> Falling leaf and fading tree
> Lines of white in a sullen sea,
> Shadows rising on you and me,
>
> The swallows are making them ready to fly,
> Wheeling out on a windy sky—
> Goodbye, sum*mer*, goodbye, goodbye,
> Goodbye, sum*mer*, goodbye.

90

What are we waiting for? Oh! My heart!
Kiss me straight on the brows! And part!
Again, again! My heart! My heart!
What are we waiting for, you and I?
A pleading look—a stifled cry—
Goodbye, for ever, goodbye, for ever,
Goodbye, goodbye, goodbye.

Single phrases taken out of that puzzling context were exciting dramatic material, and Melba made them spine-tingling. The great wooden horn into which she sang mercifully softened the *s* on *brows* and discouraged inquiry into how trees fade or what it was that the swallows were preparing for flight. I once took the record to school, where it was played for morning assembly. The principal explained how lucky we all were to be able to hear a great soprano and incidentally mentioned that the record cost three dollars.

For a year or two I studied the piano with Harmey Warner, in whose orchestra my father had played cornet. He was now an old man who sucked Sen Sens and jabbed me in the ribs with a pencil to call my attention to mistakes. I learned the names of the notes on the scale by spelling words—writing "cabbage," for example, as a melody. I practiced monotonously on a piece called "Morning Prayer," said to have been composed by Streabbog but actually, Professor Warner told me, by a man named Gobbaerts, who, for good reason, concealed his identity by spelling his name backward. My father did not think much of professional musicians and was glad to let me give up my piano instruction after about a year lest I be tempted in that direction.

RAPHAEL MILLER'S MOTHER had once painted, and presumably named her firstborn in honor of an artist. One or two of her paintings hung on the walls of their house—dark green and black forests with waterfalls rather too white. Mrs. Pritchard, the wife of the Presbyterian minister, painted china and held classes, and the living room of the manse was warmed in winter by a large kiln. A Japanese artist once came to school and painted pictures which we bought for a few cents each; brush strokes suggested blades of grass or broken reeds and a bit of color was blown on with an atomizer bulb. When my mother gave a party she sometimes ordered place cards from Miss Graves, who painted delicate little watercolors of violets, roses, and tulips.

I do not remember a single one of the pictures in my parents' or grandparents' homes. At school we bought Copley Prints in black and white or sepia, and books and magazines had an occasional illustration in color, but the color was never very good. We had, nevertheless, the materials needed to produce works of art—crayons and watercolors, pads of paper with all edges sealed, and raffia and colored yarns. The word Prang, the name of a company supplying these materials, meant Art. I tried unsuccessfully to work with *papier-mâché*, but I succeeded in making a small loom by driving nails along the edges of a square block of wood and wove mats of colored yarn and string.

I had my father's old drafting equipment. There was a thick slab of glass with a shallow depression in which I made India ink by rubbing a block of black material in a few drops of water, and I could draw perfect jet-black circles with large and small brass compasses adjustable for width of line. I had stencils, and I used a pantograph to enlarge illustrations from magazines or books. I liked to draw a holly leaf as two scalloped arcs meeting at the tips, and a landscape with a river tapering sinuously into the distance with a succession of overlapping hills along its banks suggesting depth. I must have drawn a hundred copies of the Dutch girl with wooden shoes who "chased dirt" in the advertisement for Old Dutch Cleanser. In high school my most impressive production was a watercolor copy of a full-page advertisement for Palmolive soap, showing Cleopatra on her barge. I worked over Cleopatra's face so many times that the paper became soft and a satisfactory version impossible.

I BEGAN TO WRITE STORIES and poems at an early age. I had a printing press which used standard type and printer's ink, but it was hard to set the type and only a very small text could be printed at any one time. An old typewriter of my father's was much closer to what was needed. It was kept in the sewing room, which contained, in addition to my mother's sewing machine and a large golden-oak secretary, the space for coats and overshoes which would normally have been found in an entrance hall. An oak settee with a large mirror and a seat in which rubbers and overshoes were stored served as my desk. The type-writer was an early model, and I could not see what I was typing until I turned up the platen, but I hunted for and pecked most of the right keys and typed fairly extensive things. I often tore paper along a line I had wetted with a camel-hair brush to produce a deckle edge, and I bound pages in small booklets.

The things I wrote were no more original than the pictures I copied with stencil or pantograph, but it would be harder to discover the controlling sources. Edgar Guest or Sam Walter Foss may have been responsible for a poem I published in a magazine issued by an organization called the Lone Scouts. You became a Lone Scout simply by subscribing to the magazine, and almost all the material it pub-lished was written by members. As the number in parentheses in-dicates, I was ten years old when I made this contribution.

THAT PESSIMISTIC FELLOW

By Lone Scout B. F. Skinner, 433 Grand St.,
Susquehanna, Pa. (10)

When you're getting ready for a hike
    And the weather's looking fine
And you've got your eat kit packed chock full
    With your fishing rod and line,
Who's the fellow that steps up and says,
    "It surely looks like rain"?
He's the pessimist and joy killer.
    I don't believe he's sane!

When you're planning for a camping trip,
    And you've packed your tent and duds
Who's the fellow that steps up and says
    "You'll surely die of bugs
And skeeters and snakes and everything
    That'll come around your camp"?
Don't you know him? He's the pessimist.
    That doggone, doggone scamp.

For a year or two my brother and I sold the *Saturday Evening Post* and the *Country Gentleman,* mostly to our relatives and neighbors, for a nickel a copy, and in addition to the *Literary Digest* we subscribed to *Good Housekeeping.* My mother occasionally brought a book home from the town library, and there were a few novels in our sectional bookcases, two by a Winston Churchill who was not the British statesman, and one called *The Trail of the Lonesome Pine,* which, my father complained, mentioned rhododendrons too often. Most of the space in the sectional bookcases was taken up by sets—*World's Great Literature, Masterpieces of World History, Shakespeare's Plays Illustrated,* and so on—purchased from aggressive book salesmen. I never saw my parents reading any of this, nor until my later high-school years did I find any of it of interest. I was once looking for something we could use in a small theatre we had set up in a neighbor's woodshed (admission: five pins) and I looked in vain at the *Divine Comedy.*

I enjoyed the funny papers—*Little Nemo, Buster Brown,* and the *Katzenjammer Kids.* In *Grownup Land* adults wore children's clothing and children adults', and the children ran the show, and I liked that best. We were given books like *Black Beauty,* which I never read, and Laura Richards's *Captain January,* which I kept for years before finally reading it and was then greatly moved by it. I liked *Robinson Crusoe* and particularly Jules Verne's *Mysterious Island* because of the theme of self-sufficiency. Jules Verne's characters cemented two watch crystals together with pitch, filled them with water, and used them as a burning glass to start a fire.

At one time I collected *little* books. I had a dictionary not much larger than a small matchbox. E. Haldeman-Julius was selling Little Blue Books for five cents each, and a few small books bound in limp imitation leather by Elbert Hubbard's Roycrofters were sold with miniature bookends. Though I did not care about most of the contents, I could hold several of these treasures in my hands—with a sense of possessing knowledge which, if not secret, was at least easily secreted. They were just the right thing for a small reading room which I made at that time of an old wooden packing case. The case was large enough so that by crossing my legs I could sit wholly inside it, and I turned it on one side and fitted a curtain across the open end.

I built small shelves to hold my little books within reach and a bracket for a candle. Both the isolation and the miniaturization appealed to me, but the almost fetal position was not consoling; on the contrary, it was uncomfortably cramped.

I spent many hours with a large puzzle book by Sam Lloyd, in which many solutions called for algebra and geometry, and odd bits of space were crammed with sophisticated conundrums. I read the sentimental continued stories appearing in the newsprint magazines to which Mr. and Mrs. B subscribed, and discussed each episode with them. Through them I also came to read things like James Oliver Curwood's *Kazan* and Gene Stratton Porter's *Girl of the Limberlost*.

Myrtle Reed's *Lavender and Old Lace* painted life in fresh colors. I knew what early spring was like, but I was not prepared to read that "tiny sprigs of green were everywhere eloquent with promise." I knew what early autumn was like, but not because "as lightly as a rose petal upon the shimmering surface of a stream, summer was drifting away, but whither, no one seemed to care." I thought I had been in love more than once, but love had not "made the air vocal with rapturous song or wrought white magic in my soul." Would some girl and I ever walk "by the silvered reaches of the River of Dreams" and unknowingly rise "to that height which makes sacrifice the soul's dearest offering as the chrysalis, bound and unbeautiful, gives the radiant creature within to the light and freedom of day"? The badinage between Miss Reed's lovers is a possible clue to some passages in a novel which I started to write when I was perhaps thirteen. It begins:

> The fire in the old log hut burned low. Outside the low moaning of the forest and the haunting screech of the owl gave the interior a still greater atmosphere of solitude and the nearness of—death.
>
> The monotonous crackling of the dying fire was interrupted by a raking cough from Pierre, lying on a low bed of hemlock, then followed by a comparatively deeper silence.
>
> "Joan," Pierre broke the silence.
>
> "Yes, Father."
>
> "Joan, tomorrow ye will go after supplies to Little River. Joan, Joan, art ye listening? [Almost all the "you's" in the first draft were crossed out and replaced with "ye's."] Ye know the way?" he asked for the sixth time that night.

"Yes, but I will not go till ye are better, Father."

"Oh, pshaw!" said Pierre, summoning all his strength. "It is nothing but a cold. Please get me a drink."

"Yes, Father, but I shall not go till ye are well," she said, leaving the room.

"Till I am well," mused the old man, "God knows that that will never be."

"Here, Father," announced Joan, holding a dipper of water. "Sit up."

"Ah, that is strengthening. That water will make you rich some-day, Joan," said Pierre.

"And you, too, Father."

"Yes, yes, and I, too. It is wonderful water, minerals and salt in it, with sulfur. Someday you must go to the cities and raise companies. They will come, dig wells, sell the water, and you will be rich."

Pierre dies after instructing Joan to burn the cabin and his body and to leave for the city to claim the property. But there is a heavy fall of snow and she struggles against the elements and falls exhausted. She is awakened by a fight between an Indian, Jim Cobolt, and a naturalist, John Newman. The Indian has recognized the girl and has decided to kidnap her and demand ransom from her father. He wins the fight, drives Newman away, locks Joan in his cabin, and leaves to look for Pierre, but Newman returns and frees the girl, and they set out together for town. They get lost and make a camp "under a windfall," and John watches while Joan sleeps the sleep of pure exhaustion.

As she slept John noticed the beauty of his companion. Born and raised in the forests she was slender, lithe in limb with dark hair and eyes. With her clear complexion these latter produced a contrast which was both startling and beau. Sleeping peaceably she made a pretty pic-ture. She had not as yet told her story nor he his. When she awoke he determined to question her.

"See here young lady," he started.

"Me thinks ye need not talk to me that way," she interrupted, smiling.

"I beg pardon," with a mock bow, "What I meant was that ye have never even introduced yourself and neither have I."

"Well?" she said teasingly.

"I am John Newman, naturalist. I agreed to spend the winter with Cobolt. On the way here we ran across thee and Jim was going to kidnap thee and we fought."

Joan then explains what she has done in burning the cabin and concludes:

"Ye know the rest."
"Happily I do."
"Why 'happily'?"
"Because I met ye."
Joan blushed.

John brings out some food.

"Ye are a wonder," she complimented.
"Oh, you flatter me," mocked John. "Now which will you have? Oyster cocktail, champain, or—"
Joan, laughing, smothered the rest with her hand over his mouth.

The books we were given for birthdays and Christmas, after the era of the Bobbsey Twins, were about boys who were invariably successful in their undertakings. One of them won a baseball game by making a difficult catch, falling head over heels but "holding the ball aloft." Another was separated from his companions as they explored an uncharted territory and found himself caught on a ledge of rock, where, realizing the special carrying power of certain vowels, he called "Hello" rather than "Help" and was heard and saved. Tom Swift was, of course, a remarkably successful inventor, and I read about many of his projects, and Luke Larkin, Mark Manning, and Chester Rand all worked hard, their clothing carefully mended by their widowed mothers and, as Horatio Alger, Jr., reported, their merits recognized by affluent older men.

But I wrote little or nothing about successful boys, no matter what their fields. Instead I wrote a story about a young man who foolishly mistakes a Chinese restaurant for an opium den, though I had never been in a Chinese restaurant in my life, and another about a greedy sheriff in a Western called "Wanted for Murder."

I was getting stuff of this sort from the movies, of course, and I saw no reason why I should not put it back. I bought a book telling how to write scenarios and win fame and fortune. I learned all about close-ups (CU), iris out, and long shots. In one of my scenarios a butler breaks a valuable vase, which is later reassembled and restored to its pedestal unbeknownst to the butler. Here is a sample:

(30) EXTERIOR BEDROOM DOOR—SEMI-CU—Marion comes out with vase—looks up and down hall—exits—
(31) STAIRWAY—LONG SHOT (showing portion of room at foot)—Marion comes down—sees Mr. Rocks coming—sets down vase —dusts a bit—exits as Mr. Rocks enters—
TITLE: MR. GOLD N. ROCKS WHO THINKS HE OWNS THE VASE.
(32) FOOT OF STAIRWAY—SEMI-CU—Mr. Rocks—picks up vase—looks in direction of drawing room—exits in that direction with vase—
(33) DRAWING ROOM—SEMI-CU—Mr. Rocks—enters with vase—puts it where it originally was—admires it—exits—(IRIS OUT ON VASE)
TITLE: THAT NIGHT
(34) STAIRWAY SHOWING A PORTION OF MAIN ROOM—LONG SHOT—butler enters—lowers lights—exits towards drawing room—
(35) DRAWING ROOM—LONG SHOT—butler enters—touches button near door to lower lights—a stream of moonlight lights up the vase and pedestal—
(36) DRAWING ROOM—CU—*vase*—
(37) DRAWING ROOM—CU—butler—sees vase—horrified—thinks vase is a ghost come to taunt him—

I also wrote the words of a song and sent it off in answer to an advertisement and was told that I had a possible hit and that music could be written and the song published for, I think, $200. My father was not willing to stake me to fame and fortune in that field.

I dreamed of better things—things that might appear in sets of the *World's Great Literature* in the libraries of the future. I wrote a morality play called "Christmas Spirit" with characters named Greed, Youth, Gluttony, Adventure, and Jealousy. Greed wants to foreclose a mortgage and hires Youth to delay the final payment. Here is a sample of the text:

(Enter Youth followed at a distance by Adventure.)

Greed: Here boy. I'd have a word with you.

Youth: Yes sir, pray tell what can I do?

Greed: A favor, sir, but first you'll swear
      To not repeat a word you hear?

Youth: Yes sir, I promise.

Greed: Very well
      What e'er I say no word you'll tell.
      Tomorrow night a man will ride
      Down on the lofty mountainside.
      My favor, sir (and well t'will pay)
      Is that you this old man stay.
      Hold him up! Keep him there
      Till noontime bells next day you hear.

The dastardly plot is foiled and, as the prologue had already promised,

Into this sleeping valley
There came a spirit bold
Awakening dormant conscience
And loosening crime's tight hold.
The village woke again to right
Put down all crime and greed
And since that day there's none in want
And not a soul in need.

(I was aided in my creative struggles by a rhyming dictionary which appeared as an appendix in a book in that small library at Mr. and Mrs. B's.)

I saw myself in print a second time in a Letter to an Editor. When I was old enough to drive my grandfather Burrhus's car, I often drove my grandmother into the region south of Susquehanna, where many of her relatives still lived. In Jackson there was a hotel which had an old but still functional soda fountain with an unusual number of plungers delivering syrups of various colors and flavors. I would choose my flavor for the day, and my grandmother would take Moxie. One day we went on toward Gibson to visit an Aunt Luize who lived on a farm with a large sugar bush. The sap was running, and they had tapped the trees and were making maple syrup. Small piles of snow were still about, and Aunt Luize boiled some syrup until it was so thick that it formed a kind of taffy when poured on a panful of snow. It would stick your teeth together if you were not careful, but it was delicious, and I wrote a letter about my experience to the Editor of the *Toledo Blade,* to which Mr. and Mrs. B subscribed, and it was published. Unfortunately, no copy survives.

(The trees in front of our house were sugar maples, and I once tapped them and collected sap in little tin pails. A kettle of sap simmered or boiled on the kitchen stove depending upon the condition of the fire. The syrup was sweet, but those tin pails had collected more than sap, and its color was a sooty gray.)

THE INDIANS HAD, OF COURSE, long since been driven out of the valley of the Susquehanna, and the elaborate wooden statue in front of the cigar store on Main Street could scarcely be said to have been erected in their honor, but we all had Indian costumes, including headdresses made with turkey feathers, and we occasionally found arrowheads surviving from that Stone Age.

A wagonload of gypsies would from time to time stop on the outskirts of town and women and children in brightly colored dresses would invade the stores, putting the shopkeepers on the alert for theft.

Only one "Chinaman" ever lived in Susquehanna and my father once wrote a letter to the *Transcript* memorializing him—a letter which tells perhaps as much about the writer as about the subject:

> Wing Lee's receipt for laundry delivered consisted of one half of a slip of pink paper upon which had been scrawled with a brush Chinese characters and the rule was that unless you returned the correct half of the slip which would fit the other half you got no laundry. It was Wing who coined the phrase "No tickee, no shirtee." He smoked a pipe with a stem at least a yard long and a bowl the size of a thimble. Three puffs from real Chinese Tobacco constituted one smoke.
>
> Wing never adopted American styles. His cue hung below his hips and the cloak which he wore to church was a real specimen of Chinese art. His work shoes were flat slippers which he skillfully kept on his

feet although they had no uppers except a small cover over the toe. He could sprinkle a whole basketful of clothes with one mouthful of water. This he would emit in a fine spray which if touched by the sunlight would produce a beautiful rainbow.

He grew beautiful lilies from bulbs placed on bare stones in a dish of water.

In my day there was only one black. He worked around the railroad station, and at a fair on Beebe's Flats he willingly participated by sticking his head through a hole in a sheet of canvas and allowing customers to throw baseballs at him from a distance of about twenty feet. Three throws cost ten cents. He had a certain freedom of movement and could dodge a ball fairly well, and he was seldom hit, and he seemed to think the whole thing as amusing as the customers. We all believed that blacks had very thick skulls, and that although it might sting a bit if he were hit, he could not be seriously hurt.

I played with a black boy briefly when the first stretch of macadam road was put in, between Oakland and the state line. The operator of one of the pieces of heavy equipment was black, and he boarded at Gran'ma Graham's. His wife helped in the kitchen, and they had a boy named Victor, who came over to play with my brother and me. My mother had just discarded an old mattress, and we were specializing in tumbling tricks. Victor was especially good at them, and again we believed he could not really hurt himself. During the war a Negro troop pitched its tents for one night on Beebe's Flats, and we went over and had our pictures taken with the soldiers.

There were two Greeks, Mike and George Zaharias. Mike, the elder, owned the Sugar Bowl, and his brother worked for him. They served sodas, milkshakes, and sundaes. My favorite sundae was a "Mexican"—a cone-shaped scoop of vanilla ice cream covered with chocolate sauce and sprinkled with peanuts to suggest a Spanish hat. From a kitchen in the basement George would bring up great trays of fudge cut into squares and peanut brittle cracked into irregular pieces.

There were several Jews—my mother's friend Dora Scheuer and her family until they moved away, the Eismans and Hershes, who ran the drygoods store, and the Hersh children, and Bill Ernestone, the tailor, and his wife. Mrs. Eisman was the only woman in Susquehanna who could knit socks, helmets, and sweaters for soldiers faster than my grandmother Burrhus, and Pauline Hersh was valedictorian in my father's class. Sidney Hersh married a girl from Binghamton and they moved into a new house just off Grand Street, but his wife never adjusted to life in Susquehanna. At one time she slept a great deal, and her behavior was attributed to sleeping sickness.

Bill Ernestone began to make suits for my brother and me as soon as we were old enough to have our suits made. They were usually of serviceable tweed, but during my last summer in Susquehanna he made the tuxedo that I took with me to college, and he made one suit for me after I had gone on to graduate school.

There were a few Germans and Scandinavians, including my father's business associate Frank Zeller, the brewer, and several barbers. (My father would occasionally use a mangled German expression, such as "Nix come harróws.") At one time two or three German families came to Susquehanna and rented a house on Church Street. They appeared in the streets as a German band, playing brass or woodwind instruments and a drum. They could not make a decent living and soon left. The only time they attracted my attention was when they slaughtered a pig. We heard it screaming and rushed to a back fence to see what was happening. The pig had been hung on a tree by its hind legs with its throat cut, and blood was being collected in dishpans to make, we were told, blood sausage or blood pudding.

The main ethnic groups were the Italians, the Irish, and the Anglo-Saxon Protestants or WASPs. Two or three Italian families had come to the town in its early days, and they spoke English with no accent and lived in the better sections. One of them ran a fruit store (Bob Basso, a son, played in the theatre orchestra we organized when I was in high school), and another repaired shoes. But most of the Italians spoke almost no English and lived in "Little Italy," a long block of unpainted tenements on East Main Street beside the railroad tracks. I often saw pregnant women standing in doorways with babies at their breasts and groups of idle men calling numbers and throwing out fingers in a game of *morra*. A woman in peasant dress moving across our backyard with a knife and a basket collecting dandelion greens was a familiar sight.

The Irish either started farther up the ladder or, not handicapped by a different language, moved up faster than the Italians. Among the Irish were a lawyer, a doctor (who served as Mayor for many years), a hotelkeeper, two or three grocers, the owner of the Hogan Opera House, the manager of the movies shown in it, a coal merchant, and many of the more skilled machinists in the Shop. On my way to and from school I passed the house of a prosperous young Irish family to which a new member was added every year until there were twelve. There was always one at the right age to run across the street to walk a bit with me and say, "Gimme a pinny"—a verbal response I intermittently reinforced. The older Irish had a rich brogue. I once offered to do an errand for an old woman—a matter of carrying something to a store on my bicycle—and as I started off she called out, "God bless you"—both the intonation and the expression from a different world.

The violinist in one of our amateur orchestras was an Irish girl, and I was walking home with her one night after a rehearsal in a rather heavy fog. A figure loomed up ahead of us near a streetlight, and my companion grasped my arm and whimpered in terror. She confessed to me afterward that she had thought the figure was a witch. That was not the kind of thing a WASP ever did.

We had our superstitions, of course. If you mentioned good fortune, you knocked on wood at once lest mentioning it bring bad luck; you never walked under a ladder; and if you spilled the salt, you threw a bit of it over your left shoulder. We all believed that if you stared hard enough at the back of a man's head, he would eventually turn around and look at you. Susquehanna was not far from the territory of the Fox sisters, and we sometimes sat around a table with our splayed fingers touching, waiting for knocks. But this was very different from banshees or goblins. (The town was apparently too young to have ghosts or haunted houses.)

The unchallenged leader of the local WASPs was C. Fred Wright. He was associated with the Republican machine in Pennsylvania led by Senator Boies Penrose and served as Congressman from 1900 to 1906. He refused to run for another term "because of pressing business." In announcing his decision he asserted that being a Congressman was "not, as many supposed, a sinecure" but practically a full-time job. He had had to write 30,000–36,000 letters during his first five years in office. "Pressing business" included his interest in the First National Bank, the local water company, and the remaining timber in that part of the great hardwood forest. In 1906 my father went with him to Milford, on the Delaware River, where he was involved in the sale of the timber rights on 8000 acres of land for $200,000, then a very large sum of money.

Congressman Wright had already found young Attorney Skinner useful. He never had much work for him, but a prestigious figure could play an important role as a model. My father could not have acquired any useful professional behavior by emulating his father or either of his half-uncles, but C. Fred Wright was a man of great distinction, wealth, and influence, and my father saw or heard about him every day. It is probably relevant that I was named B. Frederic rather than Frederic B.

The Wright house was the finest in town, but it was located on West Main Street, fairly near the business district, and hence increasingly subject to the smoke and soot of trains and Shops. Mr. and Mrs. Wright were not conspicuous in the community. When my mother was young, she appeared in a businessmen's carnival, and she wore "Mrs. Wright's riding habit," but I doubt whether Mrs. Wright ever appeared in it herself. Branches of the family, however, reached into the life of the town, composing almost all the small congregation of the Episcopal church, as well as the directorship of the First National Bank.

Wright Glidden, an officer of the bank, lived with his wife on Grand Street. They had two sons of the same ages as my brother and I, and there was always a subtle, slightly invidious comparison. The Gliddens had a full-scale pool table in their living room with balls and cues and green chalk, where we had something about the size of a card table with wooden rings in place of balls, which we knocked about with much smaller cues. The Glidden Victrola was larger and more swollen than ours, and they owned the sextet from *Lucia* with Caruso, which cost seven dollars, whereas Nellie Melba's "Goodbye" cost only three. Wright Glidden drove the only Packard in town, while we were still driving a Ford.

On one occasion we were invited to call on the C. Fred Wrights at Pinecrest. It was a fine afternoon, and we sat on the porch, and I think the grownups had tea. A granddaughter of the Wrights climbed into my lap. I was perhaps twelve at the time and embarrassed, but the child was four or five years old, and it occurred to me that our ages were not greatly different and that when we grew up, she and I might fall in love and marry.

At the other end of the Anglo-Saxon scale were the Cronks, husband and wife, and their two grown children, a young man who wore dirty clothes and a cap and a girl who was a slut. They lived above the laundry on East Main Street at one end of Little Italy, and nothing too bad could be said of them, but, so far as I know, their only crimes were filth and occasional drunkenness.

Also near the other end of the WASP culture were a young motorcyclist and his girl who seemed to have no friends in town but came and went frequently. They lived much of the time in a shack some distance back from the river four or five miles north of Susquehanna. At one time it was obvious on their forays into town that the girl was pregnant, but eventually that condition cleared up. There was no baby, but there was talk.

In between the Wrights and the Cronks were most of the doctors, lawyers, and bankers, and a good many of the merchants of Susquehanna. There were also the pastors of half a dozen Protestant sects and a surprising number of widows with daughters—like the Tisdells, who taught the primary Sunday school in the Presbyterian church, and the Houghtons, who lived on our street and did sewing. Almost all the farmers in the area were Anglo-Saxon Protestants—some of them affluent, most of them pious and conforming. (I was once surprised by a glimpse into their lives. One of my classmates in fourth grade was the son of a farmer, and when Miss Brosnam asked him why he had been absent, he said, "The horse died and I had to help my father grind it up for chicken feed.")

There were also a few oddballs. A native contortionist came back to Susquehanna briefly from time to time; he could lock his legs behind his neck and was said to have syphilis. The son of the Justice of the Peace went away and returned something of a fop, coming to a party in white tie and tails, for which Susquehanna was never to be ready.

Minority groups were favorite materials for jokes. There were funny stories about Pat and Mike, with plenty of "begorrahs," and on a Victrola record we had a monologue called "Cohen on the

Telephone," in which a tenant tries to explain to his landlord that a "carPENter" is needed to replace a "shuttah" which has blown off in a high wind. ("A shuttah—a SHUTTAH—No, I didn't say 'Shut up.'") On the other side of the record a monologue called "No News" poked fun at a presumably black chauffeur. Someone at Chautauqua recited a poem in Italian-English, each stanza of which concluded with a slightly aggressive "I gotta da rock." But minority groups laughed at each other, and children laughed at their un-Americanized parents, and there was nothing vicious about it. Someone once discovered an APA sticker on the back of a folding chair at the Chautauqua. The American Protective Association was an aggressive anti-immigration, anti-Catholic organization, and it was feared that Catholic support of the Chautauqua might be lost, but the sticker had clearly been attached at an earlier location, and, so far as I know, there was no local activity of that kind.

RELIGION DREW A SHARPER LINE. The Presbyterian and Catholic churches stood side by side on a promontory looking out over the river at the foot of Jackson Avenue on land given to both congregations by the same man, and the eastern half of the town was henceforth called Church Hill. Both churches were of red brick and solidly built, but the Catholic was much the larger. Their physical proximity never brought the two congregations very close even though Father Broderick, whose regime covered my entire life in Susquehannna, was a tolerant priest, if something of a martinet with his own flock. In public he wore a frock coat and a top hat and carried a gold-headed cane, though I used to see him scurrying from the rectory to the church in his priestly garb. He was a good friend of my father's and often on the speakers' platform with him, especially during the war. (When I was born, another friend, Father Hoolihan, gave my father and mother a relic to be put on a string around my neck to protect me from harm. It was contained in a disk of kidskin with a crocheted border, and my parents saw no reason why I should not profit from a foreign religion and actually kept it on me for a time.)

Most of the Italians were separated from the Protestants by their language and style of life, but the Irish were practicing separatists, and they dominated the church. Almost all Catholic families sent their children to the Laurel Hill Academy, a parochial school run by nuns, and, so far as I know, no Catholic boy ever joined the Boy Scouts, although the movement had no religious features. One year the maiden daughters of Dr. Peck, a Protestant, organized a town-wide May Festival or Kermis in which young people were drilled in various folk dances. I was eight at the time and danced as a Rheinlander. My brother was in a kindergarten polka, and there were a Japanese dance, a Swedish dance, a wooden-shoe dance, and a Maypole. It was an ecumenical enterprise, but the promoters found it hard going and did not try again.

I saw Catholic children bringing home strips of palm leaf on Palm Sunday, and my Catholic teachers turned up with dirty foreheads on Ash Wednesday. Catholic boys wore medals on strings around their necks when they went swimming, and Catholic girls wore crosses on necklaces and dressed in white for confirmation. They all called the nuns "Sister," of course, and the priest "Father," and I was never quite sure whether I should do so too—whether I would not somehow be disloyal to my own religion or, worse, mar the sanctity of Catholicism.

I once took a message to Father Broderick from my father and caught a glimpse of the rather drab interior of the rectory in which he lived, and once in Lannon's grocery store on Main Street some nuns came in to pay their monthly bill, and when Mr. Lannon gave them a generous supply of payday candy, making a large cornucopia of a sheet of paper and filling it with chocolate drops, I was rather startled by the nuns' delight, for I had supposed that their life was much more austere.

There was one convert to Catholicism—a Mrs. Demander, whose husband was a stonecutter and lettered the monuments set up in the cemeteries. She stalked through the town in the company of the nuns, with all of whom she remained conspicuously on the best of terms. My father and mother thought she was ridiculous. She seems to have specialized in Belief. My friend Bob Perrine went on believing in Santa Claus for a year or two after the rest of us knew better because Mrs. Demander had shown him a photograph of Santa Claus which she insisted she had taken in front of her very own fireplace.

Any slight crumbling of the wall between Protestants and Catholics surprised me. Father Broderick once called my attention to a traffic sign which said, "Go slow," and asked me if I approved its grammar. I was pleased by his interest, but amazed that he should have spoken to a Protestant boy in such a friendly way. When Dr. Condon, the Catholic Mayor, drove several of us Boy Scouts back from a Liberty Bond campaign in a neighboring town, we sang some songs, and at one point he said, "That's very nice, boys," and I was surprised that he would say anything good about Protestants.

I felt the barrier between Protestants and Catholics most keenly when it came to girls. There was a dance hall over a garage in Oakland, and once a week a Mr. Donnally came up from Binghamton and held dancing classes late in the afternoon. A pianist played, and Mr. Donnally danced with each of us to improve our style in the waltz, the two-step, and the fox-trot (the tango was a little too complicated).

One day Margaret Murphy, the daughter of the owner of the garage, came to dancing school, and she and I began to dance together. We had a marvelous time. She was perhaps two years younger than I, but it didn't seem to matter. There was no flirtation, no sexual innuendo—we simply laughed, talked, and danced. It was all so wonderful that we stayed on through suppertime and I paid admission to the real dance, with an orchestra, that Mr. Donnally ran in the evening.

But I never spoke to her again. The ethnic and religious barrier had lifted for a day, but only by accident, carelessness, or neglect. She was not a girl I could invite to the parties or dances I went to, and she was part of a group in which I would be equally alien. I am not sure that I ever saw her again.

I made a more determined effort to invade the Catholic culture with a girl named Lillian McGuane. Her mother was a widow who lived on West Hill. For some reason Lillian did not go to parochial school, and I therefore began to see her. An older daughter was said to be fast and to have been seen in a Binghamton hotel with a man, but Lillian was very proper, rather pretty, and I was smitten. When I decided to go to a Halloween party as the figure in the Fisk tire advertisement, showing a young boy in a nightdress with a tire around his shoulder carrying a candle ("Time to re-tire"), I asked Lillian if

I could borrow a nightdress. I went with her to her house to get one, but her mother took a very dim view of the project and made it quite clear that I was not welcome.

Nevertheless I was in love and talked to my parents about Lillian. I once asked my mother if she did not think that she had a sweet face, and she agreed, but with marked reserve. I used to play Rubinstein's "Melody in F" while thinking of her. She soon took up with an Irish boy named Red McHugh who lived on lower Broad Street and it was clear that I was permanently cut out.

There were rather similar barriers among the Protestant sects. In addition to a Presbyterian church, there were a Methodist, a Baptist, a Congregational, and, mainly for the spiritual welfare of the Wright dynasty, an Episcopalian. At one time an evangelist named Crabell came to Susquehanna. He was sponsored by the Protestant churches, and before he arrived a tabernacle was built on Grand Street. It was a large structure of unpainted pine boards, with a platform and benches, and a "sawdust trail" down the middle. A few Protestants did not approve. They called the building the Grab-a-nickel because of the ill-concealed financial aspects of the operation. My father was one of them, and in an interview he was quoted as saying that "the house of God is not a fitting environment for theatricals." Another was the father of a friend of mine who was an electrician. He was electrocuted during the campaign while working on a telephone pole, and Crabell had the bad taste to imply that this was God's vengeance on a dissenter. "He was a fool to question the work of the Lord," he said. The dissident Protestants countered with a Biblical quotation: "He that calleth his brother a fool is in danger of hell fire."

When the tabernacle was being built, I was in fifth grade and there was a girl in sixth grade with whom I thought I was in love, although she paid no attention to me. She was a Baptist and lived in a duplex near my grandfather Skinner's. One afternoon she came to drive a nail into the tabernacle to symbolize her support, and when I heard of this I was heartbroken and abandoned my suit.

Although my mother frequently sang in the Episcopal church before her marriage, and conversion might have been a useful move for my father in the direction of the Wright family, they were born and remained mere Presbyterians. Even so, that put them a cut above the

Methodists and Baptists. Once we were driving along a rather narrow dirt road when a car overtook us and honked its horn. My father slowed down and pulled over to allow it to pass, and the driver sang out, "Thank you," as he went by. It was the Baptist minister, and his passengers were some of the ladies of his church. My mother made some contemptuous comment, and my father murmured his agreement.

As for my further religious development, my historical note records that Miss Graves's class

acquired a glamour which marked it from other classes. We studied, over several years, most of the Old Testament, and reached finally the story of Christ.

We reached the story of Christ just when the sex urge had made itself felt in me. I was twelve or thirteen. Another boy and I had built a shanty on Hillborn's Creek. They were free, natural days. I was beginning to read and think and come in contact with earth. Religion and religious ideas bothered me and I thought a great deal about them. I had never associated freely with other boys and now my doubts about things and my sex shame drove me almost to solitude.

I sensed strongly the injustice in the world. I must have been jealous and resentful. It was an uneasy age. But gradually I worked out a theory of compensation: I began to suspect that punishment or reward in afterlife brought to a balance the imbalance in this world and the theory was practical so long as I believed it. For a year at least life was perfectly happy for me. I believed that all my trouble simply made way for compensating happiness. My jealousy was not discarded (I see this now) but was rather satisfied: the happiness of my companions which I envied, simply meant, I was sure, that they would have trouble later.

It was at this time that I came to believe that I had received a divine message. The fervor of that revelation is yet possible to me as I recall the day. I had lost my most valued possession, a silver watch. I was filled with the shame and self-resentment that I had been taught to feel when I made a mistake. I escaped from home and went to our shack on Hillborn's Creek. I was alone, thinking. Suddenly I thought I had a great revelation. I cannot now remember the substance. Probably the sudden complete realization of the "truth" in my theory of compensation. At any rate I became very happy and started to walk home. Along the path, carefully placed on a bed of dry grass, lay my silver watch. At that moment I felt what must have been the greatest ecstasy possible. God has spoken to me, I thought. I have heard him rightly and he has returned my watch as an indication of his pleasure.

What a blissful combination! Born and bred with the tradition of fear before God, then suddenly to become intimate with him, to have him speak to me—

I told no one. I wrote the experience, in Biblical phraseology, on a small piece of paper which I hid in a match case. I remember now that I had a second "miracle" but I have forgotten what it was.

I cannot, now, trace the dissolution of this idea. I entered high school. A senior gave me pamphlets on theosophy which I never read.

Susquehanna was close to Joseph Smith country. When Smith took the Golden Plates from the Hill of Cumorah to Palmyra, New York, he was persecuted by a mob, and it was clear that he would have to go elsewhere to translate them. Concealing them in a barrel filled with beans, he is said to have brought them with him when he came with his wife to Harmony. He bought a house from his father-in-law two or three miles from the spot where Susquehanna would later be founded. There he is said to have translated the plates, dictating the Book of Mormon to two scribes from behind a curtain.

Smith was laughed at by the local people, and a few scurrilous stories survived to my day. I heard that he had pretended to walk on water by building a platform just below the surface but had moved in the wrong direction and fallen off. That was not unlike the stories being written about perfectionist movements in the nineteenth century by Mark Twain, Artemus Ward, Josh Billings, and the author of *Aunt Samantha Among the Brethren*.

I took certain religious principles seriously. Faith could move mountains, and when I was about twelve years old I tried to demonstrate it by levitating. I stood on a beam scale and tried to make myself lighter. My failure was especially disappointing because I often daydreamed of astonishing people by flying around a room, like the Flying Yorkshireman. (In the same mood I used to imagine jumping from cloud to cloud, as if they were great balls of cotton wool. It did not seriously stretch my imagination, for I often jumped into snowdrifts, haystacks, huge piles of autumn leaves before they became bonfires, and mountains of sawdust near lumber mills.)

My only scholarly effort to prove the value of my religion ended in failure. My grandmother Skinner subscribed for a year to a magazine published by the Presbyterian Church, to which I planned to contribute an article proving the value of the Presbyterian religion by showing that many great composers had been Presbyterians. When I began to check biographies, however, I could not find any composer who had been Presbyterian. Worse still, many had been Catholics.

An important part of my religious training was the novel *Quo Vadis*. It was not assigned by Miss Graves, and I must have stumbled on it in the town library. Sienkiewicz no doubt intended it to be a convincing statement of Christian principles, and the description of Peter's appearance at Ostianum covers a great deal of ethical self-management with which I was familiar and which I continued to practice, but the book miscarried, because I admired and agreed with Petronius. After Ursus saves Lygia from the aurochs in the Colosseum and the populace insists that Caesar spare the girl, Petronius comments, "Possibly Christ saved Lygia, but Ursus and the populace had a good deal to do with it." Sienkiewicz had prepared an answer by having Ursus testify that prison had weakened him and that only a supernatural power permitted him to kill the aurochs, but Petronius's point impressed me. (Perhaps I should have been even more a pagan if I had known that the Roman general in charge of another Christian in the novel, St. Paul, was named Burrhus.) In any event, when I began to see that my new testament was to go no further, I told Miss Graves, when I met her one day in the hallway of the high school, that I no longer believed in God. "I have been through that, too," she said.

My father may have suspected that my religious faith was slipping. The master of ceremonies at Chautauqua that summer was Hunt Cook, and before he left he gave me a paperback copy of Francis Thompson's "Hound of Heaven"—

> I fled Him, down the nights and down the days;
>   I fled Him, down the arches of the years;
>   I fled Him, down the labyrinthine ways
>   Of my own mind. . . .

My guess is that my father had taken his problem to Mr. Cook and that this was his attempt at a solution.

*   *   *

WE BEGAN TO USE the Ford to go farther and farther afield, though touring was still rather hazardous. At first it was a fairly ambitious project to go to Windsor, ten miles away, even though part of the road on the Oakland side of the river was paved. Dust in dry weather was no less a problem than mud in wet. One Sunday we got stuck in the mud between Great Bend and Hickory Grove. There was a farmer leaning against the fence in front of his house, with a team of horses already in harness grazing near at hand. He connected the team to our car and pulled us out of the mud for a fee, and before we drove off we saw him leaning over the fence again waiting for the next car, the team still in harness on the lawn.

There were very few garages to supply gasoline or make repairs or pump up deflated tires, but we were sustained by our faith in the stamina of our car. We sang a song about "the little old Ford" that "just rambled right along" where more elegant cars were often in trouble. Ford owners had a kind of *esprit de corps* and tooted their horns when passing. We sometimes counted the number of cars we passed, and the numbers grew more amazing as the years went by. Speeds were low—thirty miles an hour was relatively fast—and there was time to play wayside cribbage. My brother would take one side of the road and I the other, and we scored points for the horses, cows, and other designated items we pointed out as we passed.

My father thought it was educational for my brother and me to see factories. In Windsor we saw horsewhips being made, a tapered stick of wood and leather descending through a complex weaving device which covered it with a patterned cloth skin, ending in a few inches of cord with a tassel at the end. On a professional trip with my father to Honesdale, in another county, we visited a shirt-and-sweater factory. We also went to Milford on the Delaware River and to Afton in New York State to see the county fair, and on one journey we stopped at a cut-glass factory.

There were as yet no marked routes, and on longer journeys we used a Blue Book, which gave detailed directions for getting from one town to another, describing bridges, churches, barns, and other prominent features along the route, with distances in tenths of a mile from one to the other, which we carefully checked on the speedometer.

We visited Aunt Alt and her husband first in Beerston, where Uncle Norm took us to see the "acid factory" in which he worked. Great logs were enclosed in ovens and hot fires built beneath them, and the alcohols and "acids" driven off were collected, and what remained was sold as charcoal. The factory had the acrid smell of the remains of a wooden building that has just burned down.

Aunt Alt and Uncle Norm soon moved to that pleasant house on the Delaware River in Walton, New York, where we visited them every year, taking my grandmother and grandfather Skinner with us. My grandfather Skinner, by far the biggest of the passengers, sat in the front seat, and my grandmother and mother and brother and I in back, one boy on a small folding chair between the seat and the lap-robe bar.

On one of our trips to Walton the motor stopped halfway up a hill. My father got out and cranked, but to no avail. He took a small can and went down a bank to a stream and came back with water for the radiator, but a shortage of water was evidently not the trouble. The car simply would not start, and there seemed to be nothing to be done. My father continued to crank, with time out to rest his arm, while my grandfather—not the cranking type—touched various bits of equipment on the steering wheel or dashboard. Suddenly the motor turned over briefly. My grandfather had touched the switch on the magneto, and when he held it in place again, the car readily started. The switch simply needed to be tightened. This was a great triumph. The story was told again and again that afternoon in Walton as neighbors and friends came in, and each time my grandfather responded with a chuckle.

My father was really at home at his Aunt Alt's and very much the self I seldom saw anywhere else. Aunt Alt was warm and jovial, amused by the foibles of her sister, and genuinely hospitable. I remember her buckwheat griddle cakes at breakfast, and her chicken dinners, with small glasses of her dandelion wine for the men and homemade maple mousse and ladyfingers for dessert especially for my brother and me. They raised their own chickens and Uncle Norm would catch one and chop its head off as I watched. He knew how to set it down on the ground so that it would run a few steps, headless, before falling dead.

We made a more extensive tour to Watkins Glen, where I bought postcards of the rock formations to show with my stereopticon in a travelogue. Later we drove to Albany and stayed overnight en route at a small hotel, in the lobby of which I talked with two beautiful Cuban girls who showed me how to fold a square sheet of paper to make a pigeon. It was a remarkable piece of origami, because when you pulled the pigeon's tail, it flapped its wings.

In Albany we stayed with old high-school friends of my parents, and on this occasion I was to see a bit of statecraft rather than industry. My father took me to a constitutional convention of which Elihu Root was chairman. We climbed to the balcony and looked down on the assembly, and my father pointed to Senator Root and whispered, "There is the next President of the United States."

As local attorney for the Erie Railroad Company, my father got annual passes which permitted us to travel free, and we often went to Binghamton on a Saturday afternoon to shop and see a movie. Except for the suits made by Bill Ernestone, we bought almost all our clothing at Weed's in Binghamton, and my mother and father shopped extensively in the department stores. Occasionally we drove the Ford to Binghamton and loaded it with staple groceries from a wholesaler. None of this promoted the economic welfare of Susquehanna, but my father was apparently unaware of the effect it must have had on his business friends.

In Binghamton we saw movies made by Thomas H. Ince, often in sepia, and, unlike the Hogan Opera House, the theatre had upholstered seats rising row on row from the screen and a pipe organ instead of a Miss Dooley at the piano. After the movies we went to a white-tiled restaurant near the station for supper. We always had omelets, and I had the impression that that was all the restaurant served, but I suppose it was merely the cheapest meal we could get.

After supper we went to the station and waited for No. 26. It was usually a long wait, even when the train was on time, and it was painful to stay awake sitting on the slippery wooden benches. We might enjoy two Chiclets dispensed from a machine in a glassine wrapper for a penny, and I was intrigued by a large sign reading, "Girls, Girls, Beware, the White Slave Trader Is Everywhere," but I did not want my parents to see me reading the small print and I never found out what was so threatening about the white slave trader.

No. 26 stopped three or four times between Binghamton and Susquehanna, and the pain of sleepiness continued, and after we had reached the station we still had to walk a mile or more to our house.

My closest boyhood friend was Raphael Miller. I cannot remember exactly when our friendship formed, and it would be hard to define it. He was a few months younger than I and a year behind in school and college. I called him Doc because his father was a doctor and he intended to become one too.

His father was a homeopathist. His office was in his house, and it contained great jars of very small sugar pills to which he added minute amounts of medication when he gave them to patients. Doc and I occasionally sampled the unmedicated ones. His father was a dedicated practitioner who made himself available throughout the countryside at any time of day or night. He was the last professional man in Susquehanna to drive a horse. (In the Glidden barn next door, the Packard stood alongside stalls which still contained licked blocks of salt and bins holding a few oats.) When Dr. Miller eventually got a Ford, he nearly killed himself. In trying to turn around on the road near the Blue Ridge Metal Manufacturing plant in Oakland, he stepped on the reverse pedal instead of low gear, and the car shot backward out over a concrete cellar hole and dropped into shallow water, but it remained right side up and he was unhurt.

The quality of my friendship with Doc was touched by the fact that his father and mother were religious. They not only belonged to the Presbyterian church; unlike my father and mother they went to church every Sunday. After Sunday school Doc would stay on to join his parents. Moreover, he could take communion and I could not. (My father had decided that I should not be baptized until I understood what it meant, and that time never came.)

Doc and I did many things together, but we never took any great delight in doing them. Harmey Warner gave us piano lessons at the same time and we bought and practiced a couple of duets, but our greatest satisfaction lay in reaching the last measure at the same time. Patients who came to see the doctor at night could speak to him through a speaking tube which ran from his bedroom to the front door, and Doc and I used to play with it. You blew on the tube to sound a whistle, and then pressed a lever to open it to talk. Later we set up a telegraph line between our houses. We strung odds and ends of wire along the back fence, including an enormously long spring which, when stretched, kept a slight spiral twist. The line was not very satisfactory and my father, as secretary and treasurer of the local phone company, had the company electrician run a better one down the poles in the street for our use.

Doc's telegraph had a device in which metal disks with patterns of teeth could be used to send messages at different speeds for instructional purposes, but we never developed a good "fist" or ear. In the early evening I would hear my telegraph clattering away upstairs and would go up and answer, and Doc would then send a message and I would send one in return. They were often confusing and it was not unusual for one of us to call the other on the telephone to find out what he was trying to say.

One summer Doc and I went into the elderberry business. Elderberries grew plentifully below the Lower Road from Susquehanna to Lanesboro. They tasted like bitter huckleberries and were used in pies or "sauce." We gathered them in large clusters and stripped or shook the ripe berries into a basket. But the unripe berries came off too, and we made a device to separate the green from the ripe. We bent a sheet of metal to form a shallow trough into which we shook the berries. Water from a garden hose ran down the trough and carried them into a pail. The green ones floated and were carried over the edge to be thrown away, and the ripe berries sank and were washed clean of the dust from the Lower Road. We carried the berries from door to door and sold them to housewives interested in elderberry pies.

Although the first sexual play in which I was discovered took place in the hayloft of Doc's barn, there was never anything of that kind between us again. Doc acquired a rather medical attitude toward sex from his father, and once passed on a comment about some man who was walking in an awkward way because he had engaged in some unspecified sexual activity and had picked up some unspecified disease.

Doc never went with girls or talked about girls or went to parties where games were played with girls, and somehow it added to my strong feeling of admiration and awe that I supposed him above all that. But a lovely cousin of the Gliddens used to come to visit, and as a next-door neighbor Doc got to know her. Slowly—and to the amazement of us all—a deep relationship grew up between them which lasted until his tragic death.

MANY PEOPLE ESCAPED from the heat of the city by spending a month or two in the country, which often meant simply in small towns, and Susquehanna had a fair share of summer folk. My father's uncle and aunt came from New York City with their children and boarded with relatives on lower Grand Street. Ed Dumble had all the sophistication that his half-brother, my grandfather Skinner, lacked. He dressed nattily and told slightly risqué jokes, often to the embarrassment of his beautiful wife, who carried herself with great distinction. Their daughter, Helen, was lovely but had a weak heart. Their son, Paul, was slightly older than I and did not spend much time in Susquehanna, but once when we were both quite young, we were playing horse, and I was driving him up and down the road in front of our house with some improvised reins, and he quite innocently enlarged upon his role by peeing in the road as horses so conspicuously did.

Frances Carr was a sophisticated girl from Albany who stayed with her mother's sister near us on Grand Street for a month or so each summer. Somehow or other it was naturally supposed that she and I went together when she was in town. When we were quite young, we played a game in which a girl would tickle a boy on the knee while saying, "Tickle, tickle on the knee, If you laugh you don't love me." I never laughed when she tickled me, and I was proud of my stoicism, but, so far as I know, that was my only declaration of love. Her father was a distinguished lawyer, and on that trip to Albany we went to call on him, and Frances and I swung on a great rotary bookcase in his study.

The Keffer boys came from Bayonne, New Jersey, to stay with Gran'ma Graham, and they called her Gran'ma to her face, as I did not. We spent a good deal of time together and I knew the backyard of the Graham property as well as I knew our own. One year they put up a large tent. We all had tents of various sizes and shapes, and it was not always clear what function they served. On hot days they were uncomfortable, and a heavy rain could drive a fine mist through the canvas, but they had the merit of isolating us. We could lie on cots or on the odorous bruised grass and talk about a world of our own.

The Keffers were city boys, and they brought to Susquehanna my first pre-adolescent dirty stories. Harry Keffer told one about a traveling salesman who asks a farmer to put him up for the night. The farmer has a beautiful daughter, and an episode in the middle of the night depends for its humor on the fact that the salesman's name is Johnny Fuckfaster. My brother was beginning to tease me at the time, and that evening at supper he said, "Tell them the story about Johnny." I said I couldn't remember it but added inconsistently that I wouldn't tell it if I did. My brother could not very well remind me, and my parents tactfully let the matter drop.

THE HEAVY BENCH in the woodshed behind our kitchen held a vise, a saw, a hammer, a brace and bit, and a screwdriver, and I often made things. Unfortunately, my grandfather Burrhus never gave me any instruction. He never came to our house except on special occasions, and he had no tools of his own in any of the houses he lived in. (I did not know, for example, that you first drilled a hole before using a wood screw, and I remember the strain and frustration of trying to drive one into an oak plank, the screwdriver eventually splitting the slot or leaving at least a jagged edge which tore my skin.)

The kindling wood from the grocery store included parts of boxes and crates, good for making small objects like the stools I made for my brother, and we had a large supply of boards, painted red, of seasoned white pine free of knots, from a fence that had been replaced between our lot and the cemetery. They were just right for building benches, tables, and small houses. Long oil-soaked oak planks from the Erie Shops, destined to be sawed into pieces for our fireplace, were ideal for slides, teeter-totters, and merry-go-rounds.

There was an old rose arbor in our backyard and for many years a lawn swing with facing seats which one set in motion by pushing against a slatted floor. As the years passed, my mother and father grew too busy to spend time in a garden, and my brother and I had the space to ourselves. It became a shambles. The soil was pure brown sand left either by the river or by one of the glaciers which had rounded off the local hills. You could dig holes six or eight feet deep before striking hardpan. We dug branching tunnels which fortunately did not collapse on us. We dug cellars beneath the small houses we constructed of those red boards, and once we added a second story to give three levels.

We made vehicles of various kinds. If we lost one roller skate, we made something of the other, possibly a scooter. For use on snowy slopes we made a kind of scooter of a large barrel stave. With the wheels and axles of discarded baby carriages we made steerable cars in which we coasted downhill in summer as on sleds in winter. Some we steered with our feet on the front axle, but on one I rigged a steering wheel. It had the curious property of turning the car to the left when you turned the wheel to the right and vice versa, and I never acquired the behavior needed to race down Grand Street at high speed without incident. The stored energy of the flywheel fascinated me. I would turn my bicycle upside down and pump the back wheel to a frenetic speed, and I dreamed of a car that stored energy in a flywheel as it came down one hill and used it to go up another.

I also dreamed of an endless source of energy. I designed a perpetual-motion machine in which water flowing from a reservoir lifted a float against a spring, the spring acquiring enough energy to pump the water back into the reservoir for a second cycle. I never put it to the test of an actual construction.

It was too early for good model airplanes, since the only available engines were twisted rubber bands, but we did what we could. We conquered the air most successfully with a device said to go back to the fourteenth century. We cut a propeller out of a tin Nabisco box, and punched two small holes near the center. It was slipped over two headless nails on one end of a spool, which was held on a nail on a stick. String was wound around the spool and when pulled, the spinning propeller rose off the nails and into the air. With only a slight twist of the blades the propeller hovered and whirred for a long time almost within reach; with a sharp twist it rose above houses and trees but quickly stopped spinning and fell straight down.

For weapons we made or bought peashooters, bows and arrows, water pistols, and slingshots. We made a water pistol from a length of bamboo, with a pinhole in the natural diaphragm at one end and a piston of rags wound around a small stick pushed into the other end. We read how the Indians made their bows and arrows and tried to find ash trees and season young saplings to follow their example, but we were never very successful. We tied real feathers on sticks to make true arrows, but the simplest ones we split from a cedar shingle, fastening the head on the thick end and catching a notched slip of light cardboard in a crack in the thin end. There were plenty of forked branches to be used in making slingshots and plenty of old inner tubes for the elastic bands.

Our most ambitious piece of ordnance was a steam cannon made from a discarded hot-water boiler. The boiler lay on its side in the badly kept garden at the rear of our lot, held off the ground by a few stones and bricks, and a fire was built underneath to boil the small amount of water inside. All but one emerging pipe were sealed off. We forced plugs of potato or carrots into the remaining pipe, and they shot out like bullets when the steam pressure reached the right point.

Some boys had air rifles, but my father and mother thought they were dangerous, because you could put an eye out with one. The Gliddens had a twenty-two, and I remember some carefully supervised target practice at their summer place along the river. I may have taken a shot or two myself, and if so it was the only time I have ever fired a gun.

We subscribed to the *Philadelphia Inquirer*, a good Republican paper, which carried Rube Goldberg's cartoons with his outrageous contraptions and his Foolish Questions. Goldberg's influence can be detected in a gadget I built to solve a personal problem having to do with hanging up my pajamas. I had a bedroom of my own, and in the morning I often left my pajamas lying on my bed. While I was eating breakfast, my mother would go upstairs to check, and when she found them there, she would call to me, and I would have to stop eating, go upstairs, and hang them up. She continued this for weeks. It did not make me any more inclined to hang them up before coming down to breakfast, but it was nonetheless aversive, and I escaped in the following way. The clothes closet in my room was near the door, and in it I fastened a hook on the end of a string which passed over a nail and along the wall to a nail above the center of the door. A sign reading "Hang up your pajamas" hung at the other end. When the pajamas were in place, the sign was up out of the way, but when I took them off the hook at night, the sign dropped to the middle of the door where I would bump into it on my way out.

A device concerned only with positive reinforcement was not so successful. I was not allowed to smoke, but I tried to see whether the supposed pleasures of smoking could not be enjoyed in other ways. The important thing seemed to be playing with smoke, blowing it out in various patterned sequences, and so I built a device in which a lighted cigarette could be "smoked" by drawing air through it with an atomizer bulb. I could blow smoke rings and do other tricks, but nothing seemed to be gained. Blowing soap bubbles was more fun.

WHEN WE HAD OUR SUMMER COTTAGE on the river my brother and I and some of our friends explored Hillborn's Creek. It came down out of the hills, and we drank its clear, cold water without fear. Not more than half a mile up the creek from the highway we could find dark, mossy sections completely under the cover of trees reaching out from both banks, but there were also broad ledges of rock over which the water took shallow zigzag courses and sparkled in the sun. We knew the creek in summer when it was a small stream, but its banks were strewn with the debris of spring floods—with high-water marks of matted grass and leaves caught against tree trunks, and uprooted bushes bleaching on the rocks, with an occasional board or fragment of furniture to remind us of civilization.

One spot was particularly good for camping, and we occasionally took our Boy Scout pup tents and stayed there overnight. We dammed up a small section of the creek with stones and sod and made a shallow swimming pool, in which I learned to swim. We shared the pool with a water moccasin, a kind of snake we believed to be poisonous, and which we also occasionally saw in the river, especially at dusk, as it swam with its head out of the water, leaving a long V-shaped bow wave if the water was quite still.

Somewhat later I began to see more of a new friend, a year older than I, named John DeWitt. He suggested that we build a shack on Hillborn's Creek near the old campsite. We started with the boards we picked up along the creek and on the banks of the river, and we brought other material from town strapped to our bicycles. We got a pane of glass from a hardware shop, together with a glass cutter and advice on how to use it, and a small roll of tar paper for the roof.

The shack was big enough for two bunk beds, one above the other, and a small fireplace. We put in a few staples—ground coffee, potatoes, and crackers—and we picked up frankfurters and spent a day or two at the shack on a weekend.

There was not really very much to do. We did not smoke cigarettes, because we were forbidden to do so, but we smoked corn silk and certain kinds of dried leaves, and if we could afford it, we bought a pack of cubebs, which were sold to people who had catarrh or asthma. The Java pepper from which they were made had a rich aroma and possibly some psychedelic properties.

MY FATHER HAD BEEN WRONG, of course, in pointing to Elihu Root as the next President of the United States. Root was an internationalist and had won a Nobel Peace Prize in 1912, but he was the wrong man for the hour and Charles Evans Hughes was nominated as the Republican candidate to oppose Woodrow Wilson. My father was undaunted. He began to give political speeches in favor of Hughes. At a rally at South Gibson, said the *Transcript*, "Mr. Skinner declared . . . that the country had had four years of a namby-pamby wishy-washy administration that had made men with red blood in their veins hang their heads in shame. . . . He predicted Hughes' election and was greeted by vigorous applause when he announced this." He was wrong by only a few votes. Wilson was re-elected, in part because "he had kept us out of war," but within a month after he assumed office for the second time, war was declared.

The Erie Railroad was particularly important to the war effort because it had been built as a broad-gauge track and then converted to standard gauge in such a way that it took "wide loads." It was the only railroad from the Midwest to the Atlantic seaboard that did so, and its most vulnerable point was the Stone Bridge. Troops were moved in to guard the bridge around the clock.

We were all looking for saboteurs and spies, and within a couple of months a suspect named Love was found and brought before my father, the United States Commissioner. According to a Philadelphia paper:

> [Love] was arrested in his room at the hotel last evening by members of the detail of the 13th Pennsylvania Regiment which is doing police duty in Susquehanna and vicinity. On account of the military censorship, little information is being given out. It is learned, however, that the arrest was made upon information from Philadelphia and other cities where it is charged that Love's activities have been such as to show that he is in the employ of the German Government. . . . Love was kept under military guard last night and this morning was given a hearing before United States Commissioner William A. Skinner.

Military censorship apparently did not apply to the *Transcript*, which told the story in the following way: "A well-dressed, obviously cultured man who has been about the city for several days exploiting medicines in tabloid form and securing orders from several well-known local physicians, attracted the attention of Sergeant Carlson of the State Police some days ago by his strange ways and methods in doing business." He was placed under arrest by the sergeant at the local post office and brought before my father. "An examination of his effects in the Commissioner's office revealed among various other things six green notebooks written in various languages and dialects, also several looseleaf maps. . . . His vehement explanation of his extreme loyalty to the 'Old Flag' and his many times repeated claim of his pure American blood and birth did but little to convince Commissioner Skinner that he was the extremely loyal citizen he pretended to be." It was then that he was turned over to the military authorities.

Some of the maps the man had in his possession were of the night skies, and my father brought them home and asked me to take them to school next day to see whether Miss Graves could tell whether they were genuine or were perhaps something to be used in deciphering codes. I took them to Miss Graves, feeling very important, but, alas, she thought they were genuine maps of the stars.

At a patriotic celebration at Hallstead my father urged the passing of the bill before the House authorizing Theodore Roosevelt to lead a unit to the fighting line in France immediately. Teddy Roosevelt, back in favor, was helping to save face for the Republicans, who were now required to support Wilson. We wage war, said my father, quoting Roosevelt, not to make the world safe for democracy (that was Wilsonian nonsense) but "to defeat the men responsible for murdering our men, women, and babes." And speaking to the Sons of Italy, "Attorney Skinner made a ringing eloquent speech which electrified the large crowd and reached beyond telling. . . . He told the Italians they were worthy heirs of Garibaldi. The audience stood and cheered when he described the battle of the marines at the Marne." His concluding sentence was in Italian, translated for him by Joe Radicchi, the shoe repairman. My father had written out a rough phonetic transcription and he went over it again and again before the meeting.

He spoke at dozens of Liberty Bond rallies and was, I think, upstaged only once—at a big meeting in the Hogan Opera House. A representative of the American Hardware Manufacturers Association was scheduled to speak. The band was on the stage, and my father came out from the wings to make some introductory remarks. Shortly after he began someone brought him a note. It was from the hardware man: he would need plenty of time and my father was to be as brief as possible. My father looked offstage over his pince-nez glasses, a withering gesture he had found effective in cross-examination.

The theme of the speaker for the evening had to do with the babies who had been pinned to cathedral doors in Belgium with knives manufactured by the German cutlery industry. Would we ever again buy knives manufactured in Germany? Certainly not! The speaker wanted each and every one of us to sign a pledge saying that for the rest of our lives we would always buy American knives, as well as shears, skewers, and anything else that could be used to pin babies to cathedral doors. Then he rolled his trousers above his knees to wade right in, he said, and put over the biggest subscription to Liberty Bonds in the history of the town.

As a Boy Scout I sold bonds, mostly to my parents and grand-parents and to neighbors with no Boy Scout sons, who would have bought them anyway. The government was aware of family favoritism and gave medals only to Scouts who sold to "ten or more families." I also sold and bought thrift stamps, which were pasted in books to be exchanged for bonds. We went on motor cavalcades to neighboring towns. The Erie Band played "Over There" or "Tipperary," and my father or someone else made a speech. Dennis Horrigan, the band's star tenor, or the bandmaster's son, a boy soprano, sang patriotic songs and we passed out subscription blanks. Driving home at night, we sang the more easily harmonized songs—"Keep the Home Fires Burning" and "There's a Long, Long Trail A-winding."

When a few local boys were leaving for Camp Meade, they were given a great parade. Jack Palmer rode his least controllable horse as marshal, the Erie Band marched, and so did the Boy Scouts, together with some high-school girls dressed as Red Cross nurses. Speeches were made, and the departing soldiers received small presents, among them trench mirrors made by the Blue Ridge Company.

Troop trains brought soldiers from the West on their way to the coast and Europe, and they often spent an hour or two in town, and girls gave them coffee and kisses. I think the bars were off limits, but I once saw a soldier go into a drugstore, buy a bottle of a well-known tonic, and come out and drink it down without taking the bottle out of his mouth.

My mother was active in the Red Cross and she added new economies at home. She saved fat and made a harsh laundry soap by mixing it with lye. She flattened tin cans and put them on the coals in the kitchen stove on the assurance that some additional heat was extracted from them. She canned all available food unless it could be dried; drying was a new technique and never worked very well. My grandmother Burrhus knitted—helmets, sweaters, socks, and mittens. My grandmother Skinner tried to knit too, and she used and re-used the same yarn many times without success.

Eventually it was all over. Early on the morning of November 11, 1918, word spread that an armistice had been signed, and the *Transcript* printed a single sheet of blue paper and distributed handfuls along Main Street. The brief text concluded with these words: "The ending of the World War, like the beginning of the Christian Era, marks a new epoch in the progress of man for it ends for all time the menace of militarism." Within a few hours an effigy of the Kaiser was strung up at the corner of Erie Avenue and Main Street, soaked in gasoline, and set on fire.

A month or two later my father was a member of the reception committee for returning veterans, and still later the bodies of Susquehanna boys killed in action came back one by one and were unloaded onto freight trucks at the Erie depot in their tightly sealed boxes. I was by that time a member of the band and participated in the military funerals. We marched at a slow step—a foot forward on one beat but held above the ground until the next beat; then another foot forward, and so on. We played mournful funeral marches as we moved from the station very slowly along Main Street, into East Main and Little Italy, and then up Broad and Church streets to the Catholic church. On one occasion it was bitter cold and during the long march saliva not only collected in the brass instruments but froze.

I had my first glimpse of the interior of the Catholic church. As we took our places some members of the band genuflected, and I faced the old problem—should I do likewise? And up by the altar I was surprised to see some of the tougher kids in town in lace costumes, behaving like little angels. High Mass was sung with the help of priests from neighboring communities. Mrs. Mooney played the organ, and afterward my father commented on the fact that she ran up or down the keyboard very lightly to discover how far the priests had changed the pitch.

SEVENTH GRADE WAS TAUGHT by Miss Donovan, a strict disciplinarian who disciplined herself and walked in from Lanesboro every day, no matter what the weather. She was on the point of retirement, and in eighth grade we had Miss Keefe, a redhead in her late twenties. She may have been related to the Irishman who was killed by Joe Frank; in any case she and I did not get on well. I was constantly arguing with her and, tactlessly, correcting her. In physiology she told us that the hairs in our nostrils fanned particles of dirt out of our nose while we were breathing in. I insisted that they simply caught the particles and held them until we breathed out. She took the matter to the principal and had to come in the next day and admit that I had been right. When we were diagramming sentences, she argued that we should say "He objected to me going" and I insisted that it should be "He objected to my going." Again she checked with the principal and had to correct herself. It did not make for a good relationship. Once when I was leaving the room, I tripped on the doorsill, and when I came back she bawled me out for kicking up my heels to attract the girls. Not only had I not done so, I was offended by the implication that it was the kind of thing I would have done.

The saving grace in eighth grade was our English class, taught by Miss Graves. We met in another room across the hall, and the class was always lively. It grew especially lively when I became a Baconian. We were reading *As You Like It,* and one evening my father happened to mention that some people thought that the works of Shakespeare had been written by Francis Bacon. That was enough for me, and the next day I announced in class that Shakespeare had not written the play we were reading. Miss Graves said that I didn't know what I was talking about. That afternoon I went down to the library and found a copy of Sir Edwin Durning-Lawrence's *Bacon Is Shakespeare,* which I read in great excitement. The next day, to Miss Graves's dismay, I knew only too well what I was talking about. Act V Scene 1 of *Love's Labour's Lost* contains the long word *honorificabilitudinitatibus,* and Durning-Lawrence proved conclusively, I thought, that it was a code, and that if you rearranged the letters, it became the Latin for "These works, F. Bacon's offspring, are preserved for the world."

A few days later things became even more exciting when I discovered that the *same* act and scene in *As You Like It* was also cryptic. Touchstone is disputing with the simple William (who else but Shakespeare?) for the possession of the fair Audrey (what else but the authorship of the plays?). Would Shakespeare himself have given his name to a dolt? Hardly. And the clincher was that William says he was born in the Forest of Arden, and Shakespeare's mother's name was Arden. (Oh, the lovely adolescent obscenity of that "forest"!)

I must have made life pretty miserable for Miss Graves for the next month or two, but she may very well have let me go on for the sake of the classroom excitement. In any case, in my defensive zeal I read biographies of Bacon, summaries of his philosophical position, and a good deal of the *Advancement of Learning*, the *Essays*, and *Novum Organum*. This was stretching my abilities pretty far, and I doubt whether I got much out of it at the time, but Francis Bacon was to serve me in more serious pursuits later on.

I was not always that studious. In fact, it was at about this time that I went through a silly stage. A new boy had moved onto Church Street and we began to walk home from school together. I started to carry single volumes from that set of *Gems of Humor* in our library and there were things in them by Artemus Ward, Josh Billings, and Mark Twain, and my new friend and I would read them to each other as we walked, often laughing so hard that we staggered about the sidewalk unable to go on reading. When, in something of Mark Twain's, a tenor "let out another length of his neck" we rolled on the grass, tears streaming from our eyes.

Sex remained something of a mystery for a long time. There were allusions and innuendoes that I could not understand. In seventh grade we looked up sexual and excretory words in the large unabridged dictionary, often passing the news along to our friends when we found something juicy, but there wasn't very much juice in dictionaries in those days. We saw pregnant women and pretended that we did not know what that meant. There were jokes about intercourse with animals and, as a matter of fact, my brother reported that he saw a boy we knew, who lived on a farm, actually demonstrating the act with his pony.

There were one or two men in Susquehanna whom my mother called "old fools." An attractive young wife from Lanesboro had a job in the Erie Shops and walked to and from work, a distance of about two miles. Her route lay past Jack Palmer's livery stable, which was slowly being converted into a garage, and Palmer once offered her a ride home in his car, and this became a standard routine. Her husband did not seem to mind. Another man had an "affinity" who lived above my grandfather Skinner's house on Jackson Avenue. She was also married and her husband aware of the relation. Sitting on my grandfather's porch on a Sunday afternoon, we would see him walking up to spend the afternoon with his friend, and my mother could scarcely contain herself. (Jess Haller, who boarded with Gran'ma Graham, presumably cohabited with her daughter, but they were friends of ours, and Jess was never called an old fool.)

During the war we used to hang around the soldiers who were guarding the Stone Bridge, and one day I went into a small station belonging to another railroad and saw a woman who lived not far from my grandfather Skinner on Jackson Avenue who was suspected of being a madam. She had one of her girls with her, and they were talking provocatively with a soldier. The stationmaster went to a telephone, and the officer of the day soon turned up and took the soldier away.

Girls' legs excited me. I never dared buy a copy of the *Police Gazette*, but I could look at the front pages spread out in Charley Wagner's news-store window. The *Gazette* was printed on purple-pink paper and specialized in bathing beauties with a small expanse of bare thigh above glistening stockings. I was not prepared for reality, however, and when a line of real chorus girls came on stage in a show at the Hogan Opera House with legs bare almost to their hips, I was stunned. One of the girls was young and pretty, and I went about for days imagining that if I could only get to know her, she would turn out to be a very nice girl.

During my high-school years a silk mill was started in an effort to bring another industry to Susquehanna. The intention was to employ the daughters or wives of the men working in the Shops, but it was necessary to import girls to work in the mill. Half a dozen of them boarded with Mrs. Smith, the widowed mother of a friend who lived next door to us. They were city girls, rather uninhibited by local standards. We got to know them, and at one time I worked out a way to send messages from one upstairs room to another by holding up cutout letters in our windows. That was all innocent enough, but one warm afternoon John DeWitt and I were lying around in our backyard when one of the more attractive girls came out to clean some shoes. She sat in a chair and when she saw that we were looking at her she pulled her skirts up and spread her legs wide apart. She had pants on and we saw very little, but it was pretty clearly a sexual overture, and John and I were rather shaken. I doubt whether she was interested in more than a little fun; we were young and innocent, and she wondered what we would do. But Mrs. Smith told a neighbor that she could tell from the condition of the sheets on the girls' beds that when they entertained men in their rooms, objectionable things went on.

I worried about the effects of masturbation. There was a kind of sex manual in my father's library which mentioned the subject in what, for the time, was a liberal way, but it was not encouraging because it said that every boy masturbated briefly but soon gave it up for life. The Boy Scout manual, in a short paragraph headed "Conservation," warned against practices which might "result in the loss of vital fluids." Masturbation was supposed to drive boys crazy, and I rather admired a slightly younger boy who told my brother that, whether it did or not, he liked it and was going to go ahead anyway. I once overheard my mother telling my father that a boy down the street masturbated. "It makes a boy so stupid," she said, and my father mumbled some kind of vague agreement, but he knew better, and so did I.

I didn't worry about stupidity or insanity, but I did worry about getting caught. By the time I was in high school Mr. and Mrs. B had moved to a house on Broad Street, and I used to drop in to see my grandmother almost every afternoon on my way home from school. We played Pedro, rummy, or dominoes, but I also used to go to the bathroom and masturbate, sitting on the toilet looking at a large plant in a pot of very wet soil which resembled a miniature grove of palm trees in a swamp. Since I did this every day and stayed rather a long time, my grandmother concluded there must be something wrong with my kidneys. She urged my mother to take me to a doctor for an examination. When I heard about it, I no longer had to go to the toilet in the afternoon, and nothing further was done.

When I began to play in a dance orchestra, the violinist, considerably older than I, once said that masturbation led to poor eyesight, and since I wore glasses I was alarmed. Could there be other signs? What about my pimples? I began to go to a barber near the station who gave "facials." A hot towel was thrown over the face for a few minutes and a pink Pompeian Massage Cream was then spread on the skin. A little later it was rubbed off in little rolls, the blackness of which certainly seemed proof that it was cleaning the pores and thus preventing blackheads and pimples. Later I even had one or two mud-pack treatments.

I discovered that the concealment of sex varied among ethnic groups. I was once crossing a bridge over Drinker Creek just outside of town and saw ten or twelve Italian boys who had been swimming and were now sitting naked on some warm rocks along the bank. They were handling their genitals and the oldest boy was being greatly admired for the size of his erection. The younger were doing their best to emulate him. There was no homosexual contact, and it is possible that the voyeurism, in which I was of course taking part, was scarcely more than curiosity. Nevertheless there was a surprising openness. I can remember only one comparable example among Protestants of that age. At the time I was also swimming in Drinker Creek and my attention was called to two or three boys some little distance away. I joined them and found that they were gazing in wonderment at a particularly large erect penis. The owner was embarrassed by the attention and soon buttoned his pants.

One evening in the bathroom I was cleaning my teeth while my brother was taking a bath. A shower had been installed in one corner of the bathroom, with a base of Keene's cement and a white curtain on a curved rod. I had an erection and noticed that the light was casting my shadow on the shower curtain. I stood in such a way that the erection was conspicuous and called to my brother. He made some exclamation and pulled the curtain aside, but I quickly closed my bathrobe and picked up a nail brush, which he then supposed I had used to fool him. Later in my room I told him that it was not the nail brush and that my penis had actually grown large. He wanted to see it and I showed it to him, and he started to play with it. There was no particular sexual excitement on the part of either of us. At that age, to ejaculate was to be slightly demeaned or defeated, and he was planning to put himself in a superior position. I told him that I could take that kind of stimulation for any length of time without having an orgasm, and he stopped at once, rather petulantly. It was the only sexual activity between us.

*   *   *

As THE EPISODE INDICATES, our relation was changing. He was beginning to tease me. I once read an advertisement which claimed that the little heart of each peanut was removed in making a particular brand of peanut butter because it was bitter. I brought the subject up two or three times in conversation and this was too much for my brother. Whenever we had peanut butter, he would ask me about the little heart of the peanut and roar with laughter.

My father's secretary was named Miss Sykes. I once had to telephone her, and since there were other daughters in the family I asked for "Miss Jessie Sykes." This was a new name to my brother, who may have thought I was putting on airs, and it threw him into stitches. He rolled on the floor, gasping, "Miss Jessie Sykes, Miss Jessie Sykes."

He discovered that he could tease me by repeating what I said. He would start with a remark he thought rather silly, and if I then said, "Oh, stop it," he would simply echo me: "Oh, stop it." If I tried to save myself by saying, "I don't care if you do that," he would say, "I don't care if you do that." My protests only supplied him with further material, and my silence was his victory.

Perhaps he was only getting back at me for a trick I had played on him years before. In the pasture near our summer cottage there were what we called cow pies, the droppings of cows. These baked in the sun and became quite hard. We were walking barefoot in the pasture one day when I noticed a very large cow pie. It had already developed a dry crust and I put my foot on it and pretended to put weight on it. My brother followed my example, and his foot went in up to his ankle.

Some of the things my brother teased me about were matters of serious concern to my parents. I was moving beyond their interests, and I lived much of my life with them rather carelessly. Various faults were blamed on a temporary absence of mind. In one of the Liberty Bond rallies at the Hogan Opera House a dozen of us were lined up across the stage in our Boy Scout uniforms. At one point we were to bring our right hands across our breasts and a moment later drop them again to our sides. Much too late, I discovered that my hand was still across my breast. It was the kind of thing that worried my father and mother but that my brother found hilarious.

He was absent-minded too, but he knew how to laugh at himself. One evening we were all in the library sitting around a fire. My brother went into the kitchen, and then came back laughing almost hysterically. He had got up to go to the toilet, but instead had gone to the kitchen and had found himself starting to urinate into the coal scuttle. We all laughed, but not *at* him as he laughed at me.

He was closer to my father and mother than I, and enjoyed more overt expressions of affection, in part because I was older and less demonstrative. As a younger child he was also treated more leniently. My father used to keep a revolver in the chiffonier by his bed, possibly to frighten a burglar, but certainly not to shoot one. (When he once took a few practice shots near our cottage, with a small bull's-eye fastened to a large shagbark hickory, he could not control the recoil and did not even hit the tree.) One day my brother, alone in the house, got out the revolver and was examining it when it went off, drilling a neat hole in the front of the chiffonier. My parents were overjoyed that he had not hurt himself and never disciplined him for playing with the gun.

In spite of the fact that my brother "plagued" me, I was never aware of any rivalry. We did not compete in the same fields. My father and mother were devoted to both of us, and there was plenty of affection to go around. If the lack of sibling rivalry is disappointing, I can at least report a partial identity crisis. When I was perhaps fourteen or fifteen I woke up one morning and could not find my left arm. I groped for it in panic. It was nowhere to be found in the bed on the left side of my body and my left shoulder seemed rounded off like a stump. Eventually I discovered the arm crossed under my neck and twisted so sharply at the shoulder that all circulation had stopped. It was cold and completely without feeling. With my right hand I put it in place, like the arm of a fresh cadaver, and massaged it back to tingling life.

My brother was much more athletic than I, and the favorite local sport was basketball. A semi-professional team played in the gymnasium at the YMCA. The two-handed dribble was legal then and Susquehanna had a player who could move about the court at will with the ball oscillating rapidly between his hands and the floor. He was our only local sports hero. Our school had no basketball court, but my brother and several other boys organized a team at the Y. They called themselves the Boys Five and challenged all comers from neighboring towns. In the only game reported in my mother's scrapbook they were defeated by a score of 77 to 5. If that was not a misprint, a coach was evidently needed.

MY FATHER READ ABOUT, and yearned for, a good father-son relationship, but he did not know how to enter into one. He loved my brother and me and gave us all the advantages he could, and he was proud of us, but there was never a really warm friendship. It was part of the price he paid for that forced childhood.

Except when visiting his Aunt Alt, it was only with his father and his Uncle Ed that he was a relaxed and happy man. When his uncle was in town, the three of them would go fishing for a day. They would assemble poles, lines, and bait, including minnows in a pail with an inner wire basket that could be hung over the side of the boat, and they took lunches and drove to Page's Pond. By evening they would be back laden with bass and bullheads, which they spread out according to size on the grass by the garage. They told stories of the little adventures of the day, and my father was always especially pleased to tell something to the credit of his father. But it was not long before my mother would say something about cleaning the fish or putting on some other clothes for supper.

My father had business associates, and he was probably pretty much himself with Frank Zeller or Sid Hersh, but these were not close friendships. I do not know how he behaved with his "affinities," but I never saw him at ease in mixed company. His conversation was forced and he laughed too long at his own jokes.

He hoped that his sons would play baseball, and we had all the necessary equipment—balls, bats, catcher's mask, and catcher's and fielder's mitts—and plenty of space in our backyard, where we played three-o'-cat, yet my father never played with us. He himself played indoor baseball and apparently played it well, for the *Transcript* once reported that "the feature of the game was a triple play made by the business men when Attorney Skinner caught a line drive and assisted by E. K. Owens and Carrington retired the side." But playing with my brother and me, he would have been ill at ease, praising us too much for a good play or showing us a little too didactically how we could play better.

It was more his style to take me to Binghamton to see a World Series game on one of the animated boards in use before the days of radio. We watched small figures move about on a large diamond according to information received by telegraph as the game was being played. The audience sat staring at the inactive board while the telegraph clicked away behind the scene, and then the figures began to move and the audience cheered or groaned.

We were watching a game between Cleveland and the Brooklyn Dodgers on October 10, 1920, when the system was strained beyond its powers. The telegraph clattered away and then stopped, and we could hear the operators discussing how to show us what had happened. Finally a man came out to confess that it could not be done. The Cleveland second baseman, Wambsganss, had made a triple play unassisted. With men on first and second bases he had caught a line drive, stepped on second, and then chased the runner back toward first and tagged him out. It remains the only unassisted triple play in World Series history.

I began to play tennis on the court of the Kane sisters, who lived just off Jackson Avenue about a block from my grandfather Skinner's. Madelaine and Annetta Kane worked as clerks in the Erie Shops. They were Irish and slightly older than I, and I should never have known them if a WASP friend, Ward Palmer, had not worked in the same office. Madelaine, the younger, seldom played tennis, and I never got to know her. Annetta was small, wiry, quick-spoken, witty, and an excellent player according to our standards. She was the first intellectual Catholic I had ever met, and she quoted G. K. Chesterton, often with telling effect. Both sisters eventually became postulants in a religious order, and Annetta went on to become a nun.

The Kane court was in a depression just behind their house, and Ward and I more or less took care of it. On a Sunday morning we would roll it, mark it with lime, adjust the net, and then play a few sets. We had no professional instruction and were not strong players. When Ward and I once drove to Binghamton to see an exhibition match between Bill Tilden and Vincent Richards, it seemed to be a different game. But we talked tennis, kept our rackets in presses, had them restrung when necessary, and occasionally organized a tournament. I once played against the editor of the *Transcript*. He was as old as my father and I should have beaten him, but he was very clever in placing the ball, and he eventually wore me out and won.

Ward Palmer was perhaps ten years older than I. He was small, spare, and muscular, his skin was bronzed even in winter, and he smiled easily. His father was a free-lance automobile mechanic who loved cars and was perfectly content to spend his life working on them. Ward's mother had some connection with the Wright dynasty and maintained an appropriate bearing. His sister also moved in slightly superior circles—the semi-intellectual world of Binghamton. A short-story writer who lived there was known for dining out, and Ward relayed to me one of his witty remarks: in passing a dish of peas to his neighbor at a dinner party he had said, "Do you vibrate to peas?"

In spite of the Wright connection, the family lived in an unpretentious rented duplex on lower Jackson Avenue. The small living room contained two large easy chairs and a magnificent Victrola. Ward had all the opera records then available, together with *The Victrola Book of the Opera*, which gave the plots, and we went through them many times. We were above the "best-loved" pieces like the Quartet from *Rigoletto* or the Sextet from *Lucia* and even somewhat above things like *"Celeste Aida"* and *"Vesti la giubba."* We immersed ourselves in the dramatic solos and duets which were meaningful only when you knew the story—things like Cassio's dream (*"Era la notte"*), *"O terra, addio," "Piangi, piangi, fanciulla,"* and *"Povero Rigoletto."*

I once pointed out that a theme which would shortly dominate the music could actually be heard—faintly, or partly masked, or in fragments—at an earlier stage. I told Ward, as if I knew, that the composer did this to make the emerging theme all the more effective, and I was surprised at how readily he accepted me as an authority.

I heard opera live when my parents took my brother and me to New York. We stayed at the Martinique Hotel, which was then quite posh, with a headwaiter in tails. My father got tickets—the best box seats available—for Geraldine Farrar in *Carmen* at the Metropolitan. My brother and I had just had new suits made by Bill Ernestone. Fortunately, we had graduated from knickers to long trousers, but our salt-and-pepper tweeds with jackets belted in the back were still scarcely the thing for box seats at the Met.

We arrived early, and my father insisted that my brother and I sit in the front of the box in order to get the full benefit of the opera. Two women arrived later and took the remaining seats at the back. The box at our right suddenly filled with chicly dressed girls—from a finishing school, I suppose—who were obviously amused by the country bumpkins. We held doggedly to our front seats, returning to them after being no less conspicuous in the crowds between the acts. But we heard *Carmen*, for some of which I had been prepared by Ward Palmer's records. I felt much more comfortable the next night when we saw Ed Wynn in *The Perfect Fool*.

I BEGAN TO PLAY MUSIC again a year or two after I stopped taking lessons. I drifted back to the piano and picked out bits of my mother's sentimental music—the slower and easier things like a song called "Forgotten" or Sir Arthur Sullivan's "Lost Chord." I began to do so in earnest when I fell in love because all my early loves were hopeless, and sentimental music was a great solace.

I also took up the saxophone. An Italian, Joe Demase, had had his jaw crushed in an accident in the Shops, and my father had got him some kind of compensation (not at that time a common practice). When he was well enough to play the saxophone again, he volunteered to teach me. I began with a C-melody saxophone and worked on things like the Intermezzo from *Cavalleria Rusticana*, or Handel's "Largo," or the "Evening Star" from *Tannhäuser*.

When I had acquired a reasonable skill, my father bought me a B-flat soprano saxophone and arranged for me to play in the Erie Band. In perhaps a dozen of the Shops along its route the company was paternalistic enough to give men time off for weekly rehearsals, and once a year to hold a contest. The high school let me take Tuesday afternoons off and I went down to a large room above the Carpenter Shop. (My grandfather Burrhus would hang around near the foot of the stairs to say hello.)

There were some excellent musicians in the band. We all stood in awe of an Italian clarinetist called Teddy. (He eventually lost status, but for an irrelevant reason: he came home early one day and found his wife in bed with another man and was afraid to do anything about it.) The director of the band was Art Brower, the freight-master. He played the baritone—a lovely instrument somewhere be-tween a French horn and a tuba in size and pitch—and one of our shorter selections was a baritone solo called "A Night in June," which he played while conducting. We played marches ("Washington Post," "Stars and Stripes Forever"), medleys of Irish songs or war songs, and the overtures of von Suppé ("Light Cavalry," "Morning Noon and Night in Vienna," and, of course, "Poet and Peasant").

I played in two contests—one in Hornell, New York, and an-other in Galion, Ohio. Each of the competing bands played a short curtain-raiser—say, "Night in June"—and then a major composition —say, "Morning Noon and Night in Vienna"—and in one contest the soprano saxophone was the only instrument scored to go "tweet tweet" at an important point. The meeting in Galion was in the fall of 1920, and we heard Warren Gamaliel Harding reading a "front porch" speech in his campaign for President. I worked my way up close to the platform and watched the reporters following their copies to make sure that he read it all as written.

Before I left for Galion my father got around to giving me a sex talk, but I was ahead of him on the few details he could bring himself to mention. He told me that he had once been invited to join some young men who were going to a "house of ill repute" and had refused, and that one of those who had gone had acquired a disease from which he still suffered and which would eventually prove fatal. No further details were given.

He had not prepared me for crossing another ethnic line. There was a young Irish boy in the band, about my age but already working as an apprentice, who shared an upper berth with me on the sleeper. We took off our band uniforms—they were of heavy material with gold braid and hard to store overnight without wrinkling—and it was then clear that my new friend assumed that as a matter of course we would play with each other sexually. I never discovered whether this was standard practice among the Irish boys of the town, and when we returned to Susquehanna our relationship was once again simply that of nodding acquaintances.

Joe Demase, who was beginning to flourish as an instructor on the saxophone, organized a Boys' Band, and a surprising number of boys turned up. To my embarrassment I was made assistant director. The *Transcript* gave the venture loyal support, and we marched in a few parades and played a few concerts. At one rehearsal Joe suddenly handed me the baton, and I had to stand up and conduct, but except for the first beat, at which most of the players began to play, there was little evidence that I was having any effect.

I began to take the saxophone seriously. With a piano accompanist I played at various recitals. (I could never play with my mother, even in rehearsal, because she never *accompanied* me; she played right on, letting me follow, and although I protested again and again, I was never able to convince her that it was I who was playing the solo.)

When our musical friend from Binghamton, Mrs. Taylor, came to our house, she played my accompaniments, and it was a tremendous experience. She recommended a saxophone teacher in Binghamton named Livingston. He had entertained soldiers during the war with a vaudeville act in which he wrote the alphabet forward with one hand, backward with the other, added a column of figures, and answered questions—all at the same time. It gave him a headache. He had invented a special mouthpiece for the saxophone on which the position of the reed could be adjusted with a small screw. I bought one and he appointed me his agent in Susquehanna, but I never made a sale.

It was not easy to find serious music for the saxophone. There were collections of cornet solos which I could play on the soprano sax, but only a few elementary things for the C-melody, and I searched the music stores of Binghamton for vocal solos that might serve, but in vain. I ordered the scores of *Carmen, Aida, Faust,* and *I Pagliacci,* however, and I began to work on the tenor solos. When Mrs. Taylor organized a recital for the Episcopal church in Susquehanna, she asked me to play, and I played the aria *"Salut, demeure"* from *Faust.* Apparently reassured, she invited me to play at the annual recital of her pupils in Binghamton.

It was the spring of my senior year, and I prepared several tenor solos, including *"No, Pagliaccio non son"* and *"Vesti la giubba"* from *I Pagliacci,* and *"Celeste Aida,"* studying Caruso's performances on Ward Palmer's records. My father and mother drove me to Binghamton and the performance went off without an unscheduled squeak. Someone in the audience said that she thought she could hear Caruso in my performance, and that was tremendously reinforcing.

Afterward Mrs. Taylor wrote to thank me and added a complimentary note on my *sang-froid*, and I was far enough along in French to be impressed by the actual use of the language.

Mrs. Taylor had seen the kind of sentimental stuff I was playing on the piano, and she sent me without comment a copy of Mozart's Third Sonata. I played it bit by bit, beginning with the easier bars in no particular order. Later I put it all together and much later bought all the Mozart sonatas, and I went through them each year in a kind of ritual for decades.

My interest in classical music and in the potential of the saxophone in imitating the human voice was swept away by commercialism. I began to play in a jazz band. An established institution in the dance halls of Susquehanna was Holleran's Orchestra, the established core of which was Holleran himself at the piano and Leo Sullivan on the trap drums. Other players (never more than a total of four) came and went. In my day they had an excellent violinist but needed a saxophonist. Leo Sullivan knew me because he played the snare drum in the Erie Band, and he asked me to join Holleran's group.

Holleran played with an impeccably steady tempo. There was syncopation—the great discovery—but no rubato. He thumped the keys, the fingers of his stubby hands scarcely visible, and the volume never changed. Although he played many pieces hundreds of times, he continued to read music, and this was fortunate because I could not memorize. I simply read the music over his shoulder, while the violinist moved about in enviable freedom and Leo improvised with bass drum, snare drum, cymbals, wood block, and wire brushes.

We played two or three times a week, very often until two or three in the morning, either at the Laurel Athletic Club or in the dance hall over Murphy's Garage in Oakland. My cheeks would be painfully tired by two o'clock, and afterward, if we were playing in Oakland, I had a long walk home. A cold night could be cruel because I had to carry my C-melody saxophone in its case. Coming into a house already cold, I usually went to the kitchen to get a glass of milk before going to bed. I would stir in some flavoring and sugar to make a kind of milkshake.

Bigger and better movies were coming to the Hogan Opera House, and Ryan, the proprietor, began to replace Miss Dooley at the piano on Friday and Saturday evenings with a theatre orchestra.

Three of my friends and I organized and competed for the job. The distributors sent ahead of each film a detailed schedule, specifying the kind of music required for each scene with the precise number of seconds it was to be played: one minute and ten seconds of a romantic theme, followed by twenty-three seconds of *mysterioso*, followed by fifty seconds of a military march, followed by the romantic theme again for twenty-five seconds, and so on. My friends and I took all this seriously, and we searched our limited repertoire for appropriate music. Our drummer, Bob Basso, went beyond the script, and by the second show on Saturday night he was using the wood block, cymbal, or bass drum to add blows to the jaw, pratfalls, and collisions, giving the audience an advanced taste of sound films.

My musical history in Susquehanna reached its climax when I attended a performance of the Boston Symphony Orchestra in Binghamton. I was working for the *Transcript*, and when I told the editor that I was going, he turned to his typewriter and struck off a note to the management: "Please give the bearer two tickets to the Boston Symphony Concert as per our agreement." The *Transcript* had apparently run a free notice. I picked up the tickets at the box office at the Kalura Temple in the afternoon and turned up early for the performance in the evening. My seat was in the third row center, all of which was reserved for the press. The Temple slowly filled up and eventually was completely packed except for the third row, in which I sat alone.

Pierre Monteux conducted Beethoven's Symphony No. 3, Rimski-Korsakov's *Caprice on Spanish Themes*, Schubert's Incidental Music to *Rosamunde*, and Wagner's Overture to *Rienzi*. The thing that impressed me most was the length of the pieces. Our Victrola records were limited to the four minutes or so available on one side of a disk at 78 rpm, and the pieces the Erie Band played were not much longer, but the *Eroica* Symphony seemed to go on forever.

IN MY JUNIOR AND SENIOR YEARS I discovered another small world of art. There were two news-stores in town and both had unexpected treasures in their darker recesses—sheets of colored cardboard and drawers full of camel-hair brushes and show-card pens and inks. There were shading pens that would draw a line almost half an inch wide, perhaps a third of which would be darker than the rest, and other pens that drew parallel lines. There were bats of Dennison's crepe paper and rolls of *passe-partout*.

Most of this apparently had lain untouched for years, but I dug it out and went into the business of making show cards. I bought a book of lettering styles and began to make placards for dances, recitals, and an occasional store window. Someone in town did the bigger signs and could put gold-leaf letters on shop doors and windows, but he was apparently not interested in the small jobs I had taken over.

I continued to do watercolors, and I learned a bit about charcoal drawing from Ward Palmer, who had begun to make large copies of pictures from *The Victrola Book of the Opera*. I also moved into stage design. My brother and I were occasionally taken to New York to see shows. In addition to Ed Wynn in *The Perfect Fool* I remember a musical called *The Night Boat*, Robert Benchley reading "The Treasurer's Report" in Irving Berlin's *Music Box Review*, and W. C. Fields doing the tissue-paper-with-sticky-finger bit. I had no success as an actor, but I began to build scenery for home-talent plays in the Hogan Opera House. My brother played a small part in something called *Jimmy's Aunt Jane*, and I used my stereopticon unsuccessfully to highlight a touching scene in a plagiarized version of a popular play called *Strongheart*.

In setting the stage for a kind of Chinese or Japanese extravaganza called *The Feast of Singasong*, I made many trips back and forth between the opera house and Charley Wagner's supply of crepe paper and, possibly as a result, came down with the Spanish influenza. It was the year after the great epidemic, when the *Transcript* had sent out a call for people to "help in the current health emergency," but cases were still severe, and I had a bad one. Dr. Denman was said to scare his patients and it is true that he told my parents I was developing a heart murmur and that I would at some stage go "out of my head." He was wrong about that, but I had a high fever for a week, and much of my hair came out. We had a new Victrola record, a saxophone sextet playing "*La Paloma*," and I listened to it dozens of times as I lay stretched out in bed. Near the end of the week Bob Perrine called and brought me a bag of chocolates, and I was embarrassed by the speed with which my mother carried them off into the little attic near my room, in order to keep them cool, without offering one to Bob or me.

I LIKED HIGH SCHOOL. It was the custom for students to congregate outside the building until a bell rang and the doors were opened, but I would arrive early, knock on the door, and ask Mr. Shaughnessy, stone deaf with boilermaker's ear, to let me in. He had been told to keep students out, but he would shrug and open the door just enough to let me through, as if in squeezing through I was not really coming in. Alone on the second floor, I would go to the library, or examine a collection of bottles of gum arabic, nox vomica, and various minerals which someone had given the school but which were never mentioned by our science teachers, or simply sit at my desk with my books. When the bell rang and the other students came trooping in, I would make myself as inconspicuous as possible and pretend that I was just arriving too.

Science was taught in a room containing a chemistry bench and a cabinet full of apparatus and instruments. Mrs. Sullivan taught physics. A student pumped the air out of a bell jar so that a feather fell as rapidly as a penny. We measured quantities of hot and cold water and ice and mixed them in brass calorimeters and observed the results with a thermometer. We proved that air had weight by weighing a football bladder before and after inflation. And we rolled balls down an inclined plane, or rather an inclined gutter, the ball rolling from side to side as well as down and leaving traces in a sprinkling of talcum from which we could determine both the time and the distance to prove that Galileo was right.

Miss Keefe had been promoted and was teaching chemistry, and she remained my nemesis. At the chemistry bench one day I was doing a bit of placer mining by directing a fine stream of water from a rubber hose at some debris, and I called to another boy to look. Miss Keefe thought I was pretending to urinate and reprimanded me severely. Once I deserved a reprimand. We were discussing fatty acids, and one of the more buxom girls in our class was at the blackboard. I whispered to another boy, "There is a fatty acid!" and Miss Keefe heard me and took the matter up with the principal. The curious thing was that I saw the point of the remark only as I said it.

Miss Werle taught four years of Latin—grammar, Caesar, Cicero, and Virgil. I rather liked Virgil and dug into it well enough to feel that I was occasionally thinking in another language.

We studied botany and collected and pressed various kinds of leaves and flowers. Our text, *How Plants Grow*, contained a passage about the life cycle of the radish that impressed me, quite possibly because of my father's talk about progress and my mother's about service, and I copied it out and have kept it among my notes:

So the biennial root becomes large and heavy, being a storehouse of nourishing matter, which man and animals are glad to use for food. In it, in the form of starch, sugar, mucilage, and in other nourishing and savory products, the plant (expending nothing in flowers or in show) has laid up the avails of its whole summer's work. For what purpose? This plainly appears when the next season's growth begins. Then, fed by this great stock of nourishment, a stem shoots forth rapidly and strongly, divides into branches, bears flowers abundantly, and ripens seeds, almost wholly at the expense of the nourishment accumulated in the root, which is now light, empty, and dead; and so is the whole plant by the time the seeds are ripe.

Our principal, Professor Bowles, had gone to Valparaiso College but had never taken a degree, and he often talked defensively of his early disadvantages. He was a big man who walked as if he were making his way through a crowd, and he gave the impression of being much more aggressive than he really was. His wife was a timid little woman, and his children seemed scared of him. His instructional methods evoked something of the same response.

He taught mathematics, and it was our practice to assemble for his classes in the front row of the large hall, where we waited for him to leave his office. He would weave and stalk in, and we would brace ourselves. He might march straight toward a trembling girl, point his finger at her, and shout, "What's the product of the sum and difference?" But he took us through four years of mathematics, using textbooks by Wentworth, a writer who was unaware of the need for relevance. We studied algebra, plane and solid geometry, and trigonometry, and I loved it all. Plane geometry was my favorite, because I had my father's old drafting equipment and was particularly fond of constructions. I stood up to Professor Bowles (and this was probably only what he expected from all his students), and he began to show a special respect for me. He once brought me a newspaper clipping which reported someone's solution to the problem of trisecting the angle and told me to find out what was wrong with it.

Once we were both embarrassed by a silly prank. A student was passing out tablets, and for no particular reason I managed to get an extra one and slipped it into my desk. It turned out that tablets had been missing, and on this day a careful count had been kept. The teacher went to Mr. Bowles's office, and he stormed into the room. "Someone took an extra tablet," he shouted. I immediately put up my hand and said, "Yes, I did." He was completely deflated. He knew that I had not been stealing tablets and that the wrong person had sprung his trap, and he passed the matter off as quickly as possible.

From Professor Bowles I learned the delight to be found in bringing order out of chaos. I had been impressed by a book of my father's containing a game of checkers called, as I remember it, Old One Hundred, in which all moves, or at least all reasonable moves, were analyzed and answered in such a way that if you moved first you could win or draw. So much for pushing pieces about on the board in the course of ordinary play; in fact, so much for checkers as a game. On one of his trips to Montrose my father met someone who always won a much simpler game. Pennies were arranged in rows of three, five, and seven. A play consisted of removing any number of pennies from any one row, and the object was to make the other person take the last penny. My father thought it remarkable that the man could always win if he moved first, and I was challenged. I worked out all the possibilities, starting with certain winning arrays, such as two rows of equal numbers or three rows of one, two, and three respectively. Eventually I, too, could always win if I played first, and it was then no longer a game.

Professor Bowles liked mathematics, but I am not sure he liked teaching it. In any case he escaped from doing so for part of every period by embarking upon long-winded digressions. Something would remind him of a bit of local gossip, and that would remind him of something Carl Schurz, a favorite of his, once said, and that would remind him of the shocking fact that coffins were often made with glue and quickly came apart in moist ground, and that would remind him of a poem of Sidney Lanier's, and so on. Eventually he would get back to mathematics, and he always saved face by mentioning the point which had led him into the digression. One day I jotted down the things he talked about. As luck would have it, he embarked upon a second digression that day, and when he came to the end of it he saved face by returning to the topic which had set him off on the *first* digression. That seemed to me an important discovery, and I took my records to Miss Graves. She was amused and suggested that I show them to Professor Bowles himself. I did not do so, but not, I think, because I did not dare. I thought it might embarrass him.

One of his favorite topics was petting, and he strongly advocated the principle of *Noli me tangere,* which he translated for the benefit of those who might be getting poor grades in Miss Werle's classes: "I do not want to be touched!" He was a good Catholic and frequently discussed theological points with me privately. He was occasionally rather defensive. Catholics were not encouraged to read the Bible, he said, because parts of it were not suitable (he meant too sexual) for the ordinary reader. He argued that confession was good for the soul. Like my parents, he may have suspected that I was becoming an agnostic if not an atheist, and he lent me a book called *God or Gorilla,* which ridiculed paleontology and current efforts to reconstruct the anatomy of early man from a tooth or a bit of a jawbone.

Shortly before I was graduated he called me into his office and in a very serious tone said, "I just want to say one thing. You were born to be a leader of men. Never forget the value of a human life," and he dismissed me in some embarrassment. I could not imagine what he meant. I had certainly shown no sign of leadership. I played on no team over which I could have exerted any control, I had no rank as a Boy Scout. When Joe Demase first turned the baton over to me as assistant director of the Boys' Band, I began to beat time and the band started to play, but I *followed.* With my two or three close friends I was an equal, but with John DeWitt rather a follower. My brother would have been a better bet for personal leadership, or Bob Perrine, who went on to West Point.

I suspect that Professor Bowles simply wished that I would become a leader. He had gone about as far as he could go in education, and he may have felt that his only hope of emerging as a great teacher lay in the future of one of his students. He respected me and enjoyed our brief intellectual exchanges and he may have felt that I was his best bet. Raphael Miller once said to me, "You liked Professor Bowles, didn't you? I never did."

Miss Graves taught reading, and that meant A *Tale of Two Cities, Macbeth, Ivanhoe, Silas Marner, The Idylls of the King,* and *The Last of the Mohicans.* The high-school library had a set of the Harvard Classics—not the full five-foot shelf, rather more like three and a half feet—in which I read Darwin's *Voyage of the Beagle.* (In the town library I found a battered copy of Darwin's *Expression of Emotion in Man and Animals,* and I spent a great deal of time trying to imitate that French actor who could put horizontal, vertical, and diagonal wrinkles in his forehead at the same time.) I also read the *Autobiography of Benvenuto Cellini,* and I was impressed by Cellini's zeal as he threw his best plate into the melting pot to get enough metal to finish a statue, as well as his good luck in getting a fever which, with its natural version of diathermy, cured him of a venereal disease. I did not read Adam Smith's *Wealth of Nations* or a volume by Edmund Burke bearing on the spine the surprising title of *On the Sublime and Beautiful French Revolution.*

I tried to move from history to destiny by depositing a bit of the future. The top shelves in the high-school library were filled with huge volumes about the Civil War—routine histories of local regiments, sold to veterans or the children of veterans, no longer of interest to anyone and probably given to the school in the belief that it was the most likely time capsule in which history would be preserved. In some of these volumes I planted slips of paper offering a reward of ten cents for their return. I have never received any, and I daresay the volumes have long since been destroyed.

*   *   *

MARY GRAVES AND I WERE, so to speak, promoted through grade and high school at about the same rate, so that she taught me a bit of drawing through all twelve years and reading through the last six. Her father, James Graves, had begun life as a teacher, interested in astronomy and botany. He taught briefly in the "Little Red School House" made famous by the popular naturalist John Burroughs, who was one of his pupils. Later he became a stonecutter, working in marble, and came to Susquehanna as such, but he continued his intellectual interests. He was a member of the Asa Gray Memorial Association, published articles in various journals, and corresponded widely with botanists. He championed unpopular views. He was a staunch defender of Darwin and evolution, and with the same fervor he debated lesser issues. He had insisted, for example, that the year 1900 was the last year of the nineteenth century, and that the town should wait a year to celebrate the birth of the twentieth. He was also the village atheist, a fact which the editor of the *Transcript* tactfully concealed in reporting his death:

> All his life he was a seeker of truth. His mind was ever concerned with the great question of Being and his views were based on his interpretation of nature. It is typical of his whole mental makeup that in the days of his early manhood, his interest inclined to astronomy and the vaster fields of human thought. In his prime he directed his attention to the concrete earth he saw around him; and in the evening of life he turned again to his Universe and reached out to the Infinite.

He never lost his interest in teaching. If he came across a boy or two on his way home from work, he would stop to point out features of the night sky while his wife and children waited supper. He also impressed his views on his family. His wife, ten years younger than he, is said to have resented his didactic measures, but at least one of his children accepted them and gained from them.

An early photograph of Mary Graves shows an attractive young woman with dark, penetrating eyes and full lips, hair gracefully waved before being drawn back and held with a clip at the back of her head. I remember her much later, when her eyes were still bright but her lips had grown thin and were easily pursed. She was then what was called a homely old maid. She could have sat for the portrait in the

Prado of *"La Venerable Madre Jeronima de la Fuente"* by Velásquez. She usually wore patterned shirtwaists and dark skirts reaching to the ankles of her black buttoned shoes, and her graying hair was drawn back in a tight bun.

As a young woman she kept a notebook, in which she would devote a whole page to an exact description of a caterpillar and another to an account of how it constructed a cocoon, using a leaf but only after anchoring it securely to the branch of the tree. Other pages of her notebook listed the birds and flowers she saw.

The family enjoyed an intellectual life far beyond anything else in Susquehanna. On those evenings when my father and mother were rehearsing their roles in *Esmeralda*, the Graves family was reading aloud from the Waverley novels, Shakespeare, Emerson, Goldsmith, or Thoreau. Even so, her father and mother were not college graduates, and Miss Graves seems to have been aware of shortcomings. As a teacher she attended annual enrichment conferences in Montrose and kept careful notes of the lectures she heard, recording the punctuation of foreign words and names and the definitions of unusual terms.

She began teaching in primary school, and at the end of the first year she wrote in her diary:

> A year's teaching past. A very pleasant and profitable year. Teaching grows more beautiful to me—*teaching!*—who am I that I can *teach?* I feel more and more after the year's work how responsible I am for what I teach. I commenced the work last September with a very blind feeling but the work has opened to me more and more and I have been blessed with some success, enough to make me wish to strive harder and harder for more. . . . In June the School Board re-elected me primary teacher at an increase of salary—$37.00 per month instead of $32.00. I am very glad of course. I want to spend it wisely and well. Much for the family needs, some for necessaries of my own, and a little for luxuries—a long-wished-for book perhaps; and *save* some.

That was to be essentially her program with a meager salary throughout her life. Her father was often out of work and died when she was young; her brothers went off to New York, and she was left as the main support of her mother. They lived in a house at the corner of Broad and Oak streets. (The kitchen door opened directly on Oak Street; perhaps the house was built before the street was formally laid out.) On the Broad Street side there was a large yard which needed more care than Miss Graves could give it, and in which strange trees and bushes collected by her father grew almost wild—a "leather" tree with a flexible but very tough bark, and an "iron" tree the wood of which I could not cut with my knife.

The living room had been closed off, and I doubt whether the rotting front porch which ran alongside it would have borne a heavy man's weight. I always entered by the kitchen door and almost never did so without finding Mrs. Graves there at work.

The only other room in use on the first floor was probably built as a dining room, but it now held a long table, a golden-oak secretary, a bookcase with a glass front, and a few chairs. Here I spent an occasional Sunday afternoon talking with Miss Graves—her mother, very small and gray, sitting silently at the window at the far end of the room. There were treasures in the house, and I suppose I eventually saw them all, but they were husbanded carefully, and no more than one was ever shown to me on a single Sunday. I recall an illustrated *Sinbad*, various shells and pieces of rock, and—treasure of treasures—a letter from the Prince of Monaco to Miss Graves's father offering to exchange botanical specimens. There was also an unfired clay head modeled by a brother who had gone off years before to become an artist. His wife had left him and come back to Susquehanna, to keep house for the aging photographer Delly Harding, and to serve as librarian, but Miss Graves always spoke of him with pride when she spoke of him at all. She told me once that he was a specialist in perspective and that other artists often came to him for help in laying out tile floors on their canvases. She once gave me a broken clay figure he had left behind, and I softened the clay and made a plaque of Venus rising from the sea.

On a Sunday afternoon Miss Graves sometimes took her Sunday-school class for a walk in the pasture and woods back of the Laurel Hill Academy. There was a spring in the pasture, a real spring with clear, cold, drinkable water. She taught us to spot birds and flowers, and showed us how to find sassafras (we chewed the bark and dug up bits of the root to take home) and how to identify the birch with the bark that tasted like birch beer. The world she showed us was fascinating, and she was often embarrassed by our excitement.

It more than made up for the embarrassment we all felt when we exchanged gifts in the Presbyterian church on Christmas Eve. She and her mother could not afford substantial gifts for five or six boys. One year we did get small, nicely bound copies of Charles Kingsley's *Greek Heroes* (possibly she managed to pick up half a dozen copies at a special price), but in general her presents were mere tokens, and she would wince as we opened them and simulated our delight.

She had a way of passing on curious bits of information. She told me that Sarah Bernhardt painted her ears so that they looked translucent, that a Hindu could steal a blanket from underneath a sleeping man by using a feather to get him to roll from side to side, that Robert Louis Stevenson spent as much as twenty minutes on a single sentence, and that a pianist, whose performance before a king had been interrupted when dinner was announced, remained so uneasy at the table that the king asked him what was wrong, and he begged permission to go back and play the last chords of the composition. She also told me that when a monk finished copying a long manuscript, he would add the Latin for "Finished, thank God," and I have often wondered whether she interpreted the significance of that expression correctly.

Miss Graves, spinster, loved small children. She wrote stories for her nephew and niece, and, like a fond parent, relayed the bright sayings of a neighbor's child whose older sister used to bring him to see her. Until I reread *Silas Marner*, the only bit I remembered was Silas's ineffectual discipline—the child's comment, "Effie in de toal-hole," and Silas's refusal to continue punishment—and I suspect I remembered it only because of the warmth and affection with which Miss Graves must have discussed it.

With older students she found teaching difficult. The books we read were evidently chosen to sample life over a period of many centuries and, I think, had that effect, though I was to reread most of them years later with greater understanding and enjoyment. They were not relevant to life in Susquehanna (we were not yet "ready" for them) and the tougher boys paid little or no attention. One or two were even more refractory, and the principal would have to be called in.

Her influence was felt outside the school. In that small Pennsylvania town she stood for culture. She kept up with things. She once confided to me in a conspiratorial tone, as if it were something disreputable, that she was reading "the strangest book—it is called *Lord Jim.*" She organized and ran the Monday Club, an afternoon literary society to which my mother belonged. Miss Graves carefully prepared for its meetings, looking up the pronunciation or meaning of difficult words in the things they were reading. (They spent much of one winter on *A Doll's House.*) In the town library she selected most of the new books the town could afford, and for a while on Saturday morning she read to groups of children—from *Uncle Remus* and Kipling.

She subscribed to serious magazines like the *Outlook* and brought her copies to school. I have good reason for not forgetting that fact. Once a week the whole school assembled in the high-school auditorium, which could be enlarged by opening two great doors into a side room. One morning someone who was scheduled to perform was ill, and Miss Graves and Mr. Bowles called me aside and showed me a copy of the *Outlook.* It contained a short article about an island in the Pacific which had come under the jurisdiction of the United States at the end of the war, and they asked me to read it to the assembled company. I had no time to go through the article but took it out onto the stage. I glanced at it, looked out over the audience, and in a loud voice announced its title: "Yap." Harold Craft was the first to laugh.

As early as 1903 Miss Graves had gone to a nursing home in the Adirondacks in New York State to recover from tuberculosis. There were other attempts at a cure, one of them paid for by grateful members of the Monday Club, but by my junior year it was evident that she was quite ill. She began to take a short-cut through a back lot to school rather than walk around by way of Myrtle Street and Jackson Avenue. She brought milk and snacks to be eaten between meals, and she was embarrassed when I once came upon her as she was drinking milk on the far side of the chemistry table in the science room.

By the end of my senior year she was forced to resign. Summer came and I heard very little about her, though I knew she was dying. Near the end of June I called on her for the last time. It was a quiet evening, and in the kitchen I found her mother, then eighty-four and tinier than ever. She understood at once why I had come, asked me to sit down, and disappeared upstairs. I waited for a long time, and eventually she came down to tell me I might go up.

I have said that Miss Graves would have been called a homely old maid. I was always glad to see her but almost not as a person. She was someone who listened to me, answered my questions, and almost always had something interesting to say or a suggestion of something interesting to do. Perhaps it was not until I went into her bedroom that summer evening that I really saw her as a human being.

There was no light in the room, and it was beginning to grow dark. She was sitting in a rocking chair by a window where I could see her in profile. She had on a kimono of some figured material which seemed almost festive. There was a rug across her lap, and her hands lay on it, white but very graceful. She motioned me to a chair which had been placed at the far side of the room. She may have been afraid of contagion or she may not have wanted me to see the ravages of her illness. She had, however, and possibly for the first time in her life, given some thought to her appearance. She had made herself attractive. Fever had rouged her cheeks, and her eyes shone brightly. Perhaps she knew this. Had her mother held a mirror for her? In any case she could have read the truth in my eyes: for once in my life, for a brief moment, I thought she was beautiful.

Teaching is sometimes represented as a kind of infection. We say that the teacher infects the student with an interest in art or a love of Shakespeare. As a teacher I have been required to have a skin test for tuberculosis, and I have always given a positive reaction, though my lung X-rays are clear. Did Miss Graves indeed infect me with more than a love of literature and art, with more than a sense of the Bible as literature? Somehow I rather hope she did. But where is the test that will show the other infections?

And how important to Miss Graves was her effect on me? She lived not only for others but for herself. In her notebook she copied this from Thoreau: "In proportion as one's inward life fails, we go more constantly and desperately to the Post Office. You may depend on it, that the poor fellow who walks away with the greatest number of letters, proud of his extensive correspondence, has not heard from himself this long while."

But she was proud of the role she strove so hard to play in the lives of her friends and acquaintances, and she marked this passage in her copy of *Walden*:

An elderly dame, too, dwells in my neighborhood, invisible to most persons, in whose odorous herb garden I love to stroll sometimes, gathering samples and listening to her fables; for she has a genius of unequalled fertility, and her memory runs back farther than mythology, and she can tell me the original of every fable, and on what fact every one is founded, for the incidents occurred when she was young.

But my guess is that the best clue to what was important to her is to be found in a quotation from Emily Dickinson which she copied into her notebook:

They might not need me—yet they might.
I'll let my heart be just in sight;
A smile so small as mine might be
Precisely their necessity.

PART III

S OMEHOW IT HAD ALWAYS BEEN ASSUMED that I would go to college, but neither my father nor my mother nor any of their close friends was a college graduate or knew how one went about choosing a college or getting into one. The single exception was that classmate who now lived in Albany. He had been valedictorian of his class and had gone on to become a German teacher, and when my parents turned to him for advice, he suggested Hamilton College.

When I applied for admission, I discovered that I needed two years of a modern language. The high school had thrown out German during the war and had never replaced it. Although some schools were putting in Spanish with an eye on our neighbors in Central and South America, Susquehanna High School had no modern language at all. The college said that it would accept a passing grade on a New York State Board of Regents examination in second-year French, and so at the beginning of my senior year I started to study on the side. Miss Werle knew some French and offered to help.

I bought a text, a copy of *Sans Famille*, and a rather large dictionary with pronunciations indicated in the International Phonetic Alphabet. Every afternoon I came home from school and worked for an hour or two. I sat in a new overstuffed chair in the living room, with a lapboard my mother used for sewing resting on the arms. In the light from a bluish "daylight" bulb in a new bridge lamp, the fringed shade of which was made of blue cloth, I laboriously composed sentences, translated texts, and memorized irregular verbs. I had no chance to speak French or hear it properly spoken. Late in May I went to Binghamton to a designated high school, where after considerable search I found someone who knew what I was there for, and took the examination. I passed it, but with nothing to spare. As it turned out, Hamilton College was filling out its roster that year with many unqualified students, and I suspect I could have been admitted on condition, if I had known enough to ask.

EARLY IN MY HIGH-SCHOOL YEARS I also began to study law. My father had been taken in by still another book salesman: as a leading lawyer in the community he could distribute two scholarships offered by a correspondence school, the recipients of which were required to pay only a small fraction of the usual cost of the course. Possibly because my father had read law himself when just out of high school, the proposition had not seemed too absurd. One condition was that two candidates be found, and he persuaded a boy related to his Aunt Nell Dumble to take the second scholarship. I received a copy of Blackstone's *Commentaries on the Laws of England* and a first batch of questions to be answered and submitted to the school. Abe Lincoln's life was changed when he accidentally came upon a copy of Blackstone, but mine was unaffected. My father must have realized the inadequacy of my first answers, and the whole thing was quickly dropped.

I also accidentally embarked upon another career in literary scholarship. I particularly liked one of those little Roycrofter books in limp imitation leather called *The Ballad of Reading Gaol.* (When I told this to the Reverend Mr. Pritchard, he quickly said that he was quite sure that Oscar Wilde had repented, but he did not say of what, and I was led to wonder for the first time just why Wilde had been in jail.) I happened to see an advertisement of an English bookseller in which a "bibliography of Oscar Wilde" was offered for sale for a pound or two. I looked up "bibliography" in the dictionary and misunderstood the definition: I took it to mean the complete works of a writer. I was pleased by the prospect of owning all of Oscar Wilde, and I bought a money order for what I figured to be the dollar equivalent of the price as given in pounds. Before mailing my order I discovered that I had miscalculated and was sending a little too much, but I added a note explaining that the rest was to cover postage.

In due time the book arrived. It was indeed a bibliography, edited by Stuart Mason (the pen name of Christopher Millard), and it was full of pictures and cartoons and, even though not what I thought I had ordered, quite interesting. One picture showed Oscar Wilde busily at work on *Salomé* with French grammars and books on French verbs lying about. Another showed him wearing a sunflower as a boutonnière. And so I was now an authority on two literary figures—Bacon, author of the works of Shakespeare, and Oscar Wilde, author of *The Ballad of Reading Gaol*.

In my studies of the plays attributed to Shakespeare I had, of course, read Bacon's essays. They were the easiest of his works to understand, but still much less relevant to my daily life than those of Dr. Frank Crane, which were appearing in a Binghamton paper. In a volume published in 1919, consisting of newspaper columns, Crane developed such themes as these:

> Clean up your thoughts; don't have a waste-basket mind.
> Don't believe because you can't disprove.
> Your competitor can be your friend.
> Happiness is shy; look for it.
> Be a futurist.
> Anger is poison.
> If it's impossible, let's do it.
> Tomorrow is your friend.

I was at the right age for this perennial stuff and took it seriously. I tried my hand at writing some of the same, but ran into a grammatical problem at the very start. I wanted to say that "manners are (is?) the glass through which others see us," but I could not decide between "are" and "is," and as a result this great idea was not given to the world.

I did publish one other work during my high-school years. When we were in New York, I bought a copy of either *Judge* or the old comic *Life* which was running a tall-stories contest. The assignment for the week was to answer the question: "What would you do if you found yourself locked in a room with a mad dog, a rattlesnake and a maniac?" On a free postcard supplied by the hotel I wrote, "I'd sic the dog on the maniac and rattle the snake for help," and added my name and address. Two weeks later, back again in Susquehanna, I got a check for five dollars.

There was no bookstore in Susquehanna and with the exception of those little books from the Roycrofters and E. Haldeman-Julius and my bibliography of Oscar Wilde, I was not accumulating a library. When Mrs. Taylor sent me a few dollars as a graduation present, I invaded the depths of the Williams Stationery Store again and found a copy of Palgrave's *Golden Treasury* with a padded red-leather cover.

HIGH SCHOOL USED only a small part of my energies during those four years. My father had always believed that I should work. My first job was selling the *Saturday Evening Post* and *Country Gentleman,* but I moved on to other things. I mowed our lawn, and one or two of the neighbors hired me to mow theirs. Lawns in Susquehanna were always a problem, with their steep, eroded banks. Power mowers were unknown, and it was usually impossible to push a mower up a bank or even to allow it to run down while in a cutting position. You had to mow sideways, and the mower tended to slip toward the bottom.

In high school my father gave me a serious job collecting telephone rents. He continued to be treasurer of the local company and had trouble finding collectors at a low salary. His secretary gave me great batches of pink slips bearing the names and addresses of subscribers and their charges, and I went from door to door asking for payment. It was often obvious that I was not welcome, and in any case I was always embarrassed. I began to stammer as I said, "I came to collect the telephone rent." Some people ran up bills for long-distance calls which it was hard to persuade them to pay.

To make matters worse, I mixed the money I collected with my own funds and began to find myself short when it came time to report collections and turn over the cash. I began to pretend that a payment or two had not been made. In short, I embezzled. When I got further and further behind and it became difficult to juggle the accounts, I confessed to my father that I was in trouble, though I claimed to have lost some money. He lent me $25 to cover my shortages and agreed not to tell my mother. We drew up an IOU on a slip of paper. I once repaid $10 and my father duly entered it on the IOU with his signature, but there were no further payments, and nothing was ever said about it again. I hated the job and someone else soon took it over.

Another job my father gave me was serving legal papers. I looked up a man in Oakland, whom I found working in his garden. I asked him if he were so-and-so, handed him a paper—a divorce summons, I think—and then asked him if he acknowledged service. I was aware that I had dealt him some kind of blow, and fortunately my father did not ask me to do much of that kind of thing.

At one time John DeWitt and I planned to go into business. Our bicycles took a great deal of our time, and we knew them well. We could take a New Departure coaster brake apart and put it back together again, take a link out of a chain, and true the rim of a wheel by tightening or loosening its spokes. We could mend a puncture by inserting a rubber band dipped in rubber cement into the hole with an awl-like device. (We never mastered the method in which a brass disk was inserted into the tire through the puncture, and a second disk was screwed tight on its stem on the outside.)

With this experience we decided to open a shop to sell bicycle, parts and make repairs. A small building, once a barbershop, on a side lot on Broad Street next to my grandmother Burrhus's could be rented for almost nothing because it was in disrepair and had no services. (We could go to the toilet or wash our hands at my grandmother's.) We also found that we could order supplies on thirty days' credit, or so we thought. We intended to put in a supply of parts and sell them at a profit in time to pay the bills when they came due, and meanwhile we would repair bicycles and make a lot of money.

It was not a very business-like plan, and it came to an abrupt halt. I had kept the whole thing secret from my family, but my brother heard about it and brought it up at dinner one noon by asking a few leading questions. When I finally explained what we were going to do, my father, alarmed no doubt by the thought of the bills for which he would be legally responsible, said flatly that I was going to do nothing of the sort. I left the table and went into the living room and sulked. There would be another unpleasant scene when I had to confess to John DeWitt that I was not to be allowed to go through with our carefully laid plans.

As an aspiring writer I went to work for the *Transcript*, the editor of which was a jovial extrovert named Ulysses Grant Baker. My first duty was to go down to the newspaper office before school in the morning and crib national or world news items from the Binghamton morning paper. I also did "literary" things. There were some large bound volumes of earlier *Transcripts*, and I wrote a series of reminiscences of Susquehanna. I was told not to mention the roller-skating rink because some still-remembered marital difficulties had originated there. I had office space in a small room upstairs, off the job-printing department, and felt very much like a journalist. Once in a while I would be given a story to cover, such as a concert or a meeting, and I also wrote a few advertisements, including several very swank ads for a new ice-cream parlor that I patronized.

On a day when I was not in school I could watch my stuff coming out of the linotype machine in slugs, to be locked up in the frames that ran under the rollers of the press, and later, with the noisy press shaking the whole building, I could see my very own words falling into a bin, copy after copy, in print.

I often helped out in the job-printing department. I learned to set type and knew the disgrace of having it pied. I set only small jobs —things like business cards or letterheads, or my bookplates (the first of which went into my copy of the *Golden Treasury*)—but I learned to feed sheets of paper into a job press one at a time and get them out again without smudging them with printer's ink or pinching my fingers.

A large paper-cutter was used to sheer off the edges of thick blocks of paper. You put the blocks on a flat bed and brought a plate down to put them under pressure. Then with a long iron handle you lowered a very sharp horizontal blade. The handle remained upright while you put the paper under pressure, and one day I discovered that the latch which held it in place was defective. The handle could easily have fallen and sheared off both my hands. I always recall this in my wrists.

Otis Chidester worked in the job-printing department, and he and I embarked upon a small and unsuccessful business career. We invented a game, called Tenniball, in which players batted a toy balloon back and forth across marks laid out on the floor. We printed instructions, and offered them for sale, together with a few balloons and a piece of white string as a marker, in a Sunday paper in Elmira, New York. We received no orders.

* * *

THE MOST SERIOUS JOB during my high-school years was in the Economy Shoe Store. The owner, George Harding, must have come to Susquehanna rather late, and his judgment that a new shoe store was needed was only the first of many mistakes. He was politically liberal. He admired Woodrow Wilson, whom my father could not abide, and subscribed to a weekly edited by Wilson's confidant, Colonel House. Perhaps it was a touch of Wilson's idealism which led Mr. Harding to specialize in the inexpensive, rugged work shoes manufactured by the Endicott-Johnson Company located in two small cities near Binghamton and owned by the philanthropic industrialist George F. Johnson. (There was another great industrialist in the Binghamton area at that time named Thomas J. Watson, and it has been said that the difference in their subsequent histories is to be explained by the fact that Johnson kept his eye on the welfare of his workers while Watson kept his on the welfare of his stockholders, but there was undoubtedly a greater future in business machines.)

Mr. Harding's first store was on Erie Avenue and it did not thrive, even when a laundry was added, with packages of shirts and collars processed in Binghamton filling the shelves in the rear of the store. Prohibition made it possible to move into more promising quarters when the Oakland Hotel, no longer supported by its saloon, was converted into a business building. The space was not ideal, because the windows were much too small to display merchandise effectively. Nevertheless, I helped George Harding make his move.

It was not difficult, because the back door was just across the street from the old store, and the stock was far less extensive than I should have guessed. All the shoe boxes above a certain height in the old store were empty. Since there was less shelf space in the new store, the old empties were thrown in a great pile on the floor before being jammed into a baling machine. Once, at the top of a ladder, throwing empty boxes to the floor in great abandon, I said, "I'd make a good Bolshevik." I probably remember this because Mr. Harding laughed. It was something he seldom did.

I would go down to the Economy Shoe Store before school and sprinkle oily green perfumed sawdust on the floor and then sweep it up together with the dust it adsorbed. Later, as the word "economy" took on another meaning, I used plain sawdust which I wet before strewing it about. I made a gadget to spread the sawdust—a tin can with a crank, operating a little like a coffee grinder.

After school I went down and worked as a clerk, joining Miss Dooley, who was hired not so much for her skill in salesmanship as for the fact that she was an Irish Catholic and thus gave an ecumenical touch to the establishment. Since she played the piano at the movies, she could not work at the store on Saturday afternoons or evenings, and Saturdays were therefore long, long, tiring days for me. But I got to know all about shoes—lasts, welts, counters, vamps, the difference between oxfords and bluchers, and different ways of lacing shoes.

When Mr. Harding put in a line of arch supports and foot powders, I took a correspondence course and became a Practipedist, with cards to pass out to my customers.

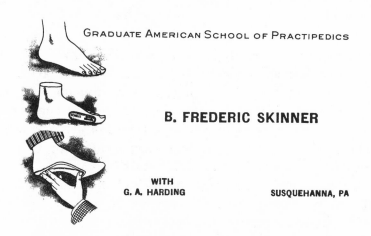

GRADUATE AMERICAN SCHOOL OF PRACTIPEDICS

B. FREDERIC SKINNER

WITH
G. A. HARDING   SUSQUEHANNA, PA

I made only one practipedic sale. When I was alone in the store, a spinster came in with her aging mother complaining that she had flat feet. We didn't have a support of the right size to fit her shoe, but there was equipment for cutting down a larger size, and although I told her it would be a gamble and expensive (something like $5), she authorized me to do the job. I hacked away at the supports, put them in her shoes, and watched her hobble out of the store. Mr. Harding added a little something to my pay that week as my share of the profits.

Empty shoe boxes were thrown into a small cellar, and it was part of my job to bale them. I hated to operate the baling machine and tended to allow the cellar to fill up. Once I heard Mr. Harding baling boxes himself, clearly angry with me for not doing my job but unwilling to complain. In general, however, I think I was a useful clerk. I worked hard and loyally. Since all the prices in the store ended in .48 or .98, the cash register had a great cache of pennies, which were never counted, and once in a while, alone in the store, I would filch five of them and dash next door to the Sugar Bowl for a bag of peanuts, but otherwise I was scrupulously honest.

George Harding was a tall, gaunt man, suffering from chronic indigestion, who stooped as if he were afraid his head would strike the ceiling, and who approached a customer with a soft "Good afternoon" which was often frightening rather than cordial. He forced himself to carry on as a businessman. When his credit with the Endicott-Johnson Company wore thin, he would get a loan from the First National Bank and order a batch of shoes. They would arrive at the depot, and the local drayman would bring them down to the store in his horse-drawn wagon. If the day was clear, we unpacked them on the curb and brought them in and put them on the shelves. New models were put in the windows on the same old off-white pedestals.

Occasionally we had a sale. I lettered big show cards for the windows, and circulars were sent to the surrounding countryside. Mr. Harding had the use of an addressograph machine with stencils covering the subscribers of the Water Company, owned by C. Fred Wright, a fellow Episcopalian, who had taken offices upstairs in the new building. I would run off a few hundred envelopes and stuff them with circulars. Once a small sample of leather was to be included to show its toughness and flexibility. The samples were shaped like the soles of shoes and had been stamped out of scraps at the factory. Some of them were indeed of very good quality but others were quite thin and easily torn. Presumably the merchant was to sort out the samples to be sent with the circulars, but it was typical of Mr. Harding that he neglected to do this.

I worked in the shoe store till the beginning of my senior year, when life became much too complicated and some simplification was needed.

*   *   *

DURING MY HIGH-SCHOOL YEARS I got to know many girls, four of whom represented rather different kinds of relations. Marion Knise (we pronounced it K-nice) was the temptress. Her father was a barber with a shop on the corner of Grand Street and Jackson Avenue. He must have cut my hair once a month for more than ten years, but I do not remember that he ever said a word while doing so. He was a chain smoker and interrupted his clipping at regular intervals to pick up and puff on a cigarette which burned on a tray in front of his mirror.

The family lived in the same building and opened a small ice-cream parlor on the Jackson Avenue side. Marion tended the parlor after school, and I was a steady visitor if not always a customer. We sat at the table in the far corner and talked about sex. The main question was how far a girl should let a boy go. With Marion this was a simple matter of geometry. Between customers I was allowed to go three inches above her knee. She wore silk stockings, which girls of her age did not often wear at that time, and she would sometimes wear two pairs to produce an interesting moiré effect. They were delightful to touch, but I never got above the line which defined my territory. What I should have done if I had suddenly been allowed to "go all the way," I doubt whether I knew. There was a suggestion that other boys had lines above and below mine.

Marion's conversation was full of innuendoes many of which I did not want to admit that I did not understand. She had gone on dates with boys from out of town who were much faster than the local boys, and one of them, she once told me, forced her to do something by threatening to scar her with a lighted cigarette. What it was she did not specify, but she said that she no longer had any respect for him. In spite of many hours on the subject, I learned very little about sex from her.

The big love of my high-school days was a friend of Marion's named Margaret Persons. She was a tall, willowy redhead who so obviously enjoyed life that it was a pleasure just to watch her. She had gone to grade school on West Hill, and I met her when she first came as a freshman to the high school on Laurel Street. I was then a junior, and we went together for about a year. I took her to parties and dances and walked her home afterward. We would stand leaning against a tree in front of her house. We embraced tightly but our hands did not move about, and we kissed but it was not what was then called "soul" or "French" kissing. It was enough for both of us just to be together.

After dinner on Sunday I would comb my hair, walk down Grand Street and the Long Stairs, stop at the Sugar Bowl on Main Street to buy half a pound of chocolates, and then walk out to Margaret's house, which was at the very end of her street on West Hill. Mrs. Persons would let me in the kitchen door (her husband was, I believe, living separately), and Margaret never kept me waiting. In good weather we might go for a walk, and when it was rainy we spent the afternoon in her front parlor. Like all parlors, it was rarely used, but there was a piano, and Margaret played the mandolin a little, and we played a few simple pieces together. She was not a good student, in music or in school, and I am afraid I tried to improve her.

Though a close friend of Marion Knise's, she seems never to have picked up Marion's curious approach to sex, and in the end it was sex that broke us up. I became more sophisticated and one afternoon when we were sitting on the bank of the river near Canavan's Glen I put my hand on her leg for the first time. She stopped me, and we embarked upon a long argument, at the end of which she seemed to capitulate. She said she would let me do what I wanted, but she added that she would then kill herself by jumping into the river, because she could never face her mother again. I was stunned and never made any further advances. ("She wouldn't have, you know," said Marion Knise, when I told her the story later.) But Margaret began telling me that I was getting tired of her, as I may have been, and there were tears. After I moved away from Susquehanna I did not see her again. She became a teacher, married the principal of the school in which she taught, and died young of tuberculosis.

Another girl whom I greatly admired but did not see very often was Leslie Gilbert. Her father was my dentist, a small, distinguished-looking man with a tiny gray beard, and she worked as his assistant. She did not, I think, come to high school, and I doubt whether she went to the Laurel Hill Academy. Her mother wrote poetry and the

Transcript reported the publication of a poem called "In the Valley of the Grand Pré." Since there were no accents on the linotype, my mother read it as "Grand Pree," and there were shrieks of laughter and unsuppressible giggles when she related this to her friends.

The Gilberts lived in an apartment over one of the stores on Main Street. This in itself was enough to set the family apart from the normal life of Susquehanna, where almost everyone lived in a house. Possibly because of the social freedom which this gave her, Leslie went with an Irish boy, and I always suspected that they had a mature sexual relationship. She flirted with me much more openly than other girls. She would make it clear that she saw that I was looking at her legs, and once alluded, or so I thought, to the fact that I had an erection as I danced with her by repeating a word I had used with a special intonation, saying "Brother?" while glancing down toward our legs.

I called on Leslie one evening. Her father and mother were in the kitchen at the back of the apartment, and we went into a small side room at the front, in which a hammock was installed as a kind of settee. She read me a poem called "Frost Tonight":

> Child, take the shears and cut what you will,
> Frost tonight—so clear and dead-still.

This was better than most of the poetry I heard in Susquehanna, and I may even have sensed some allusion to the possibilities in our evening together. Was I being exhorted to gather rosebuds? But, alas, I was still at the stage so well defined by Marion Knise. I made no effort to embrace or kiss her; it was a matter of finding out how far I could go up her leg, and the evening ended in a violent, unskillful wrestling match in the hammock. If I had abandoned the attack on her thighs, if I had shown some signs of affection—who knows? I might have married her.

A rather different relationship emerged, much to my surprise, in my senior year when I met Charlotte Bennett, who lived on the far side of Lanesboro beyond the Starrucca Viaduct. I met Chi, as I came to call her, one evening at a dance in the Odd Fellows' Hall. We liked each other immediately, danced together a good deal, and talked, and I walked her home, or rather to her cousin's home, where she was spending the night because it was nearer Susquehanna. Even so it was a walk of nearly two miles, most of it along the Lower Road.

We had not flirted while we were dancing, and we did not hold hands as we walked, and there were no sexual allusions or innuendoes in our talk. We were laughing and enjoying ourselves. Nevertheless, I had an erection all the way and was terribly embarrassed. It was moonlight but not too bright, and I turned slightly away from her as I walked.

We joined her cousin and a friend, who had gone ahead of us, on the back porch of the house, and the four of us sat around for a while. I doubt whether I kissed Chi that night, and there was certainly no necking. I began to see her almost every Sunday afternoon, and I continued to be embarrassed by sexual excitement, though I continued to maintain a romantically chivalrous attitude. A popular song at the time was called "Nona," and it was "our song." I played it on her piano, and she sang.

Some kind of mature sexuality had made its appearance, but I was puzzled by it, and I suspect that Chi was puzzled too by my extraordinary innocence and lack of initiative.

MY MALE FRIENDS and acquaintances were also of two kinds. With a friend like Raphael Miller my behavior was easy, natural, and wholly uncontrived. It would never have occurred to us to examine the effects we were having on each other. But with more distant acquaintances my behavior was rather calculated. There is a good deal of evidence of this in a diary that I began to keep near the end of my junior year.

MY DIARY

B. Frederic Skinner

Afternoon of May 27, 1921

Busy for me, these are dormant times for most of the people here. The Shops are closed, which means that a large percent of residents are without work. Many are taking advantage of their time and are painting homes or improving the grounds otherwise. But many that are laid off are doing nothing (characteristic of many). As for me, as I have said, the times are busy. To enumerate my duties, some of which are somewhat neglected, I have five "jobs" upon my hands, viz., going to school, which, however, will soon be over, working for G. A. Harding, reporting for the *Transcript*, acting as agent for F. H. Livingston of Binghamton [unsuccessful distributor of his reed-adjusting device], and playing in the Opera House two nights a week and often playing for dances other nights. Monday and Tuesday of this week I played for the moving picture "The Inside of the Cup," a powerful picture and presenting a fine chance for good music. The orchestra I play in is the "Symphony Four," composed of Bob Basso (drums), Joseph Hickey (piano), Lawrence Larrabee (violin), and myself (melody saxophone). We organized about a month ago and so far have played for three two-day features. Our rivals in this business are the "Venetian Five" organized about three months ago by Chipman. We play the first two nights in the week and they the last two. The V.V. is a windy orchestra with dress suits when on dance jobs and the greatest of bluff. . . . Our Symphony Four is to play for the roller skating every Friday night beginning a week from tonight. Tuesday night the dances are held, and I don't know what music is to play. School is busy with tests although we have not had our finals yet. . . .

This afternoon Steve Holleran came up to school to see me. Steve wants me to play in L.A.C. Hall Monday night, but I am supposed to play at the movies. I don't know how it will turn out. I would make $6 at the dance and only $2.50 at the show.

Wednesday evening, June 1st, continued
Thursday evening, June 2nd.

I passed in Cicero. Now for the other tests which come Monday. We are making the Seniors' motto for commencement. It is silver letters on old rose background reading "En Avant." Margaret Jones and Helen Jones take the honors this year. Helen's address promises to be the same old "sweet girl graduate" stuff that is sickening. The seniors were not satisfied with the way we were making the motto but we refused to make it any other way and they calmed down and capitulated. We are planning now on a canoe trip here to Harrisburg a distance of three hundred miles through fifteen counties. If we go, my dear diary, you will soon contain an interesting account. . . . I am working at the store yet but have told Mr. Harding I will quit in the Fall. I will make enough money by my music to save up some and by quitting it will give me more time to read and write. I am planning on taking six subjects next year and this means work. This year I am taking five, Physics, Geometry (Plane), English, Cicero, and American History. Next year I want to take English, Mathematics (solid Geo.), and Economics, Virgil, Chemistry, English history.

Thursday evening, June 16
. . . This is the first evening I have had to myself for a full week. To itinerate, Monday and Tuesday the 6th and 7th we played at the opera house after being disappointed at our Friday night job at Harrison's Pavillion. It was a damp night and we waited until 9 o'clock for a car from there to take us out. None came and Harrison did not even let us know that he had called the dance off. By this we lost another job for we could have played at the opera house substituting for the V.V. However, it turned out for the best as this orchestra could not get any substitute and Ryan got mad and gave us the Friday and Saturday job. . . .

Procrastination stole the time I had meant to put to studies for tests and I went to them unprepared. However I stood—Physics 83, Cicero 88, English 93, History 96, Geometry 97. Played at the Opera House Friday and Saturday night and Sunday night went to the Baccalaureate sermon. . . . Tuesday I played at the Opera House after a hard day at the store. As this was payday night I was supposed to work but got Ebbe to work for me. The boss is running a sale Tuesday, Wednesday, and Thursday and it was a busy night so I hated to leave him. He was good, though, and let me off willingly. Last night I went to the commencement, playing in Holleran's orchestra and reporting for the paper. I got 108 lines on it making $1.08 + what I made for playing.

My account of the canoe trip begins with some business details and then continues:

Monday the 11th my father and I took all the baggage down to the railroad bridge below the lower electric dam. The other four [Leonard Titus (whom we called the Admiral), Don Berkett, Doc Miller, and Bob Perrine] went to Lanesboro and brought the canoes down. Coming out of the binnacle Doc tipped over, the only spill on the trip. At the bridge we waited a long time, and finally they came, carrying the boats over the half-built dam. They paddled down, and we loaded up. I took my canoe alone and when all was set, we shook hands goodbye and sailed off never dreaming of all that lay ahead of us.

The first few miles were rather shallow and to us the riffs in some places were bad. We soon came to consider such as those mere trifles. We ate a lunch at dinner time by the riverside and at 4 o'clock arrived at Binghamton with a storm coming up. I hastily wrote a card and ran to a mailbox and dropped it in. The storm came on. It looked like a bad thunder shower, and we paddled swiftly. The rain came, but the storm had blown over, so in a drizzle we paddled on looking for a place to camp. We finally found a place on the side of a hill. We drew the canoes up in some brush and up above them set our camp. We turned in as soon as possible. . . . Next morning I cooked some bacon for my breakfast while the others went to town for theirs. They stayed over an hour looking around, but when they came back we set out. The morning brought a terrible sun, and before we could reach Owego we were all burnt. I soaked my shirt in water and put that on but to no avail. My skin was getting literally baked. Finally, after the worst torture I ever went through, we came to Owego. We stopped and three of us went into town while two stayed with the canoes. I bought a light shirt in place of my flannel one and some cold cream for my sunburn. After having a dinner I went back out Front Street toward the canoes. I found the other two fellows on the porch of a Mrs. Loring. She was an elderly lady who was being kind to us. In her house I put the cream on and then sat on her porch in misery. Later in the afternoon we left and sailed to a place a short ways down the river and made camp under some trees near on oat field. The mosquitoes were terrible, and next morning the Admiral was to be found way out in the oat field away from them. . . .

[The following night we slept in our canoes and were drenched by a sudden shower.]

The next day (Friday) we paddled on with no events until afternoon. All along the river we had gone by eel racks. These occur where the river drops rapidly in riffs. They are walls of rock built in a V shape that cause a swift current to pour out of the point. Some of them take nearly the whole river, while some are smaller. We had been going around these, which was usually in a shallow slow flow of water, and we finally decided that it was safe to shoot the V. The Admiral and I were together in a canoe at the time, and we headed for the mouth. It neared, and too late we saw large rocks in the opening. Then bang, scrape, bang, bang, bang, bang, smash. Ten small holes in the bottom. We beat it for shore and discovered that we could push the splinters back in place and get along all right with a slow leak. Farther on we dried our blankets and things on a sunny beach just above the mouth of the railroad tunnel near Shamokin. Then followed some of the most beautiful stretches of scenery on the trip. The tunnel frees the bank from railroads and all traces of population. The long curve which looms constantly ahead of you is a rare speciman of the primeval. At the right looms Mt. Mehoogany, rocky and towering. Its almost perpendicular wall bears scraggly trees and a sprinkling of shrubbery. Halfway around the long curve we scared an eagle who swooped down the valley ahead of us. Farther on to the left a white crane stood fishing and then flew away at the sound of our paddles. It was nearly sunset and we were forced to hurry through the six-mile stretch in order to make Tunkhannock for supplies. Sunset came on, gloriously and glowing. The river was swift, and we coasted lazily on the purple reflecting water till the town was reached. A few supplies bought, we rejected an island as a camping place and finally settled on a ledge of low rocks just across the river. The ledge comes up from the water and is perhaps ten feet above the river. We cooked a supper in the dark and spread our still damp blankets. Next morning each of us independently experienced a conscious phenomenon. Probably Admiral was the first to see it, but when I awoke, Don and Doc were still asleep and probably Bob. The rocks have been washed by many rains and their surface is rippled. With the early morning light upon them and with one looking from a low level, it appeared as if there was water running over them. The previous night was still distinct in my memory, and I reached out to feel of a part of my inside jacket that was exposed. I thought that it had rained and that water was running over the rocks. My blanket was wet. I raised up a bit. There were no other indications of rain but still the water on the rocks. I reached out and touched them. Dry! My blanket had not dried from the night before. It was still early morning so I turned in again, and awakening later I found that everyone had been deceived by the same thing. . . .

About two p.m. we set sail and made Nanticoke by evening. Doc and I went into town and got a telephone call through to Doc's folks. When we got back the three were having a hard time with the canoes and a lot of tough kids, but we set out finally and in due time came to the Nanticoke dam. We were forewarned and forearmed. I was alone in my canoe and somewhat behind when we came to the broken out structure. Doc and Bob went to one side and Don and Admiral to the other to look things over. They reported everything okay, and without getting out I headed toward the big opening. The water passing through the break drops swiftly for a short space, slows up in a little pool, and then tumbles over rapids of rocks and railroad ties. The first swiftly flowing current was all I foresaw, and I shot that easily, and then ahead of me I saw the rapids. I prepared for a spill. It was impossible to stop. I must go over. I entered the rough dashing area and first thing the bow of my canoe grounded on a rock. To the right and ahead of me was a swift yet deep V-shaped current that led into a maze of rock-broken streams. I planned to back off the rock and drop into the V. With a heavy stroke I backed. The stern of my canoe was caught in the current, and the boat was whipped around tail end first. It was a ticklish predicament. Above me I could see the other two canoes passing through the opening, and below me I pictured, although I could not see, the rocks and the broken stream. Unable to guide my canoe I gave up, tossed my paddle on the pack in the middle of the boat and grasping the gunwhales with my hands, I endeavored to balance the craft. Dextrously the current carried me through the treacherous maze, and I sailed out into calm water. Recovering myself I watched the others. Bob and Doc came through safely. The Admiral and Don were having trouble. They were grounded on a rock. Admiral carefully climbed out on the end of an upright railroad tie that was fast between the rocks. His shoes only went under the water until the canoe swung around and knocked him in up to his waist. The two finally came through with no other mishaps than a pair of drenched trousers, and we camped on the shore just below the dam across from a little settlement where I went for bread and water.

We reached Harrisburg but with no time to spare for an excursion to Gettysburg. We visited the state capitol, and I shopped in a bookstore, and we put our canoes on a train and came home.

SHORTLY AFTER THE END OF THE WAR it began to be obvious that Susquehanna was a dying town. Railroads were changing, and there was no longer any need for repair shops at short intervals along the route. The steam locomotive was soon to give way to the diesel, and within another ten years the great Matt Shays, never very efficient, would be dismantled. A town built on hills did not attract other industries. (The Blue Ridge Metal Manufacturing Company had been located out over the Susquehanna River on the Oakland side, and the silk mill had been squeezed into the narrow valley of Drinker Creek.) A reduced payroll in the Shops affected other businesses. Houses went unrepaired and, in spite of an annual Clean-Up Week, the town grew grimier and more littered.

Editor Baker continued to exhort his readers to "keep firm your faith in Susquehanna." Good times would return. He had once seen a ray of hope in George F. Johnson, the philanthropic shoe manufacturer, who had built up the towns of Endicott and Lestershire, in return for which Lestershire had been renamed Johnson City. He had come to Susquehanna during the war to conduct a Red Cross rally and had predicted at the start of the meeting that the audience in the Hogan Opera House would that day subscribe $3000. When the pledges were tallied, they had done exactly that, but it then appeared that Johnson himself had contributed the $1300 needed to bring the total up to the predicted amount. This was Editor Baker's cue. Why could Susquehanna not become a shoe town? The *Transcript* ran headlines across the whole of page one:

GEO. F. JOHNSON IS NOW IDOLIZED HERE.

He Came to Susquehanna, He Was 'One of Us' and Ever Will Be.
No Such Act of Generosity as His Ever Recorded Here Before

Johnson may have been tempted. The *Transcript* reported that he came back for a second visit. He arrived on No. 4 and was met by a committee that took him on a tour of inspection of the Erie Shops and local industries. He was then "tendered a complimentary dinner" at the Oakland Hotel, during which an orchestra played. "Mr. Johnson was cheered to the echoe [sic] as he was introduced and all stood and applauded him as he arose to speak." The Erie Band gave a concert in front of the hotel and then marched to the Odd Fellows' Hall, where, at a public reception, everyone had "an opportunity to meet and grasp the friendly hand of the gentleman who has brought gladness to the hearts of thousands of thousands of people." But, alas, Johnson was not to be caught.

My father remained a "booster." As chairman of the guarantors' committee of the Chautauqua he continued to work to bring culture to the town; he had been president of the Auto Club and the *Transcript* reported his remarks "favoring macadamization" at a meeting of the Good Roads Association; and when at the end of the war there was a false rumor that the Shops were to be expanded, he served on a committee to found a Building and Loan Association which would "give Susquehanna a building boom." He went to Harrisburg to meet with the Governor about the possible gasification of coal to be used in lighting, and again to promote the growth of the highway system; and he went to New York to remind the officers of the Erie Railroad that the company had been given special tax advantages when it came into Pennsylvania in the nineteenth century and therefore had good reason to maintain and even expand the Susquehanna Shops. But it was no use; the town was in decline.

The story can be read in the history of the library. In 1859 a newly founded Young Men's Literary Association established a library in a company boardinghouse, and when the Shops were built, the company set aside space for a library and later appropriated $450 for books. It also fitted out a large lecture hall for the use of the Literary Association. By 1870 the library had over 3000 volumes. When the company became less paternalistic, the Literary Association disbanded, and the books became part of the town library, which I first knew when it occupied the quarters on Erie Avenue later taken over by the Economy Shoe Store. When rents went up, it moved into the basement of a private house on Willow Avenue, which could be entered directly by going partway down the Long Stairs. It was there that I did most of my exploring during my high-school years. As subscriptions fell off and its fortunes declined, the library moved to a single room in an office building, and when that could no longer be maintained, the books were sold, and the town had no library at all.

My old boss George Harding bought a good many books at the final sale for a few cents each, and when I saw him once during my college years and recalled having read Darwin's *Expression of Emotion in Man and Animals,* he said he had it and gave it to me. He also gave me Sir Charles Bell's *The Hand, Its Mechanism and Vital Endowments, as Evincing Design* and Thomas H. Huxley's *On the*

Origin of Species: or, the Causes of the Phenomena of Organic Nature, both of which were among the first books acquired by the association. Also among the first were Thoreau's *Yankee in Canada* and his *Letters,* first editions which I bought for a few cents during the sale.

George Harding was part of the story of the town, too. His business slowly failed, and the bank loans grew smaller and smaller. One day, as he left for work, he called back to his wife: "Good luck to you today in everything you do," and walked down Broad Street and lower Grand Street to the Long Stairs and down to Erie Avenue and Main Street and his store. He put a sign on the front door reading "Back in fifteen minutes," went into the rear of the store, took a length of rope he had bought at Ned Owens's hardware store six months earlier, and hanged himself.

Ned Owens was part of the story, too. He once came to consult my father about getting a divorce from his flirtatious wife, and my father talked him out of it. Years later he found another way: he took a shotgun from one of his shelves, went into the basement, and blew his head off.

MY FATHER'S PROFESSIONAL LIFE was not expanding. He continued to take local cases which were no doubt interesting but could not have been very profitable. According to my mother's scrapbook, he represented the Commonwealth against an Italian in a stabbing case, against a man who resisted an officer, against a man accused of cheating a woman (the man committed suicide while in jail), and against four boys for stealing a car. He asked for suspended sentences for a group of gamblers and defended a yeggman. He appeared in court to oppose the granting of a liquor license in another city, but represented a friend who had been denied a license in Susquehanna. He frequently appeared before the Superior and Supreme courts of Pennsylvania and New York State, but even so his practice could not have been said to be lucrative.

A case we frequently discussed at home had to do with two families living on Oak Street. My father represented a man named Brenchley who complained that his neighbor had built a driveway which blocked the flow of groundwater and flooded Brenchley's base-ment. The neighbor was represented by two lawyers who were my father's arch rivals, and the case was bitterly fought. The jury came from Montrose to the Brenchley cellar to see that water began to flow out of the cellar when a block was removed from the driveway. The case was taken to a higher court (I was working at the *Transcript* when the "books"—the transcripts of evidence taken in the lower court—were printed), and eventually Brenchley won, but he had very little money, and my father told me afterward that his fee was only $300.

He continued to speak at political meetings, and he made one last try by running for Republican State Committeeman. It was a minor office, but one in which he would not be opposed by the Democratic Irish vote. He was jittery about the outcome and, on the evening of the election, asked me to go to the poll, in a barbershop, to ask how the count was going. The man in charge was a friend, and my father thought he would tell me. I knew it was wrong, and I am sure my mother did too, and why she didn't stop me I don't know, but I went and rapped on the door. Inside I could see four people sitting around a table counting ballots. No one responded to my knock. I knocked again and my father's friend shook his head without looking up. I turned and walked away, and two or three young people sitting on a bench outside the building laughed and made some comment about my father's likely loss of the election. And lose it indeed he did.

Since judges continued to be elected, my father would never be Judge Skinner, and unfortunately he had a taste for the office because as U.S. Commissioner he was called upon to act in a judicial capacity. He would have been a good judge and it was the kind of success he deserved, but he would never make it. In every professional direction he had gone as far as he could go.

His personal and social life had reached the summit too. He was an Odd Fellow and always hoped to be a Mason, which was much more prestigious, but someone—someone who had lost a case against him, perhaps, or simply did not like him—had always blackballed him. He had made progress in one direction, however: he had reached the level of the Wright dynasty. In December 1916 he attended a dinner of the Pennsylvania Society in New York City with C. Fred

Wright and Wright Glidden. (Senator Boies Penrose, the leader of the powerful Pennsylvania Republican machine, was at the speakers' table. Sir George Foster spoke, and he warned would-be United States peacemakers not to "butt in by advising peace to Canada . . . until those vital principles for which we strive have been fought out and won.")

My father had also drawn the will of another member of the Wright clan, Miss Clara Falkenbury, and as executor of her estate he found himself rather in command of the fortunes of a nephew, Clarence Wright, the principal beneficiary. Clarence was easy-going and moderately successful in real estate and insurance. He had married a socialite from Montrose who was never very happy in Susquehanna, and he was always short of money. He would come to my father asking him to advance more than Miss Falkenbury's trust authorized. My father followed the letter of the will and I rather suspect that he took some satisfaction in exerting this much control in the Wright family.

I glimpsed a bit of the decline in the family when a scion, Miller Wright, a young man with little ambition who worked in the bank, asked me to show him something about the saxophone. He had married a girl from Philadelphia, and together they made the best of living in Susquehanna. I went one evening to their house, which stretched along the top of a bank on lower Grand Street. In the living room there were comfortable chairs and a divan in slipcovers, with soft light from table lamps, which were not yet very common. He had bought a C-melody saxophone and an instruction booklet, and he wanted a bit of practical advice. We spent a very pleasant evening, but somehow this little world, almost completely isolated from the culture of Susquehanna, seemed pathetic.

Though my father had pulled abreast of the Wright family, he was still in awe of the social life to be found elsewhere. During the war my mother was invited, as chairman of a Civilian Relief Committee, to a luncheon at Fernheim, the estate of the Warriner family from Philadelphia, near Montrose. It was a beautiful place with many signs of affluence. My mother was nervous about her appearance as my father drove her up to the door, and in awesome tones he pointed out the importance of what we were seeing.

With little support from my mother, he promoted friendly contacts with Mrs. Taylor's daughter, Elisabeth Lamb. She took us one Sunday afternoon to call on some friends in Binghamton—a young civil engineer employed by the city and his extremely attractive wife. My father's efforts to live up to the occasion—to be witty and just a shade risqué—were embarrassing to everyone, and I sensed my mother's malaise. Mrs. Lamb came to Susquehanna once with a friend who was a dealer in Hudson cars, apparently intent on making a sale, possibly with Mrs. Lamb's collusion. He took us for a drive in a "coach"—the first enclosed car that I had ever been in. He demonstrated the beauty of the mechanism by shifting smoothly into second gear while moving at a high speed. My father told me later that he had seen that trick before, and he did not buy the car.

My parents occasionally went to Binghamton for a dinner party and a play (after a dinner in Binghamton in January they astonished my brother and me by reporting that they had had fresh strawberries), and they spent short vacations in New York City, Philadelphia, or Atlantic City, but these were excursions, not daily life. Professionally, socially, and personally, they had exhausted Susquehanna.

My mother was, of course, not untouched. She had done her part for the town. She was president of the Ladies' Auxiliary of the hospital and gave benefit teas at our house. At a meeting of the Town Council she spoke for the Civic Club "for a bigger and better Susquehanna." She did all this while managing a family in a far from convenient house. Once or twice an advertisement appeared in the *Transcript* for a girl to work during the day, but I remember no such person, and my mother continued to make the beds, cook the meals, mend our clothes, clean the house, and put up fruits and vegetables in Mason jars and eggs in waterglass.

She was overworked and showed it, and she may also have reached the menopause. She would blow up when things went wrong. A Cemetery Association was organized by a former citizen who was dismayed by the condition of the cemetery next to our house, and my mother became secretary. It was her duty to send out literature to members. She bought a crude duplicating system, consisting of a gelatin pad and a special typewriter ribbon. The typed copy was placed face down on the wet pad and the typing was thus transferred

My Grandmother Burrhus, Great-Grandmother Porter, and Grandfather Burrhus (top row), with unidentified relatives

My grandparents Ida and Charles Burrhus with their children, Harry and Grace

My Grandfather Skinner

My Grandmother Skinner

My father at his graduation

My father as General Counsel for the
Hudson Coal Company

My mother as a young woman

My mother, Grandfather Burrhus, and I

We are pretending to be driving past our house (my brother is in the front seat), but my mother's relaxed posture and the brick under the rear wheel give the show away.

Posing for the camera

With my younger brother, Ebbe,
dressed up for the photographer

My Boy Scout troop (Ebbe is second from left in the middle row; in the bottom row, Bob Perrine is second from right, and I am second from left)

At age nineteen

As a freshman, wearing my "slimer" cap

"The maker of ships on his [twenty-third] birthday"

to the gelatin. One could then lay moist sheets of paper on the gelatin and pick up copies. But the copies were scarcely legible, and my mother broke down and cried. She had tried to economize, but it had not worked out.

She complained of small details of my behavior, and I resented it. One day in the kitchen, when she was behind in her work and things were not going well, she made some critical remark, and I replied that others were guilty of the same thing. I had meant my mother, of course, and she got the point. She turned toward me, opened her speechless mouth, raised both hands like claws, and came at me. I held my ground, and she stopped before she reached me. She tore off her apron and dashed out of the room and went upstairs. My father, in the living room, quietly suggested that I go and say I was sorry. I found my mother sobbing on her bed and said I was sorry. It was upon this kind of occasion that she would say, "Someday you will understand."

For my mother, as for my father, something had gone wrong. Life was progress, but they had stopped progressing. To live was to improve oneself, and they had come a long way beyond their parents, but further improvement seemed unlikely. Instead, decay might be setting in.

They could not look for a solution by moving to another city. A successful merchant can sell out and start again elsewhere. A doctor can buy the practice of another doctor who has retired or died. But a lawyer, before the day of the big law firm, was tied to his local reputation and good will, and my father seemed caught in a trap.

SUDDENLY AND QUITE UNEXPECTEDLY he was able to escape. He was offered the position of junior associate to Mr. James Torrey, General Counsel for the Hudson Coal Company in Scranton, Pennsylvania. The offer came about through a series of accidents. In 1920 Susquehanna County increased the tax assessment on anthracite-coal properties in the southern part of the county, and the coal companies opposed the increase. Mr. Torrey came to Forest City to represent the Hudson Coal Company, and my father appeared for another company. Mr. Torrey saw my father in action and liked his energy and efficiency. It may also be relevant that Mr. Torrey had recently lost a son, also a lawyer and also named Will, whom my father was said to resemble. When, two years later, he was looking for a Junior Counsel, he remembered my father and offered him the job. There was a strong implication that upon his retirement my father would become General Counsel, and Mr. Torrey was then seventy-one years old.

The job and the salary—far more than he had ever made in a year—were precisely what my father needed to restore his faith in himself, and there was no doubt that the offer would be accepted. My grandfather Skinner beamed when my father told him about it, and my grandmother did her best to understand.

Only my grandmother Burrhus had reservations. Why should we make a change? We were comfortable and happy in Susquehanna, and we belonged there. Why could I not apprentice myself in the Erie Shops like other boys—or study law if I must—and be content with a good life?

The *Transcript* trumpeted my father's appointment and ran his picture:

W. A. SKINNER
ACCEPTS FINE
APPOINTMENT

Will Become Counsel for Hudson Coal
Company with Offices in Scranton

I, too, welcomed the change. I was never aware of the control exercised by my family or my associates in Susquehanna, but it was nonetheless irksome. During the day I was a committed scholar, but the rest of my time was not spent in interesting ways. My various jobs were routine, and playing the saxophone had become work. I had friends—but the pattern of friendship had been established in preadolescent days. I accepted all this as I had been taught to do; I had never learned to protest or complain or even to try to find out what was wrong. And so, although college would take me away from my old world for a substantial part of each year, a move to another city would make a much greater difference.

In Harrisburg I had bought a book called O. *Henry Prize Stories of* 1920, and it contained a story by Frances Noyes Hart called "Contact!" using the word as aviators used it during the war. It was a sentimental story with supernatural overtones, but I liked the flyer's account of his experience as he buckled the strap about him and laid his hands on the stick.

> It's waiting—waiting for a word—and so am I and I lean far forward, watching the figure toiling out beyond till the call comes back to me, clear and confident, "Contact, sir?" and I shout back, as restless and exultant as the first time that I answered it—"Contact!"
> And I am off—and I'm alive—
> And I'm free!

That was my mood. College *and* Scranton meant a new world!

I was second in a class of seven graduating seniors. (Both my father and my mother were second in their classes in the same high school.) The class was supposed to choose a motto, and we considered several of the old standbys, such as "*Ad astra per aspera*," without enthusiasm. I suggested "Contact!" and it was accepted. The junior class, according to tradition, lettered it on a panel decorated with crepe paper in our class colors, "gitane and white," and it appeared above us at graduation.

In the commencement exercises I played "*Celeste Aida*"—with Robert Perrine, soon to go off to West Point, at the piano.

THE MOVE TO SCRANTON WAS indeed a sweeping change. We left that old ramshackle house at 433 Grand Street, next to a graveyard, its rooms awkwardly arranged, its conveniences primitive, and its stucco turning gray in the soot of a railroad town, and moved into a clean white house in the fairly prestigious Green Ridge section of Scranton, with a laundry in the basement and a maid's room on the third floor, instant hot water at any time of day or night, a kitchen with a gas stove and a refrigerator rather than a coal stove and an icebox, a two-car garage with its own gasoline storage tank (never used), and a professionally groomed lawn and garden. We sold the old upright piano with its scrollwork over faded gold velvet and its ornately carved legs and bought a Steinway baby grand and put it in the entrance hallway with its top propped up for show. Except for a recently acquired dining-room suite and some bedroom furniture, everything in the house was new—fire screens, drop-leaf end tables, upholstered chairs and divans, and Oriental rugs. We turned in our open Chevrolet and bought a Packard sedan.

My parents joined the Country Club, which, with its eighteen-hole golf course, was within the city limits, only a few blocks from our house, and my father bought clubs, knickers, patterned socks, and golf shoes. My mother left her sewing machine in Susquehanna and turned to a Madame Berg, who selected clothes for a small clientele, and from that day forth was chicly dressed. My father continued to come home at noon but it was to eat "lunch"; we ate dinner at night. We had a uniformed maid, or rather a series of maids, toward whom my mother showed no trace of the Lady Bountiful, and to cap it all, they were to call me "Mr. Frederic" and my brother "Mr. Edward."

Most of these changes were due to my mother, who probably overestimated what needed to be done because she was frightened. In Susquehanna her place had been secure, but now everything was strange, and she approached her new life timidly. The moving van brought the pieces of furniture we had salvaged, together with pots and pans and books and linen, and delivery trucks came out from the central city with our new purchases, and the house began to look furnished; but it was still only a house. And when one day the wife of our real-estate agent came to the front door and hoo-hooed, my mother was tremendously relieved, and she often said that that "hoo-hoo" saved her life.

She was not a social climber: she made no effort to get to know the "right people"; but she wanted to be *like* the right people and so she bought the kinds of furniture and draperies described in *Good Housekeeping* and *House and Garden*, and she read Emily Post's *Etiquette* and worried about table service and what she and my father should say and do at receptions and banquets. She ordered engraved calling cards for all of us, although it was not clear how we should use them, and in place of the Monday Club she joined a book club in which once a week a woman summarized and read parts of a recent book, so that she could pass for being well read.

My father went along with this, though he felt no great need for it. He was immensely pleased with his success: he had gained an excellent position in a large company, he owned a good house in a desirable section of a large city, he drove a Packard, and he played golf with friends who talked about politics and the stock market. That was enough.

My brother was not much affected. He went to Central High and immediately made a host of friends. He played basketball much better than the score of that game in Susquehanna suggested, and he was soon elected to a high-school fraternity. Later my father bought him a small Overland runabout, which undoubtedly increased his popularity, but he was the kind of person who was instantly liked anyway, and I doubt whether anyone could have detected any great change in him between Susquehanna and Scranton.

I was exposed to our new life only briefly before going to college. I discovered that there were tennis courts at the YMCA in the central city and I joined the Y in order to play on them. A tournament was held in the Green Ridge section, and I entered that. I played against an older man, a doctor, whom I should have beaten, but he used the same strategy as U. G. Baker and eliminated me.

I spent much of the summer preparing for college. Bill Ernestone made a tuxedo, but I needed other clothes and at Samter's, a men's store in Scranton even more fashionable than Weed's in Binghamton, I seemed at once to be an old and favored customer. I bought a large wardrobe trunk which opened up to become a chest of drawers, with coat hangers on a rack. A new portable typewriter could be fitted into the shoe compartment. I bought a large suitcase, and a fiber mailing case which carried my laundry back and forth between Hamilton and Scranton for the next four years.

PART IV

MY FIRST LETTER home from college begins with some local details because my father and mother were out of town on the day I left.

> *North College Hall*
> *Hamilton College*
> *Clinton, New York*
> *Tuesday, September 19, 1922*

Dear Folks,

 . . . Monday morning I got up about seven and took Ebbe down to school, then I phoned a cart man and sent the trunk down, went down and checked it to Utica and also checked my sax at the parcel room. As that was all I had to do I spent a long morning reading O. Henry. I got to the station and got the sax but found the train about a half hour late. It turned out to be a whole hour behind time. I met a fellow from Owego on the train which was packed with college boys and girls mostly going to Syracuse.

 Changing cars at Binghamton we gained a quarter of an hour on the scheduled time and made up another on the road. [Railroading was still in my blood.] *I met a fellow on the train who was going to Colgate which is near Hamilton. After he got off I met two Hamilton fellows. One of them is a Weed of Binghamton whose father died this summer and who has studied baritone singing in New York for several years.* [He knew or at least dropped the names of many people connected with the opera in New York, including Gatti-Casazza, the impresario of the Metropolitan. I brought up the fact that I had seen Geraldine Farrar in Carmen, but he quickly spotted me as an amateur and put me in my place easily enough.] *I also met another fellow on the train named Davies. He and I got off at New Hartford and took a trolley there which was shorter than from Utica. The other two fellows took care of our trunks at Utica.*

Ebbe would have had the time of his life on the trolley car. It went quite fast—both forward and back and forth. Everybody in it would lean way over one way then fall the other. The straps slapped back and forth against the ceiling and a variety of noises came from the engine and wheels. It was worse than the Toonerville trolley.

We got to Clinton and took a taxi which took me to the Chi Psi (pronounced kye sigh) fraternity house. Paul Olver met me there and after playing the sax for a while in a get up orchestra and playing rummy I went to bed. Some of the fellows at Chi Psi are fine. One short guy with red hair that acts like Napoleon (the fellow not the hair) is really funny. At breakfast this morning someone was talking about an abandoned swimming pool at the gym. The fellow said, "The water ran out as fast as they put it in." Napoleon asked without smiling, "Why didn't they put it in faster?" Another junior there just bought a Ford. He said it was in perfect condition. One little thing though bothered, he said. That was the fact that it boiled over which was due either to the fact that the brakes dragged or to the fact that the radiator was out of commission. He also added the batteries weren't working good so I haven't figured out what part of the car was in perfect condition. [I believe I thought that these anecdotes would amuse my parents and my brother; I cannot believe that they were a reflection of my own tastes. I was playing the role of a dutiful son.]

This morning I got up at seven and took a walk around the campus and it is really beautiful, much larger and nicer than I expected. I reported my arrival and filled out my course card. After having dinner at the Chi Psi's I went for a room in a dormitory and got one in North Hall. [I went only after being abruptly pressured by someone at the fraternity. They had looked me over carefully. I had played the saxophone, told them the sports I played, and described the school I had gone to, and they evidently found me wanting.] This is the oldest hall here and of course not very modern. It is, they say, the best heated and has the best showers. I haven't eaten at the Commons table yet but will breakfast there tomorrow. I visited the Psi U house where Davies lives and I met all the fellows there. Their house is the newest and biggest here. It has a mammoth living room with fire places and a grand piano. Its dining hall is of the old Anglo Saxon architecture and is really beautiful. I have been invited to the Psi U house for lunch tomorrow so will soon know how they eat there.

At the Chi Psi they have a man chef and butler who is a facsimile of the movie butler. He is a fine fellow and they have good meals *there. I had a wonderful dinner at the Beta Kappa house tonight. A fellow I met invited me down and Stewart Brownell who wrote to me lives at this house. The meal was great and served with the neatness and care of a fine hotel. The fellows there are the best natured bunch I have met yet. I have a standing invitation to eat there again when I wish. . . .*

I am going to have a physical exam tomorrow morning.

So far everything is fine but I will be glad to see you all Christmas and would be pleased if you could drive up some day. Yet I am not homesick and I think I am going to enjoy my four years here.

Lots of love,
Fred

P. S.   The real name of North Hall is William H. Skinner hall so I feel at home.

BETA KAPPA invited me to join and I quickly accepted. The fraternity occupied a remodeled frame house at the foot of College Hill. That meant a long climb up the hill to classes in the morning and down again for lunch and up again for afternoon classes and down again for dinner and up and down again for any evening activity, but Susquehanna had prepared me for that. The living room was furnished with heavy oak furniture, a small grand piano, and two large colored prints by Maxfield Parrish. Freshmen slept in a small dormitory, and there were several studies with desks and Morris chairs, which freshmen shared with seniors.

To a good fraternity man I had made a mistake. I had joined a local (though Beta Kappa "went national" a year or two later when it became a chapter of Lambda Chi Alpha) and Hamilton was an extremely strong fraternity college. I did not immediately feel any lack of status—two or three of the national fraternities also had remodeled private houses at the foot of the hill—but certain disadvantages became clearer as my four years passed, and after I had graduated I was often embarrassed when a new acquaintance familiar with Hamilton would ask me what "crowd" I had belonged to. (Perhaps I had picked up some of my mother's social aspirations. I told an upperclassman in my fraternity that I thought I could "get into

Utica society by my senior year." I doubt whether I knew what I meant.)

My life in the fraternity turned out well enough. My so-called brothers remained friendly after I was pledged. Rather than haze or otherwise mistreat their freshmen, they helped them find themselves on campus, warning them of difficult courses and steering them into rewarding activities. The house was comfortable if not beautiful, but the food fell far below the standard I had reported at that dinner when I was being rushed. It was plentiful but greasy and unappetizing, and I developed a bad mid-morning candy habit, going into the college store for two Schrafft chocolate bars with vanilla-cream centers and three nut meats on top of each.

Fraternities compared their grade averages (another local, the Emerson Literary Society, was always at the top) but ranked themselves mainly according to extra-curricular accomplishments. I was urged to "go out" for everything within range. My only sport was tennis, and I made an abortive try for the team. I quickly discovered that I was a poor player, and that the game I had learned in Susquehanna was not a foundation upon which a skilled performance could be built. I tried out for the Charlatans, the student theatre, and was actually chosen for a part, but my performance at the first rehearsal was so bad that I was dropped. My last chance was the instrumental club. I took my saxophone one evening and went up the hill to a small building in which I could hear tryouts in progress. I could scarcely force myself to go in. I considered returning to my fraternity and reporting that I had failed, but I did try out and made the club.

FRESHMEN, CALLED "SLIMERS," were required to wear small green knit caps and to say hello to everyone they passed on pain of some unspecified punishment. There was a scheduled wrestling match with the sophomore class after chapel one morning and a tug of war across a small pond in the middle of the quadrangle through which one class or the other was dragged.

The year before I came to Hamilton there had been a tragic hazing accident, when a freshman, asleep in his bed, had been dumped onto the floor by his fraternity brothers and had struck his head and died, but in spite of this there was still some rather vicious hazing. One evening I was captured by two sophomores and taken into a classroom, where I was tied to a seat with clothesline. I did not resist; I simply let my captors tie me up without protest. Fortunately, I had secreted a razor blade in one of my rubber heels for just such an emergency, and I managed to get it out and cut myself free. (In my sophomore year I was captured by two freshmen as I left the fraternity house and strung up against a clothes pole with my arms stretched out and my thumbs wired to a crossbar. There I should have stayed all night and quite possibly lost a thumb or two if a friend, who had seen the attack, had not come and cut me down.)

Classes at Hamilton were run strictly on schedule. At the beginning of each period the bell in the chapel tower tolled twelve times. If you were not in your seat on the stroke of twelve, you were marked late or absent, and only a small number of absences were excused. A student racing to class across the quadrangle would cry, "Hold that bell!" and not entirely without effect if the student who was ringing the bell was in a sympathetic mood. Every weekday morning the bell tolled for compulsory chapel, and a topcoat thrown over pajamas was an acceptable dress, though uncomfortable and ridiculous in warm weather. Church service on Sunday was also compulsory.

All this regimentation was balanced by a surprising freedom in our examinations. Following an honor system, we signed a statement at the end of a paper or an examination to the effect that we had neither given nor received help. Taking a breather during a three-hour final examination, we might discuss the fairness of the questions and mention the ones we were finding difficult, but we never gave each other any help.

Hamilton was not at the time an outstanding college. Only a few members of the faculty had Ph.D.'s. (They were called Doctor as a mark of distinction, while all the rest were called Professor.) Only one or two carried on scholarly activities. But almost all were dedicated teachers and we got to know them personally. In a survey of comparable men's colleges in the East, Hamilton was then distinguished only by the amount of time its students spent on modern languages. In reporting this fact to the college, the President said, "It is nice to know that Hamilton is outstanding in what has always been regarded as the mark of a gentleman." But we were not there merely to become gentlemen.

I had trouble with my courses my freshman year. I went into Intermediate French on the strength of that bare pass on the Regents' Examination and was in real trouble. On the first day "Gigi" Wisewell dictated a few sentences, and since I had never heard French properly spoken, my transcription was far from adequate. "Bugsy" Morrill's General Biology was not very interesting because botany and zoology were then merely systems of classification. Bugsy saved his more interesting materials—such things as a dried, partially dissected body of a young girl and a bear's os *penis*—for his advanced courses. He was interested in the health of his students, and when there was an epidemic of colds, he would come into the classroom with an oily mixture smelling of eucalyptus and put drops into all our upturned noses. One day Gardner Weed had the misfortune to cough two or three times, and Bugsy left the room and returned with a microscope slide on which he had scooped up a large lump of Vaseline. He asked Weed to open his mouth and scraped the lump off on his teeth, telling him to hold it in his mouth as long as he possibly could. Weed was the aesthete of the freshman class, and we divided our attention for the rest of the hour between Bugsy's lecture and Weed's efforts to control himself.

I don't know why I took Greek. I had had four years of Latin in high school, but another classical language must have been required. The first year was taught by "Bull" Durham, not a very classical type, but I rather enjoyed it. Public Speaking, on which Hamilton prided itself, was compulsory for four years. Professor Lewis, known as "Cal," had written the freshman textbook, with pictures of a middle-aged female in a turn-of-the-century costume demonstrating speech sounds with her far from lovely pharynx. Our instructor was "Swampy" Marsh. The class met in the chapel and a few students spoke at each session. Once in a while someone would flick a penny onto the platform. At my first rehearsal Swampy made suggestions and noted them on the copy of the speech I had memorized. In my first paragraph I was to clarify the pronunciation of the *a* in "economic abyss" and the *o* in "European." At the beginning of the second paragraph I was to shift my position on the stage. I was to emphasize the word "incredible" and not swallow the "is" in "so far as recent American history is concerned." I was to be sure that "history" had three syllables. In all these courses I got B's, but in mathematics "Brownie," as we called Professor Brown, gave me A's both semesters. The course covered algebra and trigonometry, and I had been well prepared.

The course I enjoyed most during my freshman year was "Smut" Fancher's English Composition. Smut was a man easy to view with contempt, but he was responsible for perhaps more of the better features of Hamilton College life than any other faculty member. He was homosexual and had made advances toward a student or two, but no one would testify against him, and the administration had allowed him to stay on, doubtless with stern warnings.

He conducted the college choir and was one of those who, like "Doc" Davison of Harvard, elevated college singing above the level of "The Bulldog on the Bank." He also directed the Charlatans, the productions of which suffered because female parts were played by male students—a tradition perpetuated perhaps a little longer than necessary because of Smut's predilections.

He encouraged us to believe that he knew literary people and was himself a writer. I never saw any of his work, but he knew how to teach writing. His senior class read, criticized, and graded freshman themes, Smut himself reviewing the seniors' comments and grades and adding comments of his own. (He was a stickler for spelling and deducted one letter grade for each misspelled word.) In class he read one or two papers each day and discussed them at length. The first of mine he read was a report of a lecture on Petrarch by a visiting scholar, and I was astonished at how effectively he did it: ". . . Petrarch's life was spent in learning: and when this varied, unconventional, politically involved, yet artistically inspired career was snuffed out, they found him—with his books." Fancher hammed that last line beautifully.

A week later, assigned "One of My Interests," I wrote pretentiously about the opera, with some shameful faking.

You are in a magnificent theatre, large and richly decorated. You sink into a soft chair, glance through a program, notice the occupants of the boxes with which you are familiar [those girls from finishing school!], then, as the curtain rises, surrender yourself to the author and composer. You are his for a few hours. . . . With the least exertion on your part, thoughts and emotions are put in your mind that in no other way could become yours so easily.

Opera does not affect everyone in this manner. Before you can taste of its pleasures, you must go through tedious hours of study and tolerance of what may seem to you at first to be "noise. . . . "

The tedious hours were, of course, the hours I spent listening to Ward Palmer's records and playing bits of the scores of three or four operas on my saxophone.

THE TRANSITION FROM A SMALL TOWN in Pennsylvania to a long-established college in New York State was not without its problems. In Susquehanna the older Irish had a rich brogue, and a bit of it survived in their children and even grandchildren. Most of the Italians continued to speak broken English. My grandfather dropped his aitches and said auto*mo*bill, and Miss Graves said something close to *ruff* for *roof*, but in general we all spoke what I thought was standard English. Until I reached Hamilton College.

When I first met with Cal Lewis to rehearse an appearance in Public Speaking, he asked whether I had ever had speech therapy. Among other things, he mentioned the way I emphasized connectives. I tended to say, "What is man that thou are mindful *of* him?" and only with concentration could I say, "What is man that thou art *mindful* of him?" I used a great many unnecessary *up*'s—I did not clean my room, I cleaned it *up*; I did not wrap a package, I wrapped it *up*. Brownie's wife, who called herself Mrs. Seeley-Brown, once commented on the fact that I used *yet* for *still*. (In my diary I wrote, "I am working at the store yet.")

In Susquehanna most words ending in *-dous* were pronounced *-jous*. I grew up saying *tremenjous* and *stupenjous* and continued to do so through college. *Forehead* had two strong syllables; it did not rhyme with *horrid*. *Creek* was pronounced *crick*. Much of my vocabulary was acquired from books, especially in art and music, and when in class one day I referred to music by the composer *Du-vor-ak*, Gardner Weed whirled around and exclaimed, *"Dvorzhak!"*

Been we pronounced *ben*, and my professor in American Literature, "Chubby" Ristine, once tricked me by asking me to comment on Whittier's

> For of all sad words of tongue or pen,
> The saddest are these: "It might have been!"

He asked the class what was wrong, and when my hand shot up, he called on me, knowing perfectly well that I should have made the words rhyme. I replied that it could have been "might have *bean*," and that evoked Chubby's dry little laugh.

I was learning a new life in other ways, not all of which gave me any great assurance. My roommate, "Stew" Brownell, was a sardonic teacher. When I began to smoke cigarettes, it took me some time to learn how to hold one and once, walking on a street in Utica, I threw a butt in the gutter and stopped to grind it under my shoe. Stew was with me, and he said, "That's right, Fred. Be sure you put it out." In Albany on the way to a football game he and I went to a barbershop and I had a haircut, shampoo, and facial. As I paid and left, there were puzzling glances and smiles among the barbers, and outside Stew said to me, "I suppose you give a big tip for a job like that." I had never tipped a barber in my life.

I was slow in making another adjustment. In the Susquehanna High School our teachers were our friends; they were not out to prove us wrong, nor were we out to harass them. And we were friends among ourselves. Those who answered questions were not suspected of currying favor. We knew nothing of the leveling practices which keep members of a large class in line, and it never occurred to me that other students would censure me for volunteering an answer. But most of the freshmen at Hamilton had come from large high schools in which a student who answered too often was punished in one way or another by his peers. I was slow in discovering this, and unfortunately, sensing my inadequate preparation, I was particularly anxious to display what I knew.

One day in Freshman Composition, Smut read something from

a paper containing the expression "very interested" and looked out over the class quizzically. My hand shot up. "I was taught to say very *much* interested," I said. It was a lie. I may have read something about treating past participles as adjectives, but I had not had that kind of instruction, and it was quite true that I was advancing my own interests unfairly. The class no doubt punished me, although I do not recall the murmur or groan that the comment deserved.

The result of my insensitivity to the counter-control exercised by my fellows was a reputation for conceit. This was my father's old problem, and with him it arose from similar circumstances. I did not feel that I was superior to my fellow students; I simply wanted to make it clear that I was not inferior. And were we not *all* there to better ourselves?

HAMILTON COLLEGE was a mile from the small town of Clinton and nine miles from the city of Utica. I occasionally walked into Clinton to mail or retrieve my laundry case or get my hair cut, and I sometimes joined a friend on an excursion into Utica on the trolley —to see a movie, perhaps, and to have a good dinner at Harding's Restaurant. But it was then just a matter of taking the trolley back to Clinton and walking to the Hill. One or two of the better fraternities had social connections in Utica, but Beta Kappa was a Johnny-come-lately.

Sexual activity was largely verbal. It was confined to dirty jokes and allusions to old conquests. There were a few copies of *La Vie Parisienne* around, in the cartoons of which girls were sometimes drawn with bare breasts. There was a pulp magazine called *Captain Billy's Whiz Bang*, but the naughtiest story I remember was this: A man sits down beside a woman on a train and they both doze off a bit, and when the man leaves the train, he says goodbye and adds, "I hope to sleep with you again sometime."

Those who took advanced Latin with "Trot" Chase had access to some really juicy stuff, and I learned from one of them about the device called a dildo. We occasionally received titillating advertisements for books by Aphra Behn, de Sade, and Masoch, and I sent for one or two, but they were so heavily bowdlerized, or my understanding so inadequate, that I got nothing out of them. Later I bought a copy of Ben Hecht's *Fantasius Mallare,* in the decorative line drawings of which phalluses could be identified and in which someone was characterized as a pisser-against-the-wind. The book had drawn a jail sentence for Hecht, and the sexual hunger at Hamilton can be estimated from the fact that when I lent it to a friend in another fraternity, he returned it months later dog-eared and with a broken spine, after having gone the rounds of all his brothers.

Fall and spring house parties were almost our only chances to be with girls. Our guests stayed in the Beta Kappa house, which had been cleaned for the occasion, while students doubled up with friends in the dormitories on the Hill. For one party I decorated the hall with silhouettes of musical instruments. We were on our best social behavior. In the evening we wore our tuxedos, and I began to smoke Pall Mall Ovals, which came in a red-and-gold box and made me feel very distinguished. There was almost no drinking.

For my first party the cousin of a roommate was found as my date. As soon as I had a chance, I opened up with my leg-feeling technique but was staunchly resisted. The girl explained vaguely that she was "sick," but I did not understand her, and she did not understand why I did not. Could she mean venereal disease? It was only after the party was over that my roommate explained that his cousin had been menstruating. It was the first time I had heard of the problem.

ON ONE OF THOSE LONELY SATURDAY EXCURSIONS into Utica I wandered into a bookshop on the third floor of a building on Bleecker Street. The shelves were painted a soft blue, and on a table near the front window were current books, most of them from a world I found brave and new.

The shop was run by Mary Ogden, the wife of a Utica businessman. She was attractive and sympathetic, and she served tea. I eventually read some of my poems to her. She asked me if I had heard about a man named Freud and spelled out the name. I thought she was referring to a cartoonist in the *New York World* named Frueh, but she corrected me, and explained a little of what Freud was writing about. She also told me about the Saunders family, whom I was to meet the following year when they returned to Hamilton. Professor Saunders, she told me, went to symphonies not so much to hear the music as to observe the conductor's style. I was greatly impressed.

I bought a few books—a deckle-edge copy of some poems by Stephen Crane, bound in heavy gray cardboard, a copy of *Ethan Frome*, a boxed and autographed special edition of Willa Cather's *One of Ours*, which had just appeared, and Louis Untermeyer's *Modern British Poetry* with the editor's name inscribed on the flyleaf. I also bought a book called *Homes in America* containing a few colored plates, and sent it to my parents with a rather maudlin inscription of which I was soon ashamed. I wrote a short short story about it two or three years later:

> Father and mother had laughed at Henry's first letters. Prosaic descriptions of college, the food, and his health, but with them an occasional unguarded note of homesickness. This pleased father and mother. They felt proud and happy that being away from home was hurting their son. It proved to them something they had sometimes doubted: that he really loved them.
>
> His overtones of homesickness increased as the months passed until a book came, carefully planned to reach home on mother and father's wedding anniversary. It was a large book, a gift edition in blue and gold, called *Beautiful Homes of History*. On the first page was carefully written:
>
> "To father and mother, whose home surpasses the beauty and holiness of any of these. Henry."
>
> Mother read it with moist eyes, and hated to have father smile at it. She did feel a little uncertain about it; but then, it was so unexpected! It really *was* dear of Henry! They both felt peculiarly happy. But after it was put on top of the bookstand, father occasionally laughed at it; and sometimes mother smiled too, although it made her feel guilty.
>
> Two months afterward Henry came home for the holidays. But during the first hour when he told them his joyous history, no one spoke of the book. No one even spoke of homesickness. Mother looked at the boy before her, and wondered about *Beautiful Homes*.

There was something incongruous there, between the inscription and Henry.

That night before she went to bed she went to the bookstand and ran her fingers over the cool gold letters on the blue cover. She read the words in a whisper: "Beautiful Homes of History." Then with a little swell of feeling she lifted the cover.

But the first page had been removed with a sharp knife.

My sexual naïveté led to an embarrassing moment one day at the Book Shop. One of Mrs. Ogden's friends was there, and I was presented to her as an "aspiring young poet" from the Hill. I had been reading *The Diary of a Young Girl*, a book published, I think, anonymously which I associate with Vienna via either Schnitzler or Freud. In it the young diarist tells of seeing a couple making love, and I felt very liberated as I reported to the two Utica matrons that she said that they kissed each other "all over." I was immediately aware that I had said more than I knew.

The following summer the *Literary Digest*, to which we still subscribed, asked readers to submit lists of the ten best American novels of the first quarter of the century. The following October it reported that

> ... B. Frederic Skinner, of Scranton, Pennsylvania who is not yet out of college sends a list "mainly to cast a vote for 'Ethan Frome,'" Mrs. Wharton's most widely appreciated story. "It could easily have been cluttered with trite New England characters," says this admirer, "and made to fill over 400 pages. Thanks to heaven that it wasn't!"

I don't remember the other nine on my list. I don't believe I had *read* ten modern American novels, if you excluded *Kazan, Lavender and Old Lace, A Girl of the Limberlost*, Booth Tarkington's *Penrod*, and a few things by O. Henry.

I WAS EARNING THAT DESCRIPTION as an "aspiring young poet," for I was turning out a good deal of (albeit pretty maudlin) stuff. Nothing in Fancher's course could have encouraged me along that path. For one assignment I submitted a sonnet beginning:

> I sometimes think the everlasting pine,
> Endowed with strength and long enduring grace,
> Is boastful of its nature-favored race
> And seeks out isolation by design. . . .

Would it not exchange its ever-graceful state "for one short month of summer's ornament"? "Too many end-stopped lines" was my senior's only comment, which Smut allowed to stand.

More helpful influences were my autographed copy of Untermeyer's *Modern British Poetry* and my slim volume by Stephen Crane. In another assignment for Fancher I had written a letter to the editor of the *Dial* commending him for publishing something of Crane's, adding, "I hope that I may go on with his work, feeling, as do many of our Moderns, that conventional forms of poetry are capable of improvement." But I was far from demonstrating any capability.

Fortunately for the historian of literature, all my freshman work can be identified because it was typed with a blue ribbon, and moreover I often put down the date of composition. February 1, 1923, will long be remembered as the day I wrote:

> The wind is sad—
> Mournful is the wind.
>
> In the silver night
> Swift, winding veils of streaming snow
> Enshroud the trees.
> Caught in the agonies of death,
> They stretch
> Their arms to heaven,
> And are wrapped
> In sifting shrouds.

Only six days later I was again visited by the divine afflatus with this result:

> **HELEN**
>
> If I could understand
> The molten blood

That drips from the ladle of the moon,
Or the voiceless mists that rise
From a frozen sea;
Then, Helen,
Might I understand thee, too.

and on the same day this:

A CINQUAIN

Three things
Reflect the fire
Of ages: *   * moonlit pearls   *   *
Deep rubies near a candle flame   *   *
Your eyes.

I was looking for things to be poetic about, and winter in New
York State supplied an example:

THE ICICLE

It grew with the moon . . .
    began like a silver needle
    when the moon was young.

Each night I saw it . . .
    how each day it grew and stopped
    at dusk when the moon came.

On my floor, in the criss-cross shadows
    that the lattice made,
    it cast a figure . . .

And when the moon was grown
    it was large . . . gigantic . . .
    like a glass tree growing downward.

Then in the waning
    it withered . . . shrank all day
    and at night wept steadily . . .

Half maddened I lay . . . listening
    to the drip of its tears . . . then
    . . . a crash . . .

The shadow sped to the window
   and out . . .
   and down to itself.

"Oh, coward," I cried,
   "you were not brave enough to face
   slow death. . . . "

I was not in fact much moved by the demise of that icicle, but another death touched me deeply. In January of my freshman year my grandmother Burrhus became seriously ill. Starkweather's flannels could not save her, and she died. I went back to Susquehanna for my first close experience with death. She was laid out in the spare bedroom, and people came to call and murmur their expressions of sympathy. A friend arrived with a small daughter who had lived upstairs in the duplex on Broad Street. The child had been fond of my grandmother and was puzzled by what she saw, but everyone seemed embarrassed, and no one tried to explain. Finally I said to her, "She is asleep," and that satisfied her. I was aware that I was behaving as people behaved in the books my grandmother had read. When I went back to Hamilton I wrote a poem which, for once, expressed something I really felt—and perhaps for that reason was one of my worst:

CHRISTMAS CACTUS

Oh, ugly, loutish, selfish thing,
   She cared for you
When you were naked, flowerless,
   The whole year through.

But each Noel you gave your gift,
   A blood-red flower:
and selfish, too, it scarcely lived
   A transient hour.

Long year on year, she gave to you
   A mother's care.
Then one Noel—your blood-red gift
   You did not bear.

Oh, ugly plant, did you discern
   What was to be?

Knew you that soon she could no more
   Keep watch o'er thee?

She went, but you remembered all.
   In her last hour
You bore to her, most gratefully
   A blood-red flower.

I had written little or nothing in Susquehanna from which one might have predicted the volume or the character of the poetry I wrote during my freshman year. The chance to publish in the *Hamilton Literary Magazine*—two of my poems were judged worthy that year—made a difference, of course, but it does not explain the mawkish sentimentality. I was not homesick, nor was I, strictly speaking, love-lorn. But there were no girls in my daily life and I missed them. The few who lived in Clinton were either pre-empted by upperclassmen or closely guarded by their parents or reputed to have venereal disease. I remember walking the streets in physical pain from the lack of someone to put my arms around. Poetry may have helped.

I SPENT MY EASTER VACATION traveling with the glee club. We performed in a number of towns where there were Hamilton alumni, usually staying with Hamilton families. The tour ended near New York City, and I came by sleeper to Scranton on Sunday morning, a week after Easter. My brother and I took our parents to church (they had begun to go oftener than in Susquehanna) and then drove downtown, where we joined a friend of his, Alex Clark. We all had sundaes in a drugstore and then drove back to our house.

My brother asked us to wait in the car while he went in to the toilet. After a rather long time he came out in great distress and said he had a very bad headache and had taken several aspirins. He went back into the house, and we followed him upstairs. He was in great pain and frightened. He lay down on his bed and cried, "Get a doctor!" Since we had so recently moved to the city, we had not acquired a family doctor, but Alex knew of one nearby and phoned him, and he came within fifteen minutes. Meanwhile my brother had become unconscious. Food was flowing out of his mouth, though he was not retching or actively vomiting. When the doctor arrived, I said, "My brother has fainted." He took off a shoe and stocking, stroked the sole of my brother's foot, and said, "It's a pretty deep faint."

I told him my father and mother were in church and asked whether I should go for them, and he said I should. I drove to the church, about two miles away, and asked one of the ushers to tell my father and mother to come out. I told them that Ebbe was ill, but spared the details, and then drove them home. I drove very fast, and my mother, not knowing how serious the matter was, complained of being jounced about.

When we reached the house, our maid was standing on the front porch, wringing her hands and crying, "Ebbe's gone! Ebbe's gone!" We rushed into the house and upstairs and found the doctor arranging my brother's body. It was true; he was dead. My mother threw her arms around the still warm, soft body, and my father in a kind of trance walked from room to room saying, "For heaven's sake, for heaven's sake."

The Presbyterian minister had noticed the disturbance at the back of the church and made inquiries. He came out to see if he could be of help. He asked if we would like a little prayer. No one of us felt any particular need for it, but we dutifully said yes, and he prayed, quietly and possibly to some effect.

There was an autopsy, and the cause of death was given as acute indigestion. Vomiting was a conspicuous symptom, and there was some inflammation of related organs. But it was nothing more than a routine check of parts of the abdomen by a "pathologist," and a medical friend to whom I showed the report many years later threw it down in disgust. His best guess was that my brother had died of a massive cerebral hemorrhage, possibly due to a congenital weakness in a blood vessel.

His death had a devastating effect on us. My grandmother Burrhus's death was not unexpected; this was an entirely different kind of thing—utterly senseless and almost impossible to accept. My grandfather Burrhus and my grandfather and grandmother Skinner came from Susquehanna and were as stunned and disoriented as my parents. My grandfather Skinner was proud of my brother and me and liked to see us enjoying ourselves, but it was not in his nature to be actively affectionate. Nevertheless, he loved us, and standing by the body of my brother as it lay in its coffin, I heard him say, "If I could only change places with that boy!" I have not the slightest doubt he would have done so if he could.

Dozens of cars full of people came from Susquehanna for the funeral—even Mr. and Mrs. C. Fred Wright. A score of friends my brother had made in less than a year at Central High in Scranton came too. My father bought a plot in a cemetery not far from our house, and there my brother was buried. And when it was all over my grandparents went back to Susquehanna and I to Hamilton College.

Several years before, Clarence Wright had persuaded my father that it was only good business to take out insurance on his sons. He was going to spend a good deal of money on their education and should be protected against loss. A month or two after my brother's death my father received a check from the insurance company. Cashing it was one of the most painful acts of his life.

Poorly prepared for almost everything he did, my father was totally unprepared for sorrow. He soon plunged into writing a book, which became the standard authority on workmen's compensation law in Pennsylvania, and dedicated it:

In Memory
of
My Son Edward

This work was undertaken to afford distraction
from the effects of his untimely passing.

The following summer he came home from his office one noon when I was playing the piano. He sat with my mother on the divan in the living room waiting for lunch to be served. I began to play Rimski-Korsakov's "Song of India," and after a few moments my mother called softly. I turned and saw that my father had fallen over sideways on the divan, as a doll might fall, and was weeping.

Just as I allowed myself to be tied to that classroom seat by two hazing sophomores, so I submitted to that tragic loss with little or no struggle. At one moment on a fair Sunday morning I was telling my brother about my college experiences (he was pleased when I told him that I had let my sideburns grow, though I had shaved them back that morning in the washroom on the sleeper), and fifteen minutes later he was dead. There was nothing I could do. It was Alex Clark who called the doctor, and when he came, I could only stand by and watch. The doctors who performed the autopsy asked me about the symptoms, and I described among other things the rather strange way in which my brother vomited—with no coughing or retching. They told my father that my objectivity was helpful. With the same objectivity I had watched my parents as they reacted to the discovery that my brother was dead.

But I was far from unmoved. I once made an arrowhead by bending the top of a tin can into a flattened cone. I fastened it to the end of an arrow, and when I shot it straight up into the air, it fell back and struck my brother in the shoulder, drawing blood. Many years later I remembered the event with a shock when I heard Laurence Olivier speaking Hamlet's lines:

> . . . Let my disclaiming from a purpos'd evil
> Free me so far in your most generous thoughts,
> That I have shot mine arrow o'er the house,
> And hurt my brother.

My brother and I had never competed for the same things. Our tastes, intellectual interests, and avocations were different. He was much closer to my father and mother, but even so I had been, if anything, too close. Escape had been the dominant theme in my departure for college. And now, with my brother's death, I was to be drawn back into the position of a family boy. It was a position I had never wanted, and it was to become increasingly troublesome in the years ahead.

IN OUR FINAL FRESHMAN THEME, Smut asked us to describe the change we had undergone during one year in college, and here is part of what I wrote:

> In the fall of 1922, a boy was matriculated at Hamilton College.
> He was from a small town, reared in a sympathetic home, and trained

in a school of interested teachers. Intent upon building a well-trained brain, he eagerly anticipated the new life and the Great Change.

To this boy college was to be four years of earnest study in subjects he enjoyed. His home and school, he thought, had shown him the necessity for certain kinds of knowledge, and now the work of building his mind was before him. What a joyous task it was to be! With what interest he would watch his mental powers expand, growing proficient in the things he wanted to do!

Eight months later, indifferent to the world, the boy looked upon a broken air castle. College had proved a disappointment. The Great Change was far from the change he had expected, and bitterly he wrote:

"The only broadening one year of Hamilton has given me is the enlargement of my own self-centered microcosm; the only agility of mind I have acquired is wasting itself in a ruinous flight toward selfishness."

It needed barely one month of the first term to show the boy he had misjudged college. There was no majority of students who enjoyed study, who frequented the library voluntarily. He found that he was almost alone in his pursuit of literature, and that he was actually jeered at for spending time on a book when other boys were supporting athletics. But as he stayed longer, he began to see the cause of it all, and even began to feel his own desire for study leave him. . . . He wrote:

"They're making me do too many things I don't want to do. They say these are things that I need; yet, while they may know a lot about what the average person needs, they don't know half as much about *me* as I do."

. . . In his fight to retain his individuality, and with his mutated notion of college, the boy rapidly changed his point of view toward other subjects. He looked upon himself as isolated. He became critical, almost cynical. His tastes changed. He had fits of brooding over heavy music. He read pessimistic or morbid books. He became unable at times to appreciate humor. He came to derive his only pleasure from lonely walks and poor verse writing. . . .

The Great Change has been wrought. The college, anticipated as an incentive, has become a burden; the new world has proved too unsympathetic; the boy's view of life—

Fancher kept these papers and gave them back to us in our senior year.

* * *

I CAME BACK TO SCRANTON a total stranger, and my parents had not yet come to know many people through whom I could make friends. Mr. and Mrs. Torrey took us to dinner, but they were in their seventies, and we saw little of them. My father played golf with the company's chief mining engineer, a man of considerable distinction whose wife was brilliant but incapacitated by asthma. An older daughter was married to an expatriate in Paris whose name I was to hear again, but the younger daughter was not a promising companion. I was invited to a rather swank party at her home, and during the evening she took me to her room and showed me a small jewel case half full of the fingernail and toenail clippings she was saving.

The company surgeon, Dr. Fulton, did not play golf but we were occasionally invited to his house for Sunday-night supper. The Fultons had two daughters, one of whom, Nell, was studying the organ with Charles Courboin, and through her I met a few musical people. Courboin was well known in international circles, and it may have been through his intercession that Nell was asked to play a piano quintet with the Flonzaley Quartet when it came to Scranton. She was not up to Flonzaley standards but the performance went off without incident. (Nell had less luck the following year when she gave a recital at the Century Club and found herself trapped by a faulty memory. She kept going back to an earlier point in a piece and was finally compelled to leave it unfinished and walk off the stage.) I went to a reception for the Flonzaley Quartet the evening after their concert and made some condescending remark to one of the players about Scranton audiences, and he dismissed me quite appropriately by saying that music depended upon audiences.

My parents were far happier with their old friends in Susquehanna and they began to invite eight or ten of them down for a day, perhaps to spend the afternoon and have dinner at the Country Club. My father first met the Jewish problem when his old friend Sid Hersh asked whether he and his wife would be welcome at the Country Club. Fortunately they were, although they probably could not have joined at that time. I too turned to old friends that first summer and went back to Susquehanna two or three times. I stayed with the Skinners but saw more of Mr. B and my distant cousin who was keeping house for him. Gran'ma Graham was bedridden, and my mother insisted that I call on her. Jess Haller and Nellie Graham were taking care of her, but there were no longer any boarders.

I saw some of my old girls, especially Chi Bennett, who had gone to Pennsylvania State College. She had always been slightly more sophisticated than I, and she held the advantage as we grew older. It was she who taught me how to kiss properly. Another old girl had "had to get married," as my mother put it, and since I had never been able to make any progress with her, I was surprised and retrospectively jealous.

My cousin invited a friend to visit her, and Kenny Craft and I took them out in my grandfather's car. The friend and I sat in the back seat, and when we parked on a dark road, we began to kiss. I was still concentrating on the leg, and for the first time I met no resistance. My hand went all the way up. But it did not seem like the right occasion for copulation, and I did not know what else to do. When I saw my cousin and her friend the next morning, it was clear that the evening had been discussed and that I had been dismissed as an ignorant and fumbling lout.

I started to play golf, largely because my father urged me to do so. I bought knickers, elaborately patterned woolen socks, and shoes with soft cleats. I bought a driver, a brassy, a midiron, a mashie, and a putter, and a heavy bag to carry them in. We hired caddies (carrying one's own golf bag was just not done), and I played only with my father and his friends.

We were not yet very clear about our social position in Scranton. We were upwardly mobile but we had not yet discovered how far we were to go. Certain limits revealed themselves when we took a short vacation together. We decided to go to the seashore. We had heard about Asbury Park, and we drove there and checked into one of the large hotels. It was a noisy place; the dining room was crowded; the food was poor and badly served; and the beach was dirty. We left after a day and drove south along the coast. At Spring Lake we passed the Essex and Sussex Hotel, and my father went in and found that we could get rooms.

It was certainly not like Asbury Park. Most of the guests were women and children whose husbands and fathers spent the summer in Wall Street and came down for weekends. There was a large lounge, in which a trio of piano, violin, and cello played tea music in the afternoon and dinner music at night. The beach was not good, and no one seemed to swim, but there was a walk, of wooden slats, along the dune-like shore. Most of the guests were well known by the employees, who quickly decided not to know us.

The dining room was under the control of a despotic headwaiter. At dinner one night I noticed a rather attractive young wife with two children at an adjacent table. She caught me looking at her and seemed annoyed. When she caught me a second time, she spoke to the headwaiter, and at the next meal we were put at a different table. One evening I came to dinner wearing a buttoned sweater, and as we left the dining room the headwaiter said to my father, "Please have the young man wear a coat in the dining room." My mother smothered a cry. We had made a mistake.

There was absolutely nothing to do. There were one or two unattached girls, but they were not attractive. In any case, I did not know how to approach them, and I knew that if I did so, my parents would want to meet them a little too soon. I envied a smart young man who drove up to the hotel in a sports car and turned it over to the doorman, to whom he flipped a large coin and from whom he got an appreciative "Thank you, sir." While my mother had her nap, my father and I took our bags and drove to a golf links which was open to guests of the hotel, but that covered only a small part of the day. In the evening we walked along the shore on that slatted walk and then sat in the lobby and listened to the trio until we could decently go to bed.

I was as miserable as I have ever been, and I am sure my father and mother were scarcely less so. They stayed on because it seemed to be the way in which successful people took a vacation. It is not so easy to say why I stayed with them.

MY SOPHOMORE YEAR was a great step forward, even though only two courses were interesting. I began to get something out of Greek. We read the *Iliad*, and the text was printed in a style of Greek letter which has always seemed to me particularly beautiful. Professor Fitch's nickname—"Little Greek"—was no doubt acquired when he was a junior member of the staff. At each meeting he would punctiliously write out our assignment on the blackboard—so many lines, to be found on such-and-such a page—and at the next meeting we translated them. Some students used a "trot," but I dug out the Greek and reached a stage—as with the *Aeneid* in high school—in which I read and thought at least fragments of a classical work in the language itself. Somebody had set up a prize for sight-reading Greek. We were given a passage from a part of the *Iliad* we had not covered and were asked to translate it without benefit of a dictionary. My translation could not have been very accurate; it was certainly not distinguished for its style; but I won.

I got much more out of a course on the French theatre taught by "Bill Shep." William H. Shepherd, a specialist in Provençal, was the most distinguished scholar on the faculty—so distinguished, in fact, that *real* French scholars came to visit him. He was a lean, angular man who whistled softly when speaking French. I was recovering from my inadequate preparation and was enormously impressed by the dignity and poise of Corneille and Racine. We read Molière as well, and Marivaux with his marivaudage, and moderns like Hervieu and Bernstein. I liked the archetypal pattern of Hervieu's *La Course du flambeau*: one generation receives the torch from the preceding and passes it on to the following. That was my father's notion of progress, my mother's of service, and Asa Gray's of the radish, and it was becoming my own.

I particularly liked Rostand. I was fascinated by *Cyrano de Bergerac* and went to see Walter Hampden in Brian Hooker's translation in New York that winter. For my final term paper (*en français*) I analyzed Rostand's *La Princesse lointaine*. I usually studied during the day, almost always in the morning and almost never in the evening, but in writing that essay I stayed up all night, busily consulting grammar and dictionary to bolster my far from idiomatic French, looking a little like Oscar Wilde writing *Salomé* in that cartoon I had seen in my bibliography.

"Bob" Rudd, who taught a General Introduction to English Literature, was not at all like Miss Graves. He was a perennially boyish enthusiast who occasionally told slightly risqué anecdotes about the people we were studying. I also took a course called "Phil. 1–2, Psychology, Logic" with "Bill" Squires, who had taken his degree under the great psychologist Wilhelm Wundt, at Leipzig, but who called himself a philosopher. He dressed impeccably in dark gray, in a rather antique style, and strutted about the campus in a posture which suggested that he was just on the point of falling over backward. The only psychology in the course was a brief demonstration of the two-point limen, in which Dr. Squires applied a pair of dividers to his forearm and quickly returned them to his desk drawer. By way of logic we memorized the Scholastic mnemonic for types of syllogisms which begins *"Barbara, Celarent, Darii, Ferioque,"* and it was implied that we were thus prepared to solve any logical problem that might come our way. Dr. Squires's favorite course was on Kant, and, for all I know, he taught it well. One final examination paper was so nearly perfect that he went to Utica and had a jeweler engrave HH (High Honor—the Hamilton equivalent of A) on a small disk of gold, which he gave to the student.

MY MAIN ADVANCE in my sophomore year was extra-curricular. The student who had been killed in the hazing accident was William Duncan Saunders, the charming and brilliant son of the Dean, who was also Professor of Chemistry. After his death the Saunders family took a year's leave and during my freshman year were in Paris. When they returned, they asked Brownie to suggest someone to tutor their son Blake in mathematics, and he suggested me. I called on Mrs. Saunders for an interview and was accepted. Blake, who was then appropriately called "Frisk," was a sophisticated twelve-year-old who wore tweed shorts and roamed the countryside with the Saunders scotties. His room contained aquaria and vivaria of various sizes and kinds, and he was not much interested in mathematics, but I got to know the Saunders family and the house, and it was an entirely new world.

Because Professor Saunders taught chemistry the students called him "Stink," and somehow that unbecoming name acquired affectionate overtones. I took his course that year and it was not exciting.

Stink's great love was peonies, and the house was half surrounded by great peony beds. He hybridized many beautiful types which are still prized by fanciers. He also liked astronomy and on a clear night a long brass telescope might be set up among the peonies and we would look for Saturn's rings or the moons of Jupiter.

He also played the violin, and every week players came from Utica for an evening of string quartets, to which I began to be invited. A large music room with a fireplace at one end had been added to the house, and it was furnished in a nondescript style with pictures, sculptures, great bowls of peonies in season, books, stacks of music, and magazines I had never heard of, such as *Broom*. I remember seeing a letter from Ezra Pound about George Antheil, together with a page from the score of Antheil's *Ballet mécanique* with the words "COMPLETELY PERCUSSIVE" printed diagonally across it. Stink was an old warhorse of a violinist, and he led whatever players he could assemble through a vast collection of quartets, with an occasional piano quintet. When they tried something he had not played recently or at all, he would call out a comment on a particularly good bit or spot a resemblance to something else as he played. Once when they were playing something by Mendelssohn, he shouted, "Rotten development!" sawing away without stopping.

EACH YEAR MRS. SAUNDERS took in two or three young people and tutored them for college. One was Cynthia Ann Miller, the daughter of a Utica banker, with whom I fell passionately in love. We went for long walks through the Root woods, and when we came back we might stop in to see Grace Root, the wife of Edward Root, who taught art, and a close friend of Cynthia Ann's, or have tea before the fire in the Saunders music room. Cynthia Ann admired Katherine Mansfield to the point of cutting her hair in Katherine Mansfield's style, and she read me some of her stories. I read her some of my poems, including a sonnet about a string quartet.

An older student was interested in Cynthia Ann, and I came into the music room one evening to find Stink and Frisk singing a song Stink had picked up in a music store called "Somebody Stole

My Gal," under the title of which Stink had written: "as sung by George Perrine." Unfortunately, this romantic idyll was not long-lived. After a certain amount of unskillful sexual fumbling, Cynthia Ann wrote me a long letter breaking off our relation, and I went for months in an agony of unrequited love. I watched for her everywhere, and my loneliness was excruciating. She went on to Radcliffe the following year, and it was a long time before I saw her again.

My love for Cynthia Ann was deep and painful but it was not primarily sexual. Indeed, I must have seemed sexually backward. An episode at a house party in the spring of my sophomore year makes it pretty obvious that sex was still a kind of game. While visiting a fraternity brother in Freeport, Long Island, I had met some of the girls he knew there, and we invited two of them to Hamilton for a house party. Eleanor, a pretty but rather chubby girl, was my date. She was a devout Catholic, and Professor Bowles would have been proud of the way she observed the principle of *noli me tangere* and thus blocked the only courtship ritual I knew. Frances, my friend's girl, had more chic and was obviously more liberal. Since I had driven my mother from Scranton to be one of the chaperones, our Packard was available, and at one point I persuaded Frances to go for a short drive. We parked, and I began a kind of verbal seduction: should we or shouldn't we? Eventually she said all right, we should, whereupon I put my arms around her, gave her one dry kiss, and then released her and started the car to drive back. "Was that all you wanted?" she said, greatly surprised. Evidently it was; apparently I was simply proving that I could kiss my friend's girl.

I continued to make lonely safaris into Utica, and once I found a pretty young girl in charge of the Book Shop. I was so smitten tthat I wrote an account of the meeting the next day, somewhat in the manner of Samuel Pepys by way of Christopher Morley, whose columns I read in the *Saturday Review:*

> To Utica this morning where I spent two hours till lunch with Claudia Hatch in Mrs. Ogden's bookshop. I had never met her but we fell to talking easily. She has read widely and evidently hurriedly and talks on everything whether she knows about it or not, but she is so frank that it is delightful superficiality.

She is slim and attractive though rather young. Talked very seriously about the "aristocracy of intellect" and assured me that from personal experience she knew there was no "pure love." She said she was in love now but wasn't true to him.

She makes herself attractive to the occasional patrons of the shop with such a naive affectation that it is delightful to hear her. I listened intently each time someone came in and once found that I had been listening to her and making out at the same time to be intensely interested in some children's book.

I sketched Cyrano for her, since she has not seen it, and I read a couple of short lyrics I have just written. At the end of one she said it was very good and asked me if I didn't think so. She was very anxious that I should because she had admitted that she herself was egoistic and wanted company, so I said I thought it was very good. The truth is, I do.

As we became acquainted, we grew less guarded. She became very frank about sex literature and remarked that her mother was very mid-Victorian, comparing her to Stuart Sherman's Cornelia. She said she thought Sherman "laughed" at his Cornelia but upon my suggestion changed it to "smiled." I told her I wanted a book very "Russian" to read. She seemed to interpret that freely and recommended *Jurgen*, which, as I have never read it, I took.

Joined John Gregory at lunch and over the orange pekoe he told me about Claudia. Was so charmed I walked up and down the street afterwards for a half hour trying to think up an excuse to go back to the shop.

IN THE FALL OF MY SOPHOMORE YEAR I had several attacks of what later proved to be appendicitis, a high incidence of which at Hamilton was popularly blamed on the very hard water. I would lie on my bed in agonizing pain, foolishly pounding my gut. In Scranton at Christmastime I told Dr. Fulton about it and he examined me and took my appendix out. As a result I missed my fall-term finals and had to take make-ups in the months which followed. Under the extra work I developed tachycardia; my heart would suddenly begin to beat 130 to 140 times per minute. I called my father and, no doubt moved by my brother's death, he urged me to come home at once. "Come home and be my chauffeur," he said—a curious suggestion but I think an affectionate one. I stayed at Hamilton, however, and got through the make-ups and back on schedule during the spring term.

Fatigued by extra work and possibly concerned about my health, I began to reconsider my bold announcement to Miss Graves that I no longer believed in God. I heard bits of the King James Bible read every morning in chapel, and some of the Sunday sermons were interesting, though seldom theological. I liked many of the hymns. Kipling's "Recessional"—"Lord God of Hosts, be with us yet/Lest we forget, lest we forget"—was as meaningless as Nellie Melba's "Goodbye," but almost as spine-tingling. Inevitably I argued religion with other students. In one of my papers for Smut Fancher I denounced the cowardice and deceit of that religious man Friar Lawrence in *Romeo and Juliet*, but he was a Catholic. Bugsy Morrill, a scientist I admired, taught Sunday school! Uneasy about all this, I went to Bill Squires, who often took morning chapel in his most pompous manner. With a voice quivering with emotion I said that I was worried because I had "lost my faith." He did little to help.

The Saunders family led me out of the difficulty. Stink could enjoy a chorale, oratorio, or cantata as secular music, and he "took" morning chapel and read bits from the Bible as literature. It was said that he himself had conducted a secular funeral service for that brilliant son killed in the hazing accident. I recovered my strength and the issue gradually faded.

IN MY FRESHMAN YEAR I had contributed only to the *Hamilton Literary Magazine*, but students could also publish original work in the *Royal Gaboon*, specializing in college humor, and a column in the student newspaper, *Hamilton Life*, called "*Carpe Diem.*" In one of my Public Speaking assignments I criticized both of these, and near the end of my sophomore year or possibly at the beginning of my junior year a rejoinder appeared in "*Carpe Diem*," with an allusion to Cynthia Ann. It was signed by Jay Kay, the nom de plume of John K. Hutchens.

Sir Burrhus Goeth Forth

And he cometh upon a fair ladie. And the ladie was Farina, the Miller's daughter. And Sir Burrhus was fain to speak, thus:

"Dromoundes maugre percloos poynt paltockes rechate."

Whereate first of all, the ladie Farina blusheth exceeding, for Sir Burrhus had spoke ille indeede . . .

I countered by submitting to "*Carpe Diem*" a manual on how to write puns for the *Royal Gaboon*. The battle line was drawn, and there were skirmishes between Jay Kay and Sir Burrhus de Beerus during our junior year. An account by a third party appeared in "*Carpe Diem*":

> Loud clanks armor as the stout knight rides,
> Deep sink his rowels in his charger's heaving sides,
> Gold rimmed spectacles bouncing as he goes,
> Upon the freckled bridging of his literary nose,
> Deep eyes flashing 'neath his forehead pale—
> Burrhus is seeking his imaginary Grail!
>
> Burrhus is challenged, as he learns right soon,
> Jay Kay charges with a "Till Death, Gaboon!"
> Forward rushing on his gaily mottled ass,
> Fool's bells dragging through the campus grass;
> Poet and Jester clash on Carpe's Field. . . .

I was writing fewer poems, and the themes were changing. My unhappy love affair had given rise to a certain cynicism:

LYRICS OF HATE
I. C.A.M.

> I came to you with a weary heart
>   Faithless, and in fear.
> I thought, "This is a place apart."
>   I thought, "Love wanders here."

You were to me a holy place
  With a white god above—
Until upon the pavement's face
  I read, "Here lieth Love."

II. Triolet

You had the right to kill
Even so coldly.
Bitter the death—but still
You had the right to kill.
Love's fate was yours to will,
Killing so boldly.
You had the right to kill
Even so coldly.

In my freshman year I had sent some poems to a little magazine and received an encouraging reply from a young woman on its board of editors (it may have been Babette Deutsch). Another note, in the spring of my sophomore year, was more exciting:

College Hill

Dear Fred,

    On Saturday afternoon (the 17th) Edna Ferber, Alex. Woollcott and F.P.A. are to be here for tea. Hope you will be able to come in then as I think you might be amused by them and I certainly know I should be glad to see you.

                                    Sincerely yours,
                                      Grace Root

14 May 1924

I was about to meet some great writers personally! I had run into Woollcott briefly when he was staying at the Saunderses', but Edna Ferber and F.P.A.! Of course I went, and shook hands, and balanced my teacup successfully. There was no very stimulating conversation and I had no witty remarks to pass along to my friends, but at last I knew what it was like to be "in."

＊　　＊　　＊

FOR A VACATION in our second summer in Scranton my parents rented a cottage in Columbian Grove. It could scarcely have been less like the Essex and Sussex. The Grove had once been a rather pleasant spot on the bank of the river, but it was now heavily wooded and dark and damp, and the cottages were rotting, moldy, and uncomfortably furnished. The one we rented had a "backhouse" as a toilet, opening off the kitchen.

I am not sure how much of this my father knew when he took the place, but it would not have greatly mattered because he was insensitive to differences between his past and present styles of life. He was not only loyal to Susquehanna, he remembered it with uncritical pleasure.

The vacation was again a disaster. At my parents' suggestion, I invited two girls who had been friends of my brother's to come for a weekend. Not only were the house and its facilities primitive, there was no boat or beach on which one could swim comfortably, and the girls had scarcely arrived before I discovered the problem of having absolutely nothing to do. I drove them into Susquehanna for a sundae at the Sugar Bowl, proud of being known there, and then in the other direction to Windsor, but the whip factory had gone out of business. Most of the time we simply sat around disconsolate. I was embarrassed by the ease with which I sped my parting guests when they left.

IN MY JUNIOR YEAR I took Introductory Spanish, in part because my friends liked Professor Super, who taught it. "Supe" was an eccentric bachelor who lived at the Faculty Club. He could be drawn from the day's assignment by questions about certain well-known events in his life, and he enjoyed the digressions as much as his students. I needed the course for a minor in Romance Languages, and I took English Literature of the seventeenth and eighteenth centuries with Bob Rudd as part of a major in English Language and Literature.

With some vague idea that I might go into law I took Political

Science 1–2. It was a happy choice. The field was American government, and a teacher from Brooklyn was replacing the regular professor, who was ill. He gave me my first glimpse of a political liberal. We took out student subscriptions to the *New Republic* and he assigned liberal books—one a discussion of the misuses of "national honor" during the war. He described ward politics, and told us how he had been tricked as a watcher at the polls when ballots for his man were invalidated by someone with a concealed stub of pencil while they were being counted for a different candidate. When I relayed some of this to my father, he began to fear that I might be moving in the direction of socialism, and a month or so later I received a paperback defense of capitalism called, as I remember it, *The Things That Are Caesar's.*

Early in the year it was clear that my major interest was literature. I was not a great reader, in part because I was a slow one. I did not take Cal Lewis's course in the novel because I could not imagine covering the assignments. But I was learning to write.

My skill at that time was evaluated—favorably but rudely—by Cal Lewis himself. We were to submit an original paper to be read in Public Speaking 9 (Junior Discussion), and I wrote a personal essay called "The Confessions of a Puzzle Eater." It began

> My friends noticed a change: I was becoming indifferent, I went about my work lost in thought, I kept to my room. When finally one of them spoke to me about it, I confessed. I had become addicted to Crossword Puzzles.

At the end I signed the usual declaration, "This is my own work," and left the paper in Cal's box in the chapel. When I got it back, I found he had made a few editorial changes on the first page—good changes—but had then stopped and in large letters on the last page had scrawled, "See me about this. Bring its original with you. I read it just the other day. Apparently you have cut generous chunks from it and transplanted them bodily to your paper."

He may well have read something of the sort, but it was certainly nothing I had ever seen. I am inclined to believe that the paper was better than he expected and that he claimed to have read an original in order to see how much I had indeed plagiarized. He was accusing me of a gross violation of the honor system, and if his charge had been valid, I could have been put on probation or expelled.

I went to see him, and told him that I *was* a crossword-puzzle fan, that I had read what others had written about crossword puzzles, but that the essay was my own. He accepted my explanation and apologized.

During my junior year I spent most of my Christmas and spring vacations in New York seeing plays. Walter Hampden's *Cyrano* had been a highly reinforcing experience, and it had brought my course in the French theatre together with the real stage. Since I had not yet made many friends in Scranton, there was nothing to keep me from checking into a New York hotel and picking up tickets for a bout of theatre-going. A matinee made it possible to see two plays in one day. I saw *What Price Glory?* and Jeanne Eagels in a revival of *Rain*. I saw Lunt and Fontanne in *The Guardsman*, and Joseph Schildkraut in *The Firebrand*. I saw Congreve's *Way of the World* at the Cherry Lane Theatre and Katharine Cornell in *Candida* with Clare Eames as Prossy. I saw George Arliss in *Old English* and Blanche Yurka in Ibsen's *Wild Duck*. (I saw *Candida* again the following year with Peggy Wood, who was married to a Hamilton man, John V. A. Weaver.)

A curious result was a sudden bout of dramaturgy. In a single day, scarcely leaving my room in Carnegie Hall, I wrote a three-act play. I had not planned to do so, nor had I been speculating about the theme. I simply came back from breakfast one day and began to write —in pencil on unlined paper. A few parts of the third act are merely sketched in—I was running out of steam—but otherwise it is complete. It is a blend of Ibsen and Shaw, on the theme of the clever wife who promotes an affair between her husband and an old school friend who has come to visit her; it is done for the sake of her husband but only the friend is aware of what is happening. It was very close to automatic writing, and I was not to experience anything like it again for many years.

* * *

I WAS PUSHED FURTHER in the direction of literature as a career by John Wright, an alumnus of my fraternity, who occasionally came back to the Hill on his travels as an insurance agent. He tried hard to be a successful businessman, but he wanted to be a writer. We discussed literature and the literary life, as well as life in general, which he found difficult. He lent me Upton Sinclair's *Book of Life* and told me about a place in New England designed as a recuperative environment for neurasthenics, with the implication that he and I were the kind of people who needed such an environment from time to time.

He was much attracted to the daughter of the president of his company, which was based in Vermont, and he told me about the Summer School of English at Bread Loaf, which she attended. He urged me to go there the following summer, and I applied and was accepted. I met Jack in Rutland, and he drove me to the school.

The property had been given to Middlebury College by Colonel Battell, an eccentric bachelor who had built a summer hotel on a 30,000-acre tract of land. It was a large wooden building with a veranda on two sides, to which an auditorium and a few small classrooms had been added. Battell had resisted the automobile and for many years had brought his guests from a point nine miles away by horse and carriage, but now cars were allowed. One of the conditions of his gift was that cornmeal mush be served once a week in the dining room. Accordingly it was available as a side dish every Sunday evening, and we all loyally ate it and said we liked it. Battell had written a book called *Ellen, or the Whisperings of an Old Pine*, copies of which were to be found in all the rooms. It consisted of the musings of a romantic old man as he explained various things, including mathematics, to a charming young girl.

I took a course in stagecraft with Donald Oenslager, of the Provincetown Playhouse, shortly to begin teaching at Yale. I took a course in creative writing with Sidney Cox, who, like John Hutchens, came from Missoula, Montana, but was teaching at Dartmouth. Other interesting people on the staff were available for discussions, and a series of guest lecturers turned up from time to time. I played a game of croquet with Rollo Walter Brown, and he gave me some helpful advice: a whole paragraph, he said, could be made or destroyed by one word. (When I went back to Hamilton I mentioned him to Chubby Ristine, who spoke of him rather contemptuously. They had been students together at Columbia, and Chubby thought that Brown was hanging around Cambridge in the forlorn hope of joining the Harvard faculty.) A former Middlebury professor *recited* from memory an hour's worth of Browning's "The Ring and the Book"—interesting as a *tour de force* but as a recital dull.

Carl Sandburg came and Sidney Cox cornered him for an evening with some of the more liberal students. Sandburg told a story about Jesus Christ and St. Peter in a Chicago saloon. St. Peter suggests rolling dice to see who will pay for the drinks and when Jesus puts six dice in a cup and rolls six sixes, St. Peter says, "Now, wait a minute, Jesus, roll them again and none of your God-damned miracles." I found that story a new and refreshing kind of religious freedom.

John Farrar was a visiting lecturer, and so was Kenneth Murdock, whom I was later to know at Harvard. Another was Louis Untermeyer, whose autograph adorned the flyleaf of my copy of *Modern British Poetry*. Jean Starr Untermeyer, whose poems were to be found in his *Modern American Poetry*, was with him, languid and bored. I was one of a small group who met with the Untermeyers and was struck by the number of words he used (like "morganatic") which I had never heard before.

Living nearby was William Hazlett Upson, who wrote the Earthworm Tractor stories for the *Saturday Evening Post*, and Jack Wright spoke of him with awe as a man who supported himself with his typewriter. There was another man living nearby who was unable to do so. Robert Frost had been associated with the Bread Loaf school for many years, and Sidney Cox was a close friend, and when Frost came to the school, Cox asked me to have lunch with him.

My first contact with Frost had been embarrassing. I had gone to the empty lecture hall the previous afternoon to play the piano. I had played only a few bars before someone broke through the door at the back of the hall and hurried toward me. "Stop playing," he cried, "Robert Frost is reading poems." I followed him back into a small conference room where there were twenty or thirty adoring students with Frost holding a book in his hand. As we sat down, he started to read and then broke off. "I'm sorry, I've lost it," he said, and turned to another page. But at lunch that noon with Sidney Cox he was friendly. He asked me about my work and my plans and suggested that I send him some of my stuff.

Extra-curricular life at Bread Loaf was equally exciting. The daughter of the president of the insurance company was registered, and she had made friends with a beautiful Southern girl with whom I quickly fell in love. I wrote an account of the affair shortly after the summer school closed:

I first saw Ellen as I drove up to the Inn with J.W. She was standing in a doorway looking curiously at me. She wore a black and white striped dress with a black bodice-like jacket with a soft white shirtwaist with long sleeves and a ruffled collar. I noticed her hair, black, drawn tightly in a knot in the back curving gracefully along each side of her head. I was busy with arriving and I saw her only as one of the many things about the place which struck my eye. I mentioned her to J.W. with a remark about Bohemian atmosphere.

I soon discovered that she was by far the most attractive of the women there. The fellows talked about her a lot, especially the young men who worked in the office of the Inn. She would stand and talk with them for long periods and seemed to be generally affable and agreeable. Then I discovered that she was married and had a boy four years old with her. One of the fellows talked with the boy and learned that he had no father. This was eventually proved a fiction. The child was unattractive at first, almost repulsive. He had a pugnacious nose and broad forehead. His hair was dark but in no other way did he resemble his mother.

At dinner the first evening I sat with J.W. and two other fellows in such a position that I could watch Ellen. She was wearing a yellow dress, flowered with red and black, and her attitude at the table was perhaps matronly. She paid little attention to the chow and had a way of looking at other guests without lifting her head. I talked about her to the fellows exclaiming how beautiful she was, with which they agreed. Not once during the meal did I catch her eye.

I did not meet her that evening but saw her a lot as I followed her half consciously. It was afternoon of the next day before I met her. She was in a room next to the office telling fortunes to the Reynolds sisters. With each new discovery the three would laugh loudly but the most distinct laugh was Ellen's, a high-pitched clear laugh that later affected me in various ways according to my mood. I knew the Reynolds girls and as I approached they introduced me. In a moment she was telling my fortune. The touch of her hand was glorious and as she drew a slender finger along each line I was faint with ecstasy. She discovered that my love arises from jealousy and that I am stubborn. We talked for some time and later she began a letter to her husband. "Dearest," it began, "it was so thoughtful of you to send the cigarettes as there are none obtainable here."

That evening I started a bridge game with Ballou and Louise H. I made occasion to ask Ellen and she gladly accepted. For several evenings we played together up until school began; I was furious when Ellen suggested we change partners so that she and Ballou could play together. In a day or two we changed back. She liked Ballou at first but later he made some remarks about the impotency of the South which stopped any intimacy there. In the meantime Ellen was just as friendly with the office fellows and other students as with me. Either she suspected that I was in love already or else my persistency brought us together too often for she avoided me for a time.

When registration time came I persuaded her to take the courses I was taking so that we might be together. She agreed but it showed, I think, no special desire to be with me. We had had moments together when we had discovered common likes and we gradually found each other's company satisfying. In the meantime I had got to like the child, Bradford, rather well. He finally made friends with me in order that I might swing him around and give him piggy back rides as often as he desired. This I think helped my case with Ellen since she had a real affection for Bradford.

Shortly after school began Ellen agreed to go walking with me to "Widow's Clearing" across the sheepfold from the school and along a climbing wooded path up the opposite hill. I found numerous occasions to take her hand to help her and usually insisted on keeping hold of it all the time. She laughed as though the idea were foolish, but permitted it. We reached the clearing and tried to go back another way. With my conscious effort we succeeded in getting lost. In a pine grove on swampy ground we were forced to stop. I drew Ellen to me and tried to kiss her but she would not even let me put my arms around her and she started back immediately. Uncertain of my actions I followed. She, however, was not angry; we talked lightly on the way back, picked flowers and laughed. I felt peculiarly relieved and happy. As we neared the Inn Ellen said, "We can't go walking any more together." I persuaded her to take back the statement even if she wouldn't change her mind then. I wanted her to feel free to change it later without being obliged to explain away so positive a statement.

About two days later we went again. As we started she went in for a hat and came back pulling it on her head. It was a black straw hat and I suddenly realized that she looked like my mother. Almost immediately the thought occurred to me. I behaved very well on the trip, did nothing but hold her hand. When we returned I went to my room and wrote this note:

TRAGEDY

He waited for her, leaning against a pine, with his face toward her door. She had gone back for a hat, but she would be out again in a minute. Then they were going to walk together. He had so much to tell her!

"You poor boy . . . " Oh, but he would show her how absurd it was to call him that! She must forget that he was only 21, and that she was married. They must forget everything but themselves—and that he loved her! . . .

She came out to him, her heels striking a little heavily on the steps as she came down them. She was pulling on a black straw hat.

Strange, but she reminded him of his mother. . . .

I gave it to Coxy, my creative writing professor, that evening, and the next morning he said, "Have you any objection to my reading this?" Foolishly enough I said, "No, of course not." Ellen was in the class but she was not the only one who recognized the implication. From then on she never wore the hat. I think she wanted to be angry with me but she had a strong sense of humor and rather excused me on my age. I protested that I had had the subject noted in my notebook for three weeks but for a long time she amused herself with acting very maternal toward me and saying, "And I remind you of your mother?" Almost a month later we were sitting together before a fire with several others singing, and someone began a song, "You remind me of my mother." Ellen whispered to me in a soft whisper, "That was what you said about me, wasn't it?"

The first two weeks went by and we had become nothing more

than friends. Ellen spoke often of her husband and I, who by this time protested my love almost continuously, said I was not jealous of him. This annoyed her; and later when I confessed I was jealous she was triumphant and pleased. I would wait for Ellen to come from the dining room after each meal, talk with her and follow her with my eyes. She would sit in the high backed bench on the veranda, and usually a little group collected there. The talk about us was becoming so thick that we were compelled to stay apart some of the time and pretend to be indifferent. I occasionally turned myself to A. McK. or Louise H. to ward off suspicion, but I was undoubtedly lovesick and the fact was generally known. I would stand in the gate to the sheep-fold for hours at night without moving a muscle. I would hear people on the veranda talking about me.

The account breaks off at that point, but the story was not quite finished. Ellen made it pretty clear that I should abandon hope. At times she was very considerate of my feelings, but at other times rather careless. Of course I wrote poems, and again there was a touch of cynicism.

But cynicism could not save me from the sheer physical pain of being in love. I would lie awake at night suffering acutely. We eventually spent some time together in the evening, although our sexual behavior remained largely verbal. She asked me, rather timidly, if I masturbated after being with her, and I learned from her that girls did that sort of thing too. We planned to spend the last evening at Bread Loaf together. My roommate had spent the summer finishing a long novel, and Sidney Cox had arranged to have it read continuously by several readers, the audience coming and going as it pleased. Ellen and I planned to attend the reading but to leave early in the evening. We left at separate times, but our friends and a few gossips no doubt knew it was by arrangement.

Jack Wright had come to drive me back to Rutland, and I borrowed his car, and Ellen and I went for a drive and parked. It was a cool evening and she was wearing a rather heavy coat. I struggled with one of the buttons, and she said, "You can break it if you want." I was still inexperienced, alas, and Ellen did nothing to educate me, and after some not fully consummated action, I drove her back to the Inn.

*　　*　　*

DONALD OENSLAGER, who was to become a leading stage designer in the New York theatre, lectured on modern stagecraft. We heard all about Gordon Craig and *Jessnertreppen* and Max Reinhardt, and we built scenery, made costumes, memorized parts, and put on plays. I wrote a one-act play which Oenslager staged. It was a comedy about a doctor who has discovered how to control temperament through the administration of hormones, a subject which was just then coming to the attention of the press. A man arrives to ask the doctor for something to cure his wife of being flirtatious, but it appears that his wife has previously seen the doctor and has given him something to make him jealous. Now she arrives to ask for a prescription to cure his jealousy. Another patient enters who so conspicuously agrees with everyone that the others suspect that she has been treated for a tendency to argue. Her husband arrives and confirms the suspicion. He demands something to counteract her present submissiveness. There is a general melee, and the disillusioned patients take powders and syrups from the doctor's cabinet and mix a large potion which they force down his throat. "He sinks into his chair registering as meaningless an expression as possible, as the curtain falls."

On the last day of our course in Creative Writing, Sidney Cox read something of mine and then went out of his way to point out that all my contributions during the summer had been deeply moral. He was no doubt trying to offset rumors, and he may have had in mind the attitude of Professor Davidson, director of the school. A prissy bachelor, worshiped by the aging schoolteachers who attended Bread Loaf to pick up credits toward an advanced degree, he seemed to believe that Ellen and I were casting a shadow on his school with what, erroneously, he took to be adultery.

We flung our last defiance at him as we left. Ellen and her son needed a ride to Rutland, and Jack and I asked her to join us. We loaded our baggage in the back of Jack's car, and all four of us crowded into the single seat, with the child on Ellen's lap. Professor Davidson was standing on the porch as we drove off, and we waved and gaily called goodbye, but he did not acknowledge our friendly salute.

*   *   *

AFTER I RETURNED TO SCRANTON, my parents organized a kind of house party. My father's old friend John McGinty, who had closed his hotel with the advent of Prohibition, had converted a large brick farmhouse on the road to Windsor into a kind of hotel and had put in a nine-hole golf course. My father gave him a good deal of advice about laying out that course and, as the *Transcript* reported in Editor Baker's best style, was the first man to lose a ball on it. We went with two couples who were friends of my parents, and their daughters. The hotel was not particularly convenient or the golf course very good, but as usual my father was blinded by his loyalty and no doubt to some extent by his desire to have his friends in Susquehanna see some of his more affluent Scranton friends, one of whom was a multi-millionaire. While we were there I dropped into the office of the *Transcript*, and the next day the paper reported that I was planning a literary career, the editor noting that I had got my first experience on the *Transcript*.

The decision was by no means final, but when I went back to Hamilton I clearly moved in that direction. I had signed up for Bacteriology with Bugsy Morrill—a course given primarily for pre-medics—but Hutch persuaded me to shift to Smut's Senior English Composition. I hated to tell Bugsy that I was making a change. I owed him a great deal, for he had given me a lot of personal attention. (One day I jammed my finger in a microtome, exposing a bit of the bone, and when Bugsy saw that I was growing faint, he hastily prepared a laboratory cocktail of equal parts of absolute alcohol and distilled water, which he offered to me in a small beaker.) When I went to tell him of this last-minute change, I found the class already assembled, and there was nothing for it but to announce my decision before the whole class. Bugsy winced as he tried to tell me that he understood.

In Senior Composition we corrected freshman themes and submitted work of our own, which we discussed in class. I discovered that Smut lacked a sense of humor. He had complained that my stories, though a sensitive commentary on life in general, lacked plot, and so I submitted a story called "The Klondike Kills." Two prospectors have accumulated a great hoard of gold, but find themselves trapped in their cabin for the winter. After a bitter quarrel, neither man dares to go to sleep because he is afraid the other will murder him. They both struggle against sleep and when one finally gives in, the other immediately does so too, and the fire goes out and they both freeze to death. It was an obvious parody, but Smut took it seriously and read it to the class, to the barely concealed amusement of my friends.

I took Anglo-Saxon, Chaucer, and Shakespeare with Chubby Ristine. It was rumored that Chubby's courses were simply second-hand versions of the courses he had taken under Brander Matthews at Columbia, but he was a meticulous teacher and had evidently kept good notes. For a term paper in Chaucer I wrote a translation of "The Pardoner's Tale," using a shorter line to allow for the syllables which had grown silent with the years. Naturally, I talked about the Baconian theory, and Chubby asked me to take one meeting of the class in Shakespeare to present it. I worked up a very convincing case. It was Parents' Day and there were several parents in the room. Chubby explained that I would take over and then added, "Of course, no sensible man today takes the Baconian theory seriously." I lacked the courage of my convictions and explained to the class that I was going to present the theory as it would be presented by one who believed it.

HUTCH HAD BEEN ELECTED editor of the *Royal Gaboon*, and I was associate editor. The name came from a call often heard late at night on the quiet campus: someone would sing out, "Roy-al Ga-boo-oon," the "—oon" falling to a minor third, and someone else might echo it from a distance. The magazine had published typical college humor, but we decided to make it more intellectual, combining it, indeed, with the old *Hamilton Literary Magazine*. The undertaking soon ran into financial difficulties.

I wrote book reviews—of *The Professor's House* by Willa Cather, *The Venetian Glass Nephew* by Elinor Wylie, and *Replenishing Jessica* by Maxwell Bodenheim—and a short note about Mrs. Ogden's bookshop, which was just moving into new quarters. My main contribution was a long article on Ezra Pound, a "great Hamilton alumnus" practically unknown to Hamilton men. I could quote Carl Sandburg that someday the college would put up a tablet reading "Here came Ezra Pound." I printed excerpts from a letter of Pound's to Stink Saunders about his last appearance at Hamilton, when he, like everyone else, was taking his turn in Public Speaking. "[I] produced a near riot. Heine White, I think, pitching pennies on the platform floor (or perhaps that is a fantastic detail). I believe I disparaged 'orrratory.'" I could relay Robert Frost's story of Pound's quarrel with Lascelles Abercrombie. Pound became thoroughly disgusted with Abercrombie, and finally wrote to him: "Stupidity, carried to a certain point, becomes a public affront. I champion the public in this quarrel. My seconds will wait on you." There was an anti-climax. Amy Lowell claimed that she asked Pound if he supposed Abercrombie would choose swords; and when he replied, "Of course," she pointed out that Abercrombie knew Pound was a clever swordsman and would undoubtedly choose pistols. Pound, according to Miss Lowell, was so frightened he nearly left England. I argued that Pound's *l'homme moyen sensuel* might well be a Hamilton man, quoting:

Tell me not in mournful wishwash
Life's a sort of sugared dishwash!
(Let him rebuke who ne'er has known the pure platonic
    grapple
Or hugged two girls at once behind a chapel.)

—though why I thought that was characteristic of Hamilton men I cannot say.

ONE EVENING EARLY IN THE FALL TERM Hutch and I were in my room making plans for the new magazine. We were talking about Smut Fancher, who loved to drop names in the world of the theatre and who claimed to be involved with playwriting, and we thought up a hoax at his expense. We designed a poster, and I sent it to Otis Chidester, who had taken over the newspaper in Windsor, and he printed up a batch on bright orange paper. The poster read:

SPECIAL LECTURE

CHARLES CHAPLIN

THE FAMOUS CINEMA COMEDIAN

In Person, Will Deliver His Lecture

"MOVING PICTURES AS A CAREER"

In the Hamilton College Chapel

FRI., OCT. 9

AT 8:15 P. M.

. The College regrets that previous notice has not been given, but Mr. Chaplin has been compelled to advance the date of his lecture (which was originally set for Nov. 13) on account of a hurried departure for Europe.

The lecture has been arranged thru the courtesy of Prof. Fancher.

THERE WILL BE NO CHARGE OF ADMISSION

At two o'clock on the morning of October 9 Hutch and I went down to Clinton, moved around the square out of sight of the constable, and pasted the posters on telephone poles and shopwindows. We threw a few in the doorways of apartment houses and came back and went to bed. The next morning Hutch phoned the *Utica Observer-Dispatch* to say that the President had announced the lecture in chapel that morning. The paper dug out an old photograph of Chaplin and ran the story, including Hutch's embellishments, as follows:

America's fun maker comes to the college through the efforts of Professor P. A. Fancher who became acquainted with him at the time of the Hamilton College Choir Recital at the Booth Theatre in New York. At that time Alexander Woollcott, Hamilton '09, invited most of the literary, stage, and screen celebrities to hear the concert. The audience included besides Mr. Chaplin, Ring Lardner, Percy Hammond and Heywood Broun. A promise given Professor Fancher by the comedian at that time is now to be redeemed.

News reached the campus before noon, and the administration reacted promptly. Police were stationed on roads approaching the Hill to advise all drivers that the lecture was a hoax, but about four hundred cars got through. A Friday-night football rally was in progress around the gymnasium, and the visitors assumed that the crowd was waiting to see Chaplin and naturally joined it. Hutch went into the chapel to turn on the lights, hoping to get the crowd in there, but the authorities were waiting for that move, and he escaped through a window. The next day we ran an editorial in *Hamilton Life* saying that "no man with the slightest regard for his alma mater would have done it."

When I quite openly admitted to Stink Saunders that Hutch and I were the guilty ones, he exclaimed, "Oh, for heaven's sake, Fred, keep it quiet. The President is up in arms and is planning to expel the students who did it." A detective was hired and I began to worry. Had we covered our tracks? Windsor was a long way away, and it was not likely that the source of the posters would be discovered, but we had neglected to say that the lecture would be free, and I had typed small slips reading, "There will be no charge for admission," and pasted them on many of the posters. Could my typewriter be identified? It was early in the term and I had not yet submitted any papers, but I would be submitting some soon. I decided to disguise my typewriter. I bent several letters slightly out of alignment and filed corners off one or two with a nail file. Fortunately the detective got a wrong scent; the trail seemed to be leading to Jack Chase, Trot's son, and the matter was dropped.

Hutch and I had not correctly foreseen the effects of our plan. The story and poster had seemed to us so obviously phony that no sensible person would be taken in, but we had misjudged the local climate. And there was one result of which we were both ashamed: the Utica paper had guessed at Chaplin's schedule, and at train time the station was full of children waiting to see him.

IN MY SENIOR YEAR I occasionally took over the "Carpe Diem" column. There were certain standard themes to be found in all college magazines—girls, necking, speakeasies, and spiked beer—but there were local topics as well. Though I had criticized Jay Kay and the other contributors to the Royal Gaboon and "Carpe Diem" for their reliance on parodies and puns, I was not above seeking the same kinds of help as Sir Burrhus de Beerus.

> The shades of night have fallen fast
> And now are wholly gone at last,
> To Commons then, with weary feet,
> To find in place of Shredded Wheat,
> Excelsior!

This was followed by a far from exaggerated parody of Cal Lewis commenting on the performance of a class in Public Speaking:

> I wish you men would put a little more time on your . . . discussions. . . . I can remember the day when men . . . men like you . . . no great literary ability . . . no great literary capability . . . used to feel that a chapel oration . . . or a chapel declamation . . . was more than . . . was something to be . . . something to . . . Now you men can put your rubbers on when I'm through . . . and not until. . . .

*   *   *

Hamilton College was almost an adjunct of the Root family. The Chairman of the Board in my day was Elihu Root, the man my father had pointed out to me in 1915 as the next President of the United States. His grandfather had taught mathematics at Hamilton, and the students had called him Square Root. His father also taught mathematics and was called Cube. The Root homestead was across the road from the campus, and beyond it the family owned a large tract of land.

In my junior year I took a course in art with Elihu Root's son, Edward, whom I had first met through Cynthia Ann Miller. He had built a small studio near his house, and we met there for our class. He collected modern art, but most of the pictures we studied were the indifferent colored prints available at that time. Nevertheless, we learned to spot schools and painters, and to talk about color and light.

In my senior year Edward Root encouraged me to paint and offered me space in his studio and the use of his equipment and supplies. I had my own easel, and I began with charcoal on beautiful (and expensive!) sheets of hand-laid paper. He taught me how to put canvas on stretchers and to clean brushes. He set projects; one of the first was to paint a tin cup, and I was still naïve enough to ask him about paint that looked like metal. One day I grew expansive and tried a winter landscape with snow drifting around a gnarled tree trunk, painting all the shadows in gray, but he warned me against overlooking the essentials and brought me back to set projects. I never told him of one project—a life-size charcoal nude on the wall of my room at the Lambda Chi Alpha house copied from a print of Titian or Giorgione.

There was little about Hamilton at the time to promote an interest in music. The string quartets at the Saunderses' were, of course, an exception, and so was Smut's choir. Once or twice a year there was a musical program in the chapel. (I remember Georges Barrère playing the flute.) But the phonograph was still primitive, and I knew no one with a collection of records. I once took Cynthia Ann to hear the Utica Symphony Orchestra—paying for a taxi both ways—but I remember only that I had just had my hat dry-cleaned and that because the night was cold and the windows were closed, the taxi filled with a strong odor of cleaning fluid. In my senior year my fall house-party guest was Helen Olheim, who later sang at the Metropolitan. She was the sister of one of our freshmen and she came and sang, and I played her accompaniments, and it was all quite wonderful.

Throughout all four years, in the name of physical education, I was forced to play games. Good players were allowed to play basketball with us, ostensibly to show us how, but in fact to improve their own game by throwing us over their hips in defense or bouncing balls off our craniums before shooting baskets. On the hockey rink, pursuing a puck with wobbly ankles and leaning on my stick for additional support, I would have my shins cracked by sticks that got to the puck ahead of me. I rather liked fencing, but it was only "single-stick"; the class never advanced to épée or saber.

Soccer was one of the games I had to play, but fortunately no one insisted upon football. In high school I had written a story about an unathletic boy, possibly crippled, who sent his school's football team on to victory by analyzing plays mathematically, calculating the time it would take each player to reach a given position and the time it would take an opponent to reach the same position. (I am not sure I was not anticipating the future of the game.)

My fraternity brother Dietrich Towne was one of Hamilton's stars. He was thickset and powerful and could plow doggedly through an opponent's line. He was equally good on defense, and that was important because one set of players played the whole game (a player who left the game was not allowed back during the same half). As a freshman I learned the Hamilton cheers and yelled my lungs out whenever it was Towne who had made a first down. But Hamilton won very few games, and after another year the coach was threatening to resign. Towne had been elected captain, and he asked me to write a letter, to be signed by the whole team, giving the coach their solid support and pleading with him to stay on. I wrote a suitably emotional appeal, and it was successful, and thus in a way I played out my fantasy of the unathletic athletic hero.

*   *   *

I WAS ONE of four seniors who were attracting attention as writers. Jack Chase, Trot's son, was the editor of the newspaper *Hamilton Life*, and he had a brother, Cleveland, in the literary swim in New York. John Hutchens edited the *Royal Gaboon*, and had worked on his father's paper, the *Missoulian*, in Montana. Joe Vogel was contributing to a communist magazine, the *New Masses* (and also doing pen-and-ink drawings, much more original than anything of mine, with Edward Root). I had at least my summer at Bread Loaf as a credential. The four of us met frequently, controlled the local media, and were active in what could be called political discussions.

Stink Saunders, Brownie, and Trot Chase thought that this intellectual activity deserved some extra-curricular support and they sponsored weekly meetings. It was an ecumenical step, designed to bring faculty and students together, and hard to evaluate at this distance. Hamilton's faculty was good-natured and well disposed but it was not *friendly*. Now we were meeting a few professors man to man—as if the generals had dropped in to have dinner with the troops. One evening in the music room at the Saunderses' we were discussing sex, and I said that it was a mistake to make a moral issue of it; it should be looked on in the same light as a good meal. "What," said Brownie, "three times a day?" and we all laughed a little too hard.

I have a different reason for remembering a dinner meeting at the Chases'. Dr. Fulton, Nell's father, had tried to interest me in medicine, and he had lent me two books on the medical aspects of outstanding figures in history. In one of them Joan of Arc was said to have had some kind of hormone problem, and I brought this up at the Chases', forgetting that Mrs. Chase was a devout Catholic. She went into action at once, saying she had read all the original protocols of the trial and that there could be no question of a neurosis or psychosis in St. Joan. I made no attempt to defend my authorities. I do not remember the other issues we discussed at these meetings; we were emulating the Round Table at the Algonquin, with results which were probably no more productive.

One of the more conspicuous figures at the real Round Table was Aleck Woollcott, a familiar visitor at the Saunderses', who padded about the house in dressing gown and slippers without attracting attention. Other well-known people came for an hour or two following a lecture. I saw Sandburg again and, to my delight, he remembered me from Bread Loaf.

I continued to write poetry, my verses becoming free not only in form but in content:

VACANT STORE

Behind your dusty windows,
Like the second meaning in the eyes of an abandoned
    woman,
Your beckoning:
For Rent.

I cannot now remember whether I was aware that the following dealt with masturbation. I had not yet read Freud, nor were the literary critics I read writing about psychoanalysis. (It was said that the *New York World* had reviewed James Branch Cabell's *Jurgen* without spotting the sexual symbolism.) I believe that my title indicates, however, that I knew what I was doing.

CONCUPISCENCE

An Old Man, sowing in a field,
Walks with a slow, uneasy, rhythm.
He tears handfuls of seed from his vitals,
Caressing the wind with the sweep of his hand.
At night, he stops, breathless,
Murmuring to his earthy consort,
"Love exhausts me!"

I also wrote a skit of about 150 lines to be given at a fraternity banquet. The subject was Salome and some of my compatriots carried out the action as I read about Salome's request for an unusual part of John's anatomy:

Oh, joy to Salome, oh bitterest hate!
Oh, pity for John for his terrible fate!
With a flash of her eye and a curl of her lip,
She stands before Herod with disjointed hip,
"Oh, king, thou hast spoken, now hear what I wish":
So saying she speaks in a whisper: "Pish, pish."

Old Herod at first gives a grunt of surprise,
Then strokes at his beard, then closes his eyes,
And thinks till it hurts of the words she hath quoth,
Then looks for a moment, then says to her "Both?"

I began to write *An Anthology of a Small College*, patterned after Edgar Lee Masters. I changed names but I was talking about real people. Hamilton had once had a small observatory and a real astronomer, about whom I wrote the following:

SAMUEL WINTERS—ASTRONOMER

I lived an eternity of nights
With the stars.
I was a discoverer;
But though I searched the heavens
And found new stars and asteroids,
There was one thing
I never found in all space:
When a student asked me,
"Do you see God out there?"
I could answer only,
"I see—Law."

During the year I occasionally contributed an editorial to *Hamilton Life*. I wrote a long criticism of the Phi Beta Kappa "key-chaser." "The college man," I contended, "knows perfectly well that a man of very ordinary intelligence may win a key. . . . If a man elects those courses in college which he considers most necessary for his development, and in the pursuance of those courses does such work that he is elected to a Fraternity which honors genuine scholarship, that is one thing; if he elects those courses which will make it easy for him to obtain high marks, and devotes his time and energy to his courses with the sole outstanding purpose of getting a Phi Beta Kappa standing, it is quite another thing."

I FOUND that Jack and Hutch had another interesting connection— with Utica's famed red-light district. They invited me to join them, and one evening we drove into a quiet residential area in their battered car and went to the door of a darkened house. We rang, a light appeared, and a little old lady opened the door. She was holding a large angora cat and she greeted us pleasantly, and we went in. She went immediately to the telephone and I heard her say, "We're having a little party. Would you care to join us?" She gave us very small glasses of Prohibition wine, and in a few minutes a buxom, rather attractive girl came in. She might have been a waitress or a salesgirl now engaged in a bit of moonlighting. A record was put on the Victrola, and we danced briefly with her. Then Jack went upstairs with her, and when he came down, I went up. I asked her, rather apologetically, if she minded my using a condom, and she replied brightly that it was much the best for her too, and she took my two dollars and stuck them in her purse.

This was my first unencumbered sexual intercourse, and it was over fairly quickly. The girl said that I had obviously enjoyed it more than my predecessor, but it had been surprisingly unexciting. I was no doubt a little scared, but was this indeed what I should have found if I had been successful in all those attempted seductions? Was this what lay at the top of Marion Knise's leg? Would this have been the prize if I had won my wrestling match with Leslie Gilbert or had persuaded Ellen to have an affair with me? I dressed quickly and went downstairs, pleased that my absence was attracting no more attention than if I had gone to the toilet. Hutch took his turn, and we all drove back to the Hill.

On another trip we found that the nice old lady already had a guest—a tough, middle-aged woman who drank a glass of wine with us and who, I was afraid, was to be offered as our fare for the night. But another girl was on the way. She was young and attractive, but evidently supposed that her first duty was to seduce us, because she danced in a most lascivious way and whispered words into my ear that I had never heard a girl say before.

On another occasion we tried a regular dive. Two girls came to our table and we ordered drinks, and as we took them up the long, well-lighted stairs, the regular customers watched with amusement.

* * *

As I ENTERED THE LAST TERM of my senior year, I could no longer postpone a decision about a career, and I wrote to my family telling them that I should like to spend a year writing a novel. I would live at home, and the novel would have Scranton as a background. It was a decision my father had no doubt feared. He talked it over with my mother and then wrote me a long letter in his strong, clear, energetic, economical hand.

Dear Frederic,

Your very interesting letter has been read and discussed by mother and me. We naturally are deeply interested in your future. In no circumstances would we want to say or do anything to discourage you in following out your ambition. I am convinced and have been for many years that a young man should if possible follow out the line of work which appeals to him. No one makes a success of any business or profession in which he is not deeply interested and one cannot do good work at a job which he dislikes. I have witnessed too many failures among boys who have been forced into professions by their parents against the inclinations of the former and because the latter wanted to do the thinking for the boy. We do not propose to do this.

On the other hand we want to give you the benefit of our observation and experience. You will find that the world is not standing with outstretched arms to greet you just because you are emerging from a college—that the real rough and tumble world is not the world pictured by college professors who are constantly dealing with the theoretical and not the practical affairs of life. I am yet to be convinced that it is possible for you to make a living as a writer of fiction. I thought that you had become convinced of that from your contact with writers at Bread Loaf. Not that I am thinking of any cost to me but for your own sake I want to see you become self-supporting.

You will someday have to rely upon yourself for the necessities and luxuries of life. By luxuries I do not mean yachts, costly estates, and so on, but some of the things which people fairly well off are in the habit of having, some of the things we have enjoyed in a moderate way.

Now if you don't equip yourself to get into some line of work where you can make enough money to have these things—and they don't come easy—what will you do?

I don't want you to become one of those hermits who live in a garret on a crust of bread in order to revel in the beautiful (?) thought that his art, his music, or his ideals are so far above the comprehension and tastes of the common people that he will not condescend to get down to earth and mingle with the common trash or be as others are.

You must bear in mind that for the past four years you have been away from us most of the time. Your first two vacations home were spent under circumstances where we did not have the best opportunity to think things out and get to thoroughly understand each other after you had grown up. The third summer was spent in Bread Loaf.

We are very proud of you and have no doubt that you have been a splendid student and followed our instructions to "get out of it all there is in it." While the studies you have pursued were not calculated to fit you for any particular occupation (except writing) I did not object because after all such things are mostly for mind development. I believe you are versatile—I believe you have the ability—to study and master about anything you care to undertake. We have lots of confidence in your good judgment and common sense and in your character. But even if I was a good critic I have no way of judging your literary ability except a few small samples of your writing which I have seen and the reports from college. These reports seem to back up your idea that you have special talents. Mr. Welburn [the Presbyterian minister] was in yesterday and he reported what had been told to him by some of the faculty. Everything looks splendid and I don't want to appear to be throwing cold water on your plans but do think it highly desirable that the matter be considered from all angles.

Suppose for instance that your dream does not come true. Are you going to be disappointed and feel sour and enter other lines with lack of interest and distaste?

Have you stopped to consider that at the present time there are so many nationalities represented in this territory and so many conflicting interests that no single class or number of classes are typical—a picture of which would represent the community or industry? The predominant race (according to Mr. Welburn) is Irish—and mining does not make them any different than railroad work in Susquehanna.

Have you made up your mind to work on your book as earnestly and religiously as you would at a regular job and not treat the writing as a thing to do when you feel like it and when it does not interfere with other things you would like to do? How are you going to account to your friends for a year's apparent idleness and the impression that would give them that you were lazy, etc.?

Are you willing, if business doesn't go very good with me, to get along on a small allowance?

How long will it take and when it is finished what will you do? Unless you produce a "best-seller" you cannot live by writing books alone. If you will not write short stories, columns, nor articles which pay, how are you to get along?

It seems to me you ought to look beyond the first book—What is to follow? If it is a success, all OK but if notwithstanding your own satisfaction with it it doesn't happen to "take," then what?

These things I wish you would think about and we will talk them over when you come home.

I still think you are tackling the job wrong end to—I can't feel that if you have the talent and genius to write something worthwhile that you would lose it by writing lighter stuff for a while. Maturity cannot help but be beneficial.—If you establish a reputation as a writer of short stories and so on then this would help at once in the reception of something bigger and provide the wherewithal while you were doing the big thing and do away with the feeling that you must hurry —We are not in a position where we can retire and devote our time to literary pursuits.

I repeat I am not thinking of the money cost to me. All I have is for mother and you. I am thinking of your future. You have acquired a taste for the finest literature—this will be a source of joy for you as long as you live—but you will find that this must be enjoyed in your moments of leisure, but that other hours must be spent on the most practical things. Appreciation of art, music and literature is a great asset for college professors, librarians, and teachers generally but it will not put any "butter on your bread."

Please do not view this letter as a mere composition! Nor pass it off because it is made up of old-fashioned platitudes, nor because it reads like "Letters from a Self-made Merchant to his Son."

While writing this letter mother telephones me about your letter saying you had been elected a member of the journalistic branch (?) of the PBK and that you want a check for $15. Enclosed. This is fine and we congratulate you. All of these things go to prove that you have talent and increases our wish to give you the opportunity to develop. The only and big question is how is it best to be done. Let's go slow and sure. Let us figure out not only what is the best way to put it over but what must be done in the way of casting out an "anchor to leeward" to provide for your future financial necessities and independ-

ence. Let us arrange some plan whereby you can support yourself, get married when the fever strikes you, have a good home life, and when these things are provided for then go to it and if your talents enable you to do something big and startle the world no one of course will rejoice more than your mother and I who have our whole life centered in you and your success.

> *With love,*
> *Father*

Naturally I showed the letter to Stink, who was very careful about the advice he gave me. When I told him that my father was a Babbitt, he reminded me that Babbitt longed for a better life too. I suggested that if I were to live in Scranton I might be able to improve it culturally, but he was doubtful of anything to be gained in that direction. Should I first become a successful lawyer and then turn to writing? He wondered whether my interest would survive or whether I would find myself trapped.

I had never made an important decision about my life, and it appeared that I was now about to do so. It was not long, however, before I received another letter which left no doubt of the course I should follow.

I HAD RESPONDED to Robert Frost's offer to look at some of my work by sending him three short short stories when I returned to Hamilton. In April I received an answer:

> *Ann Arbor, Michigan*
>
> *Dear Mr. Skinner:*
> *My long delay with these stories has given you time to think of some things about them for yourself, alternating between doubt and confidence. It has probably done you good: so I won't apologize for it.*
> *You know I save myself from perfunctory routine criticism of ordinary college writing on purpose to see if I can't really help now and then someone like you in earnest with the art. Two or three times a year I make a serious attempt to get to the bottom of his work with someone like you. But it's all the good it does. I always come a long*

way short of getting down into it as far as the writer gets himself. Of course! You asked me if there is enough in the stories to warrant your going on. I wish I knew the answer to that half as well as you probably know it in your heart. Right at this moment you are very likely setting your determination to go on, regardless of anything I say, and provided only you can find in a reasonable time someone to buy and read you. I'd never quarrel with that spirit. I've a sneaking sympathy with it.

My attempt to get to the bottom of a fellow writer's stuff this time put this into my head: All that makes a writer is the ability to write strongly and directly from some unaccountable and almost invincible personal prejudice like Stevenson's in favor of all being as happy as kings no matter if consumptive, or Hardy's against God for the blunder of sex, or Sinclair Lewis' against small American towns, or Shakespeare's, mixed, at once against and in favor of life itself. I take it that everybody has a prejudice and spends some time feeling for it to speak and write from. But most people end as they begin by acting out the prejudices of other people.

Those are real niceties of observation you've got here and you've done 'em to a shade. "The Laugh" has the largest value. That's the one you show most as caring in. You see I want you to care. I don't want you to be academic about it—a writer of exercises. Of course, not too expressly, overtly caring. You'll have to search yourself here. You know best whether you are haunted with any impatience about what other people see or don't see. That will be you if you are you. I am inclined to say you are. But you have the final say. I wish you'd tell me how you come out in thinking it over—if it isn't too much trouble— some time. I ought to say you have the touch of art. The work is clean run. You are worth twice anyone else I have seen in prose this year.

Always yours,
Robert Frost

Belief, belief. You've got to augment my belief in life and people mightily or cross it uglily. I'm awfully sure of this tonight.
April 7, 1926

The letter was waiting for me when I came down the hill at noon, and after lunch I went directly to the Saunderses' and showed it to Stink. It was very different from my father's, of course, and carried a different message. I thought it was all the evidence my family had any right to ask for. I should be allowed to try my wings. Stink was inclined to agree. I knew something about Frost's own history, his long struggle for recognition, his success in England before he was appreciated by his own countrymen, his continuing financial troubles. It was not easy. Was I prepared for something like that, too? I thought I was. (I did not know then the depth of his bitterness.)

The letter also seemed to show that I was mining a promising vein. The three stories were "psychological," with traces of Chekhov, Maupassant, and Katherine Mansfield. The one Frost liked best, "The Laugh," began as follows:

As Edsel Brock approached the door of his farmhouse, he saw his wife scrubbing the wooden step in front of it. When he was so near that his rubber boots and tucked-in blue overalls caught her eye, she stopped scrubbing without looking up and held her brush in the middle of a stroke. Then in a voice harsh from deafness she said, "I seen you talking with Jim. What's he want?"

Instantly Brock was angry with her. She held her brush as if she meant, "Well, go on, walk on my step if you're going to, and let me get cleaning it up!" Then asking what Jim wanted—as if he and Jim had a secret, as if he was doing something with his money unknown to her!

"Frank Sykes's wife's got a baby!" he said contemptuously.

"Frank Sykes?" she asked sharply. "You say a baby?"

Brock went in, closed the door, and pressed his face against the screen.

"Yes, a baby!"

"Can't have!" she said. "I saw Zelda day before yest'd'y. . . . She wasn't going to have no baby."

"Well, if you know all about it . . . God, I never seen a woman like you, Ide. Call me a liar. Like Jim never told me that. Like I made it up."

"Mebbe you did."

"All right, then. A-all right. Only don't ask me again."

He left the door and went to the far side of the room where he put his back against the wall and stood, legs spread, watching Ide scrub. After a minute she took the pail of dirty water and with all her force threw it against the step to rinse it, her shrunken arms twitching with anger. Brock was amused.

People, Brock knew, called him a hard husband. No one said he beat his wife, or starved her, or worked her to death; no one ever named one thing he did to her. Everyone saw simply that she was miserable, and that she hated him. But a good many people hated Brock—because of his big jeering laugh, a laugh that made people uncomfortable, made them lose their temper, and lose an argument. It was not surprising that his wife too hated him because of it.

Just then Brock wanted some excuse to laugh.

And he is lucky. Sykes turns up with the news that his wife has had *twins*. Brock can scarcely contain himself, but he must hold his laugh until he can be alone with his wife. Sykes stays on, however. There is talk of a golf course and money to be made from their land. Will Brock agree to hold out for a price? Brock is slow in getting rid of him. Then—

He was gone at last! For a minute Brock stood looking from the door. Twins . . . a good joke. Yes, he told himself, it was a good joke on Ide. A good joke.

He turned and sauntered out to the kitchen. He saw his wife looking into the oven, crouched as if waiting for a whip lash. He put his hands on his hips and drew a deep breath through his teeth. But it was too late; to save him, Edsel Brock could not laugh!

"Damn Frank Sykes!" he said aloud.

At Bread Loaf I had not only practiced the art of writing, I had talked about writing as a craft. I continued to do so, but with very little profit. Fancher was not strong on analysis. Mr. Torrey had given me a copy of *The Genius of Style*, written by a classmate of his named Brownell, and I read it doggedly but to little effect. In the college library I found Percy Lubbock's *The Craft of Fiction*, which I read with the same determination and no greater profit. Edgar Allan Poe's *The Philosophy of Composition* was more concrete, but scarcely more helpful. Robert Louis Stevenson's principle of the sedulous ape, according to which the aspiring writer was to begin by writing in the manner of various well-known authors, had been the heart of Cal Lewis's Junior English Composition, but I had not taken that course.

Herbert Spencer was helpful, though I did not care whether the English or French order of adjective and noun was psychologically superior. Polti's *Thirty-Six Dramatic Situations* was advertised as describing all possible plots, but I found that it applied to the works of men like Corneille and Racine rather than the writers whom I intended to emulate.

I never actually planned my stories. I began with a quick impression—of a character or an incident—and developed it to make a small point, often not clear to me until I looked back upon it much later. That was particularly true of my most ambitious story, which began with a fragmentary personal contact. Nell Fulton, resigned to spinsterhood, had worked out an elaborate rationalization. She once lent me a book called *Apologia pro Vita Monastica* which expounded the virtues of an essentially monastic, though not religious, life. In practice she collected friends who specialized in simple living. She once took me to a farm near Stroudsburg, Pennsylvania, where two or three couples and their children ₁aised gladioluses. We went into one of their houses, in which the tiny living room was almost filled by a grand piano. On another occasion we visited a young couple who had left the city to run a small farm. A great deal was made of the simplicity of their lives, but it seemed to me that "simple" often meant "inconvenient," and my impression that the young wife was not happy grew into a story called "Elsa." The theme was already dominating my life and was to become critical within the year, though I was not to discover the relevance of the story to my own problem until many years later.

The setting is just such a farm. It is late afternoon and Elsa has spent the day canning vegetables. Will, her husband, is haying in the back field and will be home soon for his supper. Suddenly three old college friends of Elsa's turn up for a surprise visit, anxious to see how her strange life is working out. Will returns, and he and Elsa show off their house. In the kitchen—

> Mary Lou had gone to the sink, and she began to work the pump.
> "Selma, look!" she cried. "Isn't this the quaintest thing! Watch out! It splashes!"
> "You pump it backwards when you want hot water," said Will dryly.

"You do?" Selma turned quickly.

"Don't let him fool you, Selma!" said Elsa.

"But where *do* you get hot water?"

"Here," said Elsa, opening the reservoir in the stove. "You dip it out."

"Elsa!" said Mary Lou with real enthusiasm. "I think this is just wonderful. You have a lovely little home. You must be very happy."

Elsa felt suddenly in love with her!

"But you must remember," said Will, as if this made all the difference in the world, "the water is *never* hot in the morning!"

"Think of it!" said Elsa dramatically. "We have to wash in cold water. Isn't that terrible?" Will's humor was delightfully subtle, but sometimes it was best to help it out a little.

That night Elsa stays up after Will goes to bed. She is tired and unhappy. Her life is by no means as bright as she has told her friends and she now decides that she cannot go on. But she is afraid to face Will, because he will argue too persuasively. And so she starts to write a letter which she will leave for him after he has gone off to the back field the next day. In it she tries to tell Will the truth, but she feels that she is being unfair, and, weeping, she tears up the letter. She will write it properly the next morning before she leaves. The next morning:

It must be very late, Elsa thought. Will was up, and the bedroom was already warm and dry. Nine or ten o'clock, perhaps.

She slid out of bed and went to the window. The barn and sheds glared in the sunlight and hurt her eyes. Yes, it was late; Will had let her sleep. She dressed quickly, half ashamed of herself, and hurried down to the kitchen. Will was outside, working on the car—whistling, off-key.

Elsa pumped water into a basin and sprinkled her face and neck with it, shivering in the sharp chill. Then she washed more thoroughly, and dried her face with a rough towel until it glowed comfortably. She saw Will at the door, pressing his face against the screen.

"Hello, Will," she said.

"Morning, Elsa. Cold water seems rather good in weather like this, doesn't it?"

Will was right. Will was always right, wasn't he?

That year Alexander Woollcott and Grace Root established the William Duncan Saunders prize for creative writing, in memory of the boy killed in the hazing accident. The prize was $200—then a substantial sum. I submitted "Elsa." One of the judges was Cynthia Ann Miller's father, who told me that my story made him realize how much he had imposed upon his wife when they were first married. Hutch also submitted a story, and it was generally believed that one of us would win, with Joe Vogel a dark horse. Hutch and I decided to reduce the anxiety and agreed that the winner should pay the loser $75. I got the $75. I was not shaken; there was no doubt that Hutch was good.

I WAS CHAIRMAN OF THE CLASS DAY CEREMONIES and worked out a program that was clearly designed to make a joke of the college. In Edward Root's studio I made a series of charcoal caricatures of members of the faculty. I emphasized Smut's ovoid head and called the cartoon "The Triumph of an Egg," after a story by Sherwood Anderson. I was working on it when Edward Root walked in, and he immediately said, "Have you quarreled with him?"

A freshman, Alf Evers, a far better artist who later became a well-known illustrator, added some less vicious portraits. I mounted them all on the walls of the gymnasium in which the Class Day ceremonies were to be held and assembled a three-piece orchestra which played a single selection, "Ach, du lieber Augustine," at intervals during the ceremonies. A Chinese student gave a Salutatory Address in Chinese.

It was customary for the class to give the college a present, and a large crate on the stage was opened with a great deal of trouble and found to contain nothing. The caricatures were auctioned off, ostensibly to pay for the orchestra, and were sold at figures which could be taken to represent the values we placed on the professors they depicted. The first amount bid for the picture of Cal Lewis was snapped up as if the bidder were out of his mind.

My mother and father came for commencement, and the Saunderses invited us to tea. It was the first time my father and mother had met the Saunderses, about whom I had so often spoken, and it was a difficult moment for all of us. Stink showed my mother a few peonies in the garden, and then we went into the music room and sat near the fireplace, where tea was served. My father tried to say the kinds of things he supposed appropriate. He was naturally very curious about the Saunderses' way of life, but he did not try to conceal his own. He remained himself. My mother, on the other hand, tightened up and spoke rather airily. The Saunderses recognized the situation (it was old stuff to them) and did their best, searching for suitable things to talk about.

I found it very hard going. I had developed two verbal repertoires, appropriate to very different audiences, and now the two audiences had come together and there was little I could say that was appropriate to both. I did my best by telling them about the role I was to play that evening in the Clark Prize Exhibition, giving them a sample of my oratory, with a few key sentences and gestures.

The exhibition was an important event in a college which boasted of its emphasis on public speaking. Each year seniors were encouraged to submit "orations," and six were chosen for the exhibition. The participants memorized their contributions and drilled under the direction of Cal Lewis, picking up appropriate gestures, working on timing and pacing (always start with the right foot when moving to the right), and so on. It was my understanding that Jack Chase, Joe Vogel, Hutch, and I were to turn the evening into a hilarious farce by submitting orations which could at the last moment be converted into sheer bombast. We were to "disparage orrratory." But something went wrong and I was left holding the bag. Jack and Hutch were on the program with standard orations, and I was stuck with an impossible travesty. One of the suggested titles was "Plymouth Rock and Ellis Island in American Life," and my oration consisted of an ultra-conservative attack on immigrants. I pictured the old Puritan coming to America in search of religious freedom and contrasted him with recent immigrants lured by the almighty dollar. My last sentence was: "The doors to Ellis Island must be *shut* if Plymouth Rock is to remain the heritage of American life." With the help of Cal Lewis, I worked out an appropriate gesture: I took a step forward with my right foot and, on the word "shut," threw my arm straight out at the audience with the palm up like a traffic cop's. I demonstrated this stirring conclusion together with a few other passages at the Saunderses'. But my father and mother were rather puzzled by the laughter.

That evening, when it came my turn to speak, Dean Saunders rose from his accustomed place in the left front balcony and quietly retired into the shadows. I must give Fancher his due. He was one of the few who saw the joke. When I passed him as I was leaving, he looked at me and shook his head. Trot Chase, who knew me well enough not to be taken in, nevertheless said, "Skinner, I thought you'd do better than that."

The Chaplin hoax, the Class Day caricatures, the Clark Prize Orration—these were a kind of intellectual vandalism that I never stopped to analyze. My college education proved to be surprisingly useful, and it had made no taxing demands upon my time, but I had spent four years under moderately irksome conditions, such as compulsory attendance at all classes and at morning and Sunday chapel. (As one of the monitors who took attendance at chapel during my senior year, I would mark an absentee present in exchange for a pack of cigarettes, and I felt no guilt because I thought attendance was an outrageous requirement.) There was little entertainment on the Hill apart from sports, and very little "culture," and the Hill was a long way away from the rest of the world for those who had no cars. We had girls only at fall and spring house parties and then under strained conditions. Fraternities strove for social prestige and I belonged to one at the bottom of the totem pole—which, by my senior year, meant the bottom of College Hill, because the other fraternities that had been there my freshman year had moved to new quarters at the top.

Today I should no doubt be protesting. I should be storming the President's office carrying placards reading: "Down with Morning Chapel!" or "Voluntary Attendance at Classes!" or "Make Hamilton Coeducational!" or "Decent Quarters for Non-Fraternity Men!" But that was not the fashion, and I was to leave the college without ever trying to tell myself or anyone else what was wrong with it.

Commencement morning was lovely and the campus as beautiful as ever, and the chapel was soon filled. The seniors sat in the first rows, their families and other students in the rest of the hall and balcony. Some members of the faculty had seats facing the audience, and in one of them sat old President Melancthon Woolsey Stryker, who had composed "Carissima," one of the loveliest of college anthems. He was now almost stone deaf, and as the audience grew quiet before the ceremonies began, he turned to his companion and in the hollow voice of a deaf man boomed out, "It's a lovely old *hall*, but it's getting a little *small*." The audience laughed sympathetically.

It was my lot to open the proceedings with a Latin Salutatory. I had written it in such a way that at least a few phrases would be understood by non-Latinists. I addressed the President as *"Praeses suaviloquens,"* a characterization repeated many years later when his successor described him to a friend of mine as "a mealy-mouthed son of a bitch," and I continued, *"Ave, Caesar, nos morituri te salutamus."* I called the trustees, among other things, *"possessores automobilium fulgentium."* We had a college song with the phrase, "Out, out in the cold, cold world" and I pictured our professors weeping as their favorite class *"in mundum frigidum frigidum exit."* And inevitably, of course, I addressed *"virgines dulcissimae,"* admitting that *"ad oppidum sub colle venimus, vidimus, sed vos ipsae vicistis"* ("to the town below the hill we came, we saw, but *you* conquered"—a generous tribute considering the fact that during my four years at Hamilton I had never had a date with a girl who lived in Clinton or Utica). It was all as pathetic as it was predictable.

There was a good deal of unseemly spirit during the first part of the ceremony, and the President sent word during the intermission that we should quiet down or risk losing our degrees, and we returned to our places somewhat shaken. We had rehearsed the procedure for getting our diplomas. A student's name would be called out, and he would go up the steps at the left of the platform, cross over to the Dean and the President, who would hand him a rolled diploma and shake his hand, and then leave by the steps at the right. When a few students had done this, old Prexy Stryker turned to his companion and boomed, "Why don't they make a bow?" A little later he boomed out again, "Why didn't *some*one tell them to make a bow?" When my turn came I took my diploma and bowed deeply. The audience, I am ashamed to say, laughed at this cheap joke. When it was all over, and the ceremonial applause had died down, Stryker turned to his companion and boomed, "Only *one* man made a *bow*."

There was an alumni luncheon that day at which my father's hero, Elihu Root, spoke, but I was just barely an alumnus, and we did not attend. Instead, we went back down the hill to the Lambda Chi Alpha house, stashed my belongings in the back of the Packard, and drove off.

EARLY IN THE PRECEDING FALL, my father and mother had driven to McGinty's for a week's vacation, but news had come that Mr. Torrey was seriously ill, and they had immediately returned to Scranton. Within a day or two Mr. Torrey died. My father had always regarded himself as a kind of understudy who would take over as General Counsel upon Mr. Torrey's retirement or death, but now it appeared that that was not the view of the company. He had been in Scranton only three years and his experience in corporation law was not extensive. Workmen's compensation was only one field, and a minor one at that. Rumors began to circulate that a Judge Kelly was to take Mr. Torrey's job and that my father would remain a junior member of the legal department. He went to New York to talk it over with company officers and came back with a distressing story. They had indeed made it clear that he was not to be appointed in Mr. Torrey's place, and when he hinted that he might be compelled to resign, they had simply said, "We must accept the situation as you make it."

My father talked things over with his friends. He had been elected to the Kiwanis Club and went to all the weekly meetings; he had been made a director of the Scranton Trust Company; and he and my mother had begun to make other friends, some of them affluent. He got the impression that there was a good deal of law business going around and that some of it might be turned his way. It was no doubt hazardous to start a private practice on his own again and to give up a handsome annual salary, but if he stayed on as a junior member, he would lose face. And so he resigned.

The *Transcript* did its best in reporting what had happened. "Following the death of Mr. Torrey," it said, "Mr. Skinner was offered a number of legal positions, but declined them to re-enter general practice. With his added experience gained in Scranton, coupled with his training and natural ability, his future in general legal circles in Lackawanna County seems bright." This was no doubt what he had told his family and his friends in Susquehanna, but there had been no other offers, and his future was actually quite obscure. (His letter to me about my own career is remarkable for having been written when his own career had taken this ominous turn.)

He had good luck in finding an office. Three lawyers about his own age—Ralph and Leon Levy and Frank Lynch—had a suite in one of the better downtown buildings, and they were looking for someone to take the space left by a man who had just died. They maintained a joint library, and this was particularly attractive because my father had sold some of his books when he left Susquehanna. He moved in, taking with him his secretary from the Hudson Coal Company, and on January 1, 1926, opened an office for the practice of law.

His associates seem to have understood him and his situation and to have treated him remarkably well. He appeared in a few cases jointly with the Levy brothers and Frank Lynch. Judge Smith, back in Montrose, appointed him receiver for a company in bankruptcy. But he was not busy. He had managed to save money on his Hudson Coal Company salary and was in no immediate danger financially, but he spent hours sitting in his office simply waiting for someone to come in with a case. He continued to play golf and see his friends, but their assurances of business to be turned his way—assurances he may very well have exaggerated—never bore fruit.

He was fifty years old and a newcomer to the city, and he began the long process of attracting attention in an ethical way. During the year he spoke at a rally at the Second Presbyterian Church and gave his old speech on the trial of Jesus to two church groups and the Lions Club. He addressed the Abington Men's Club and spoke on Prohibition enforcement at a Bible class of a Methodist church. He addressed a group of high-school parents, and spoke on compensation law at a meeting of the Northeastern Pennsylvania Society of Engineers. The *Scranton Republican* published a long letter from him on criminal law, in which he argued that laws favoring defendants were responsible for the failure to convict. He wrote a letter to the paper complimenting those who had kept a baseball team in Scranton, though he almost never went to a game himself, and he became an elder in the Presbyterian church and participated in a special canvass of members. The society page of a Scranton paper reported that my mother gave a "large bridge luncheon" at the Country Club.

News items about my father often referred to a law degree but he had never, of course, completed the requirements. He was evidently disturbed by this dissembling, and he went to see the Dean of the N.Y. State University Law School, which had taken over the college he had attended. He took a copy of his book and presented other credentials, and asked whether he might not now receive a full LL.B. degree. He was dismissed out of hand. The Dean may have thought he was proposing that they give him an honorary degree, and my father knew so little about academic matters that if he had been asked, he may well have said that that was what he was suggesting. He also proposed that his publishers call his book *Skinner's Workmen's Compensation Law* in the manner of the classic legal texts, rather than *Workmen's Compensation Law* by William A. Skinner. They refused at first, although they came around by the third edition.

At one point, desperate at having nothing to do, he turned to a lawyer he had known for many years and said essentially this: "Look, I am not under any financial strain at the moment, but I simply can't stand being idle. Have you got some case that I can work on?" The friend dug up a case that had been lying around for a long time in which he had very little faith. It involved a rather large sum of money, and my father spent a good deal of time on it and concluded that something could be done. But this did not bring in any new business, and by the time I had graduated from college, he was thoroughly depressed and would come home at noon, eat his lunch silently, and go into his bedroom and weep.

ALL THIS WAS OF COURSE hard on my mother, who had not yet fully adjusted to Scranton. She developed some kind of stomach pain, which she began to believe was a sign of cancer. Unfortunately she not only worried about her husband and herself, she was being sorely tried by her father.

The letter my grandmother left to be read after her death no doubt disturbed my mother, with her strong views on sex, and the rumors which now began to circulate must have been very painful. The niece who had come to keep house for my grandfather was not the companion he needed, and he had taken to seeing a Mrs. Craft. She was a widow who had supported herself and her two sons, friends of mine, by taking in boarders. She was cheerful and uninhibited, but when I was young there was a rumor that she was the "woman in black" who had been seen on the streets late at night.

My grandfather began to see her every evening, often having supper at her house, and there was, of course, gossip. U. G. Baker, hoping for a scoop, perhaps, or just out of curiosity, once asked me whether they were going to get married, and I am afraid I made some rather cynical remark such as, "Why should they?" But the only evidence of sexual behavior was meager. My cousin Lynn Burrhus and Mrs. Craft's son Kenny used to take them for rides in my grandfather's car. They sat together in the back seat, and since it was an open car, a lap robe was in order, and Lynn once told me that he and Kenny suspected that something was going on under the robe. From evidence I later collected, it could not have been much.

The problem was solved at the time of my graduation. Just before my father and mother came to Hamilton, Dr. Fulton removed my grandfather's prostate, and when we returned to Scranton the patient was moved to our house. A fistula had been made a little below the navel through which urine slowly flowed, to be absorbed by cotton pads. The pads had to be changed frequently, and that was my job. According to Dr. Fulton's calculations, the fistula would eventually close and my grandfather would then be able to urinate normally, but little progress was made. By mid-July he caught a cold and came down with pneumonia. I spent a good deal of time with him. Near the end he "babbled o' green fields." He pointed to a clothes tree on which his bathrobe was hanging and asked, "Why has that woman been standing there all day?" Soon his cough became a rale, and my arm was around his shoulders holding him up when he died.

He may have been killed by his lechery, or rather his lack of it under that lap robe, because in his wallet I found two advertisements for pills guaranteed to increase potency and among his effects some unused pills. A pill of one color was to be taken on Sunday, followed by one of a different color on Monday, and so on. They were probably strong irritants of the urogenital tract, possibly cantharides or Spanish fly, and they may have been responsible for the inflammation which led to the operation and the subsequent pneumonia.

When I picked up his effects in his office, I found a few girly pictures under the glass on the top of his desk. I had never discussed sex with him, but he once defended himself against some rumors by telling me that they had been circulated by his son's mother-in-law, Mrs. Outwater. But it was she, he said, who had invited him to her house and had pulled her dress up above her knees.

I SET TO WORK to become a writer. My first move was to build a study —the space in which I would write. Our house had a third floor with a maid's room at one end and an enclosed attic at the other. In between there was an area with a south window, and a wall and a door were put in to convert it into a room. I bought lumber and made myself a small bookcase and a work table, which I covered with green felt. I bought a filing case for the manuscripts I was going to produce.

I fell into a routine. After breakfast I went to my attic study. I forced myself to work on a story in progress or rework something I had thought I had finished. In a short time I would turn to reading "literary" things which, I could argue, would further my productivity. I had been, I think, a charter subscriber to the *Saturday Review of Literature*. I also subscribed to the *Dial*, the *American Mercury*, Ezra Pound's *Exile* when it appeared, and Samuel Roth's *Two Worlds Monthly*, which began to pirate Joyce's *Ulysses*. A writer's monthly kept me in touch with my putative market. I took a weekly newspaper, edited by the E. Haldeman-Julius of Girard, Kansas, who published the Little Blue Books. It was strongly anti-clerical, with Joseph McCabe carrying on the tradition of Robert Ingersoll, "the Great Agnostic." Near the end of the morning I would escape from my study and go downstairs—to play the piano, perhaps, or go out to the garage for a spot of carpentry, making something I could argue I needed for my work.

After lunch, when my father had gone back to his office and my mother was taking her nap, I would settle myself in a comfortable chair in our living room. One of the things I had made was a rack which held a book in a convenient position across the arms of the chair. I sat close to our new radio—the volume turned low enough not to wake my mother—and while reading I listened to KDKA from Pittsburgh or WEAF from New York City, both stations so weak and so far away that the signal faded a good deal. When I grew bored, I would take the Packard and drive to a neighborhood drugstore for a chocolate soda. There were three stores nearby and I used them in rotation to avoid being too conspicuous as the young man who had no job.

It was not easy to get books. The Scranton library had almost nothing I wanted, but later I found that I could borrow from the Hamilton College library by mail. A secondhand bookstore was not very productive and new books were expensive, but I bought and read *The Brothers Karamazov*, *Tristram Shandy*, Wladyslaw Reymont's four-volume *The Peasants*, and Proust's *À la Recherche du temps perdu*, beginning with the volumes available in English and moving into French for the rest. By this time I had become a pipe smoker and had acquired a large meerschaum with a brass cap over the bowl. In my study I occasionally took a small nip from a bottle of cognac that I had found in my grandfather Burrhus's cellar and smuggled home. To all external appearances, then, I was a writer.

But nothing happened. Anything as ambitious as a novel was out of the question. I wrote or started to write a few short stories like those I had sent to Frost, but I finished only one or two of them. Nothing in my history had led me to take a position on any important current issue, and the topics I wrote about continued to turn up by accident. In the courthouse square there was a statue of John Mitchell, a labor leader, standing with friendly hand outstretched, and I wrote a sonnet eulogizing him. I did not show it to my father, who was anti-labor, but I also wrote a parody of a poem by Louis Untermeyer about miners in which I ridiculed the demands of their

union. The truth was, I had no reason to write anything. I had nothing to say, and nothing about my life was making any change in
that condition.

BY THE END OF THE SUMMER it was clear that I had made a terrible
mistake, and I eagerly seized upon a chance to escape. It would mean
a substantial change of plans and I explained it in a note:

WHY I AM DESERTING WRITING FOR SEVERAL YEARS

The opportunity offered me to make a great deal of money in the
next, say, three years, is exceptional. I shall not find the same chance
again, and I need money. I need money because my family ties prevent my living simply alone, "struggling to write." I am not avoiding
a stringent mode of life.

My family ties prevent me, not because I have a great deal of
devotion and respect for my father and mother, but because they have
suffered very much in the last four years and because my leaving them
would increase their present anxiety to an unbearable degree.

Thus they are unwittingly forcing me into my present course.

True, they have offered me a year to stay at home to write. But
if the first three months of that year are exemplary, this will be the
condition:

My father and mother will be patently ashamed to explain to
friends what I am "doing." I have already felt the sting of implied
"You ought to go to work. If you were my boy—." My father will
assume that I am doing nothing. He will come home at noon and
scowl at me in my smoking jacket and slippers. He will tell me to do
this around the house or that with the car with the implication: "You
have nothing to do—."

Mother will say at least once a day, "It's going to be pretty hard,
son, for you to settle down to work when you can't play the piano for
an hour after breakfast, or read all afternoon."

If I go for a walk Mother will ask meaningly: "All alone—?" To
be alone in Scranton is a sin.

Father will laugh with half-veiled disgust if I make a date to go
walking with a girl at half-past eight in the morning to discuss Dostoevski.

I will accept an invitation to a piano recital with tea afterwards and Mother will say, "Don't you think that's so effeminate?"

I will ridicule a sermon, with the parental rebuke, "It isn't right for you to do that! Those are the men who get things done in the world."

Without ever inquiring into my ideas father will flutter his hand in the air and talk of my "highfalutin theories."

I will spend evenings being civil and courteous to people with whom I have nothing in common and whose only claim upon me is that of guest to host.

I will make plaster of paris plaques and paint them. Upon my showing them to Mother she will exclaim, "Frederic! Do you think you ought to waste your time like that?"

I could go on. But that would be pathetic.

It is enough to say that Scranton and my Scranton in particular is ready to quench any ideas of my own I may have. It is exceedingly inhospitable to anything new, and takes pains to make itself unpleasant.

I am too sensitive to my surroundings to stand it.

I could do little or no creative work during a year here. It was a big and important mistake that I ever thought I could. At the end of that year according to my agreement I would admit (outwardly) failure and go to work.

As I say, I could not equal the present opportunity then and since I see failure ahead I might better go to work now, spend three years in acquiring money, and if at the end of that time I am yet spiritually alive, then begin to live.

I do not remember what that "opportunity to make a great deal of money" was, but it vanished as suddenly as it had appeared, and I found myself committed, with no hope of reprieve, to what I came to call the Dark Year.

WHETHER OR NOT I COULD WRITE, I could at least write about writing, and some rather turgid analyses of what literature was all about began to appear in my notebook. Here are some examples:

DESIRE TO WRITE

I am convinced that an essentially false desire-to-write is necessary to any author. Whether it be the desire to make money, the desire to be known as a genius, the desire to get one's name in the paper, or some mystical desire to "express oneself," it does not bear analysis without resolving itself into a mean satisfaction of a mean instinct. By "false" and "mean" I do not intend to condemn exactly. I mean simply that the same desires quite as often prod a man into big business or eccentricity or acrobatics or driving automobiles at excessive speeds or marriage. . . .

The facile liar has a great deal in common with the artist who is expert in embroidering detail.

OBJECTIVITY

Is Dostoevsky's *The Brothers Karamazov* subjective?

Can a writer be entirely objective? I have read about 250 pages of Miss Garnett's translation of *The Brothers Karamazov*. I attempted to read it two years ago, understood nothing of it, and dropped it. This time I am reading it with as great an interest as I ever gave to a novel. Perhaps this is because I have become Russian in my habit of thinking so much about life and find in these real people someone to talk with about God and death and sorrow. Ivan's confession to Alyosha is wonderful.

The thing which has gripped me most strongly, however, is Dostoevsky's technique. Have I found at last a near perfect compromise of sub- and objectivity . . . Chekhov claimed to be objective. He could produce little more than short stories which, considering them as a whole, expressed no philosophy of life. If he succeeds in expressing anything it is that nothing exists which is worthy of serious expression. It remains for someone to produce a great amount of interpretation or philosophic thought by the objective method. Flaubert, as Hutchens says, could not help being subjective. True, in several senses.

MRS. FISKE'S "GHOSTS"

Yesterday I saw *Ghosts* with Mrs. Fiske as Mrs. Alving. It was probably played exactly as Ibsen would want it—highly dramatic, beautifully modulated tempo, a great deal of importance put upon Dr. Manders's self-deception and upon the sham of ideals in general

... probably an Ibsen performance at its best. [Mrs. Fiske was idolized by my fellow Hamiltonian Alexander Woollcott.]

But what of Ibsen? Important? Yes—for his time. He saw the cruelty of convention, of old ideas and ideals; and he strove to supplant them with his doctrine of freedom. This freedom was not a matter of degree. It was a real identity. A man had it or had it not. This substantializing of an abstract quality is the fate of any idea in the hands of a zealot. Philosophy deals with or rather plays with objects of its own creation. Ibsen was essentially a philosopher in his habits of thinking. The desire for order led him, as it leads all of his ilk, to defining, to delimiting, an aspect of life into a word and hence to deal with the word rather than with the aspect. . . .

But life is far too subtle to be defined and explained and illustrated. You do not know life, you feel it—with all your senses. Art should be vicarious experience; if Ibsen, by experience, came to feel some vague injustice, why did he not, as the Russians do, put life before us, turn our eyes to it, and let us come to feel as he has felt?

. . . One can only feel; one can make others feel. The *tragic question* is *why should we make others even feel?*

THE LITERATURE I was "philosophizing" about in this way could scarcely have been farther from the "literature" I was producing. The morning paper ran a column called "This Foolish World," and I began to contribute to it as I had contributed to *"Carpe Diem"* in *Hamilton Life*, signing myself Sir Burrhus. One issue contained a poem of mine (of ninety lines, but fortunately very short ones) called "Romance in Hogan's Alley"—an ethnic piece consisting of a conversation between a Mr. O'Grady and a Mr. O'Toole. Another had this:

> White with rage a college youth paced
> In and out the bathroom door,
> While a crumpled tube of toothpaste
> Lay dejected on the floor.
>
> "You may use my dental cream," he
> Cried, (I quote him literatim.)

"But if you at all esteem me,
Press the damn tube at the bottom!"

I tried to develop a standing feud similar to my interchange with Jay Kay. I brought up the fact that the editor of the column was a Colgate man and I referred to Colgate football scholarships and, of course, toothpaste. My sallies were heavy-handed, and were turned against me with devastating effect:

It appears that we did Sir Burrhus (Hamilton, '26) grievous wrong in assuming that his first letter was written in a spirit of badinage. He is in deadly earnest; and here he comes riding astride a hummingbird, with his little lance in rest and his horn rimmed spectacles glaring defiance.

—clearly a demotion from my role as the stout knight in that poem in "*Carpe Diem.*"

In desperation I played my last blue chip—and lost. I had never worn my Phi Beta Kappa key. I really did not believe in displaying supposed signs of superiority, but I almost certainly got something out of not wearing a key, because I could then fancy myself superior to those who did. In one of my heavy-handed challenges to the editor of the column I proposed that we should list the number of keys we were entitled to wear but had never worn! I was boasting of not boasting.

I was an anonymous contributor, but later in the year, when I had given up, the column contained a thinly veiled allusion to a local figure who was devoting himself to the production of the world's great literature in his attic study.

The *Writer's Monthly* conducted contests, and I won three dollars with my characterization of a flapper: "Age withered her and custom staled her to infinite satiety." I contributed two "Americana" to the *American Mercury*. One was from the *Scranton Republican*. A subscriber had written in to ask why such a big word as "television" was used for the new (still experimental) medium, and the editor had explained that "tele" stood for the part told and "vision" for the part seen.

Toward the end of the year a second evening newspaper was

started in Scranton, and because I knew Nell Fulton and, distantly, Charles Courboin, I was asked to serve as music critic. I was utterly unqualified, but that did not stop me, and I attended a number of concerts and sent in my copy. Of an aspiring young tenor I wrote:

> Mr. Jones possesses a strong, clear voice, used with ease and grace. His attack is confident and accurate, his enunciation careful. If he sings perhaps too continually in full voice, it is because he cannot, apparently, resist the sheer joy of singing. While he showed his greatest ability in the work from the oratorio, he appreciated accurately the operatic manner, and although last night gave no indication of dramatic ability except for a good stage presence, it is clear that Mr. Jones can turn to the fields of oratorio, opera, or concert, at his own choosing.

It did not take any musical expertise to write stuff like that.

I began to write a column, called "Ends and Odds," for Otis Chidester's newspaper in Windsor. Perhaps half a dozen of these, in my best imitation of Christopher Morley, were published. They contained some of the poetry I had written in college:

> She let me take a book on love;
> She told me she enjoyed it—but
> She must have read it hurriedly:
> I found some pages yet uncut.

This was dredging up the past, not writing anything new, and what was new was sorry stuff. I invented a character named Colonel Splashton and went farther than my mother had ever gone in being amused by people who mispronounced words and misunderstood literary allusions.

I lacked an audience for anything better than that. I wanted to write for people like Robert Frost, Stink Saunders, and a few literary friends, but where could they read what I wrote? I thought of publishing an occasional private letter, which I would duplicate and send to what I hoped would be a growing list of subscribers interested in reading what I had to say about books and life in general. But that was simple fantasy.

*　　*　　*

I INDULGED BRIEFLY in a different fantasy. We still subscribed to the *Transcript*, and one day it reported that Robert Sherman, the distinguished playwright, had retired and was returning to Susquehanna to spend his last days in his birthplace. He was planning to develop the old homestead on upper Jackson Avenue. I visualized him at once as the kind of writer I had occasionally seen lecturing at Hamilton College—distinguished, cultured, a lover of quiet living. I began to imagine that he had a daughter just a bit younger than I. She and I would walk along country roads in the late afternoon, returning for tea before a fire in the library of the refurbished Sherman home. All this was nourished by the *Transcript*'s subsequent romanticized accounts of Sherman's activities.

When I went to Susquehanna to visit my grandparents, I called him up. I told him I was interested in becoming a writer and asked if I could come to see him that evening. He set an hour and I was on time. The "homestead" was a small, nondescript frame house, and he had developed it to the extent of planting some bushes, putting some large whitewashed rocks along the edges of the driveway, and building a small concrete retaining wall. He met me at a side door in his shirt sleeves. We sat down beside a dining-room table bearing the remains of a supper and had coffee. There was nothing very distinguished about him nor, as it turned out, about his plays. They were written for traveling stock companies and amateur audiences and were sold in pamphlet form to schools and clubs. He was proud of his sales and said that New York playwrights had chosen the wrong market. If I wanted to get on, I should follow his example.

There was no daughter, but there was a wife, said to be a former actress, who, after an hour or more, called to her husband from the kitchen, where by arriving on time I had unwittingly trapped her, evidently *en déshabillé*. She now wanted to go upstairs and would have to pass through the dining room. I solved her problem by taking my leave, all illusions dashed.

A fragment of my literary past turned up in a letter from Rollo Walter Brown asking if I knew of any Scranton organization that might be interested in having him come to lecture. He had apparently kept lists of useful names, and mine was one of them. I was not above taking advantage of the same tenuous connection. I called the program chairman of the Century Club and asked whether or not she would be interested in a lecture by "my friend" Rollo Walter Brown. She was, and he came and gave a lecture, but I did not see him, because he made no effort to look up his old friend.

Brown's lecture was probably typical of the current literary fare in Scranton, for the Century Club was at the mercy of the lecture bureaus. I heard Hugh Walpole give for perhaps the hundredth time a lecture on the English novel, tossing off an apostrophe to that great novelist Sir Walter Scott with just the right style and timing to bring a round of applause.

I heard something much better from a young Frenchman who had come to Scranton in the forlorn hope that he might make a living by teaching the language. Someone had tried to be helpful by organizing an afternoon lecture in French. He and his wife had taken a rather dingy furnished apartment near the center of the city, and the curtains had been drawn to conceal the shabbiness of the furniture. The lecturer greeted us cordially *en français*, and his wife came out from a bedroom and timidly shook hands, her eyes red with weeping. There were perhaps a dozen of us (I was the only man) and we sat down on folding chairs.

The lecture was excellent. It was a discussion of the French novel from Benjamin Constant to Maurice Barrès and *le culte du moi*. Some of the older women in the audience probably followed the French more easily than I, but I enjoyed it and was led to read Constant's great novel *Adolphe* and to buy Barrès and two or three of the other modern writers he mentioned. It was like old times—Bill Shep, in fact—and I was desperately hungry for intellectual stimulation. It was only too clear that my world in Scranton was as drab as that darkened room.

I WAS EASILY DISTRACTED from my life as a writer. Anything that yielded quicker and more substantial rewards took possession of me. There was a bench in our two-car garage, with a small vice and a few tools we had brought from Susquehanna, and I began to make ship models. I bought some small C-clamps, some glue, and a few small cans of Duco paint, and I made a fairly large model of a Barbary Pirate ship with a tier of oars and a lateen rig. I also built a rather arty model of the *Santa Maria*, painted to simulate copper patina. Nell Fulton took a photograph of me sitting by the pirate ship smoking my meerschaum pipe and gave it to me with the inscription, "To the maker of ships on his birthday."

I made more plaques of plaster and gesso and covered them with gold paint and touches of color. Stink had liked J. M. Barrie's *My Lady Nicotine*, and I made up a packet of my best tobacco in heavy tinfoil and lettered a wrapper "The Arcadia Mixture" and sent it to him.

Alf Evers came to visit me in Scranton, and on a trip to New York I went to see him at the Art Students League. I asked someone where I could find him, and when I opened the door I found myself about five feet from a nude female model. I must have been rather conspicuously startled because there was a good deal of laughter from the students at their canvases. Alf quickly rescued me and we went to Greenwich Village. It was as unlike Scranton as possible, and I began to talk of moving to the Village, perhaps opening a small ship-model shop in a basement hole-in-the-wall.

Later that day I bought pastels, a few blocks of linoleum with a set of gouges, and oil paints and brushes—but brushes, Alf pointed out to me later, such as no artist ever used, because they had varnished handles. Back in Scranton, following a suggestion of Edward Root's, I bought some very fine sandpaper to draw pastels on, and with the oils I painted a portrait of Lindbergh, based on the well-known photograph showing him in a leather helmet.

A friend asked if I would help her with the decorations for a Christmas party at the YWCA, and I went into action on a grand scale. There was space for a number of large panels, and I bought rolls of paper and thumbtacks and show-card inks and brushes, and painted rather stylized Biblical murals featuring the star of Bethlehem.

Music was also an avenue of escape. I spent a good deal of time playing that grand piano—the Mozart sonatas, a number of things by Debussy, and some little preludes and fugues and two-part inventions by Bach. We had not brought our Victrola from Susquehanna. The phonograph was improving, although reproduction was still mechanical, but my memories of Ward Palmer's records had been dimmed by a comment of Stink Saunders's. When I first told him that I liked Verdi (no doubt pronouncing it Vurdy), he had agreed that he was a talented composer, but as for the phonograph he did not like "canned music." I settled for the radio, primitive as it was.

I was hearing good organ music, and a concert series was held in a downtown theatre. One evening I went to hear Wanda Landowska. There was a large harpsichord on the stage, and when a woman in a period costume came out and went to the instrument, we all began to applaud wildly, but it turned out that this was Landowska's companion, checking the height of the stool and the position of the instrument. Landowska herself eventually appeared and was wonderful. (In a similar series several years before, I had seen Pavlova dancing *The Dying Swan*.)

Another useful distraction was the Drama League, which staged three or four plays during the year at the Century Club. We put on *The Romantic Age* by A. A. Milne, and I was one of the Christians in Shaw's *Androcles and the Lion*. It was a walk-on part, but I was scheduled for the male title role in a play called *Adam and Eva*. An attack of influenza saved me from what would have been a disaster. I spent a good deal of time designing scenery, and I constructed a particularly elaborate set for a scene in Barrie's *Dear Brutus*. It included a large mossy bank on which several birch trees were growing. The trees were realistically round, but the mossy bank creaked slightly when the hero of *Dear Brutus* sat on it.

I also spent two days helping Jean Gros and his company with their marionettes. They did Maeterlinck's *Bluebird* and *Alice in Wonderland*, in the pepper scene of which the head of the Duchess was Mme. Gros's, grotesquely large in comparison with the other figures. I learned how to operate marionettes and to appreciate a good performance. Jean Gros did not think much of his audiences: a clown juggling three or four balls in the air was applauded as a great achievement, but it could not compare, he said, with getting just the right inclination of the head of Mytyl or Tyltyl at a particular point in a dialogue.

*　　*　　*

MY SOCIAL LIFE was only occasionally rewarding. Big parties were in full swing at Christmastime (the stock-market crash would put an end to them soon), and the professional party arrangers called on me as an eligible male. Families of marriageable daughters gave *thés dansants* at the Country Club or larger evening parties at the Century Club. The most lavish were those of the two daughters of Worthington Scranton. Name bands were brought from New York, and elaborately catered suppers were served, amid masses of flowers freshly supplied each evening lest something be recognized as left over from a previous party. You signed for dances, and I usually found the books of the few girls I knew already filled by friends who had known them longer, or had gone to dinner parties with them, or belonged in more exclusive circles. I spent most of my time in the stag line with a few other young men with the same problem.

My father took me to Kiwanis Club luncheons and introduced me to his friends with great pride, but there was nothing I could talk with them about and my efforts to find something must have confirmed their suspicions that I was not a chip off the old block. I once found myself sitting next to an officer of the telephone company and tried to make conversation by asking him whether people requested certain kinds of numbers because they were easily remembered or easily dialed; but that question was not raised in his branch of the company, and he dismissed me with, "Yes, I guess there's something like that."

Dr. Fulton and his wife remained friends of ours after my father left the coal company, and they occasionally came to call. A serious problem arose because my father was growing deaf and the doctor mumbled. For two or three hours he would tell stories of which my father heard very little. We all struggled with fatigue on those occasions, and when, of an evening, my father saw the Fultons approaching our house, he would groan.

Alone, however, I found Dr. Fulton reasonably good company. He had wanted a son, and I was a substitute. It was his habit to go for a walk with his Scottish terrier or hole up in his den as a gesture of independence from his wife and daughters. (He often complained that women were trying to move out of their natural sphere, and he suspected that this was true of dogs because he had seen a bitch lift her leg and urinate on a tree.) He began to invite me to join him. We would take his Packard coupé to Lake Scranton, a beautifully wooded part of the city's water supply, not far out of town, and time ourselves as we walked around the lake, a distance of about four miles. The scotty went with us, darting in and out of the woods.

Dr. Fulton was rather careless about his appearance, and he once told me with a laugh that a woman patient whom he was about to examine had said, "Now you wash your hands!" As a surgeon he was said to be not only careless but irascible. When a nurse handed him the wrong scalpel during an operation, he threw it back at her in a rage. And once when an intern started to leave the operating room without excusing himself, he went after him, caught his arm at the door, and turned him around, resuming the operation with his now unsterile hand.

He tried to interest me in becoming a doctor, and one strategy was to invite me to watch him operate. The first operation I saw was for osteomyelitis. I washed up with the doctor, had a gown and mask put on, and went into the operating room. The patient's leg was exposed, and the doctor took a scalpel (not too sharp, he explained to me, because a sharply cut wound does not heal quickly), and cut a great arc from knee to ankle, blood spurting out to be mopped up by a nurse. I had already been affected by the ether, and this great cut was too much. I turned away and the doctor nodded to a nurse to take care of me. When I came back, a great flap of skin had been drawn back exposing the tibia, at which the doctor was hacking away with mallet and chisel, like a sculptor. It is hard to staunch the flow of blood from bone, and the operation was a bloody affair, but I stuck it out and at the end watched the doctor sew up that great flap, obviously proud of his skill as a seamster.

The operation he performed on my grandfather was not a common part of his repertoire, and I knew him well enough to detect a certain reservation when he told me that the fistula through which urine was leaking onto those pads would eventually close.

I spent some time with a girl who was a graduate of Goucher. Her mother was dead, and she lived with her father, who was a doctor. She was small, athletic, highly verbal, with a sense of humor and great style. She drank heavily and liked to tell about the night she came home and fell into some broken glass and her father had to pull glass slivers from her fanny. She was a sun worshiper and acquired the darkest possible skin every summer. She stood for the personal freedom of the twenties, but there was nothing particularly warm about her, and I do not remember ever having kissed her.

She decided to redecorate a room on the top floor of their house, and we painted it together. We ran the floor color up on the wall in one corner and brought the wall color down onto the floor in the opposite corner and painted the ceiling to match. The walls were off-vertical stripes, and the room appeared to be tilted. The only furniture, a number of large cushions, gave no conflicting cues. Our intention was to make the available supply of Prohibition alcohol as effective as possible.

In spite of having read *Jurgen* and *Fantasius Mallare*, I lacked the sophistication needed to appreciate many literary allusions. One day an old friend of my mother's who had moved to California came to see us with her niece, who was not only attractive but extremely intelligent. I had left some *avant-garde* magazine lying around, and my mother's friend picked it up and read a bit of verse aloud. My mother was flustered and exclaimed, "Oh, these young people!" and hastened to talk about something else. Later, alone with the niece, I said I was puzzled by my mother's behavior. "I suppose it was this," she said, and she read the line: "There shall be no hot ichor shooting through my veins." I then saw the possible allusion, and I also immediately regretted that my new friend would be leaving so soon. She was obviously emancipated; a sexual advance might not be repulsed.

My FATHER WAS MOVING into his second year in private practice and still spending a good deal of time waiting for clients. He never had any secrets from my mother, and now he also took me on as confessor. One day he came home unusually disturbed. A lawyer in another city had referred a case to him for which he had been paid by the client, and that morning the client had stormed into his office and accused him of reporting the fee incorrectly and of sending less than the proper amount to the other lawyer. He was apparently quite abusive and talked of instituting disbarment proceedings. His figures were correct, and my father protested that it had been a mistake and that he would adjust the matter at once, but he was shaken. He was in no desperate need of money, and I doubt whether he had been openly unethical, but the situation was no doubt one in which it was easy to make that kind of mistake.

My mother continued to be his main support, but there was little she could do. Her assurances had once been plausible; she could alleviate his sense of failure when he lost a case by telling him, "You can't win them all," but what could she say now? At times she fell back on open criticism, as she had done successfully when they were young, but the only result now was that my father tended to withdraw from her.

My presence made matters worse. When I was a child my mother had occasionally rubbed my head, and she still did so from time to time. If I was lying on the sofa in the library when she was sitting in a chair at the head of it, she might start to massage my scalp. It was quite possibly a kind of affection which she no longer gave my father; indeed, she may never have given it, because it would have led in a direction she found distasteful. Once when we were alone and she was rubbing my head, she said that she thought my father was jealous, and she giggled, but it was not a giggling matter.

My father still dreamed of a good father-son relationship but still did not know how to achieve it. It was clear that I never really enjoyed playing golf with him and his friends. Dr. Fulton was obviously a rival. I once spent a good deal of time polishing his car and cleaning out the interior; it was something I never did with our Packard, and I made a great show of this devotion. Why did my father not inspire something like it? That I was miserably unhappy only added to his growing despair.

He made a few efforts to bring matters out into the open. He noted that I played Mozart sonatas a great deal, and he once asked me rather hesitantly why I preferred such—well, childish—music. And one evening sitting in the library he commented on the fact that I had remained completely motionless for at least fifteen minutes. I could not tell him why because I did not know. I was in fact displaying two curious "symptoms" on those long evenings. Sometimes I would cross my legs and with the toe of my free shoe describe a pattern a little like the profile of a pipe with a curved stem. Sometimes I would, as my father had observed, sit absolutely motionless in a kind of catatonic stupor. I finally said that I thought I should see a psychiatrist, and I am afraid that my father's first response concerned the cost. He told me that his old friend Sid Hersh had once gone to New York to a "life extension institute" and had been advised that he needed psychiatric help. He had spent a lot of money and got nothing out of it.

My father never complained; he never raised his voice. When a girl I was interested in asked me to drive her to a fairly distant city for the day so that she could do an errand (look up a boy she could not reach by phone, as it turned out), he did point out how much the trip with the Packard cost, but said nothing more. And once when I drove over to Dr. Fulton's, I was unaware that one of the back doors of the car was swinging open, and as I drew up alongside the curb, the door caught a telephone pole, and an expensive body job was needed to repair the damage. My father's reaction was closer to despair than anger. One day when he had gone into his bedroom after lunch and was weeping on his bed, I went in and told him that I would go out and get a job and start to earn money, but he protested that he would work it out somehow himself.

Life was almost too much for him. The move to Scranton had been a great mistake. Ebbe had died, he had quickly lost his prestigious position, he might never acquire a reasonably lucrative private practice again, and now his other son, whom he had never really understood, seemed to have lost all interest in life. My mother was afraid that he would commit suicide. "Others have done it for less," she said to me, and she was right. But other men had not believed so strongly in progress or had been so richly rewarded when they proved to their parents and friends that progress was possible. My father was too proud to kill himself; he could not confess failure that way.

Before the year was out his luck had changed. The president of a small coal company had found him useful and put him on an annual retainer. It was probably not entirely irrelevant that when the president had dined at our house he had noticed our buxom Polish maid and that he later met her in the street and began to telephone her when he knew we were not at home. She was amused and flattered by his attentions, but she was afraid that either her boyfriend or the man's wife would find out. Nevertheless, she finally agreed to go to his house, and I wrote down her account of the visit.

"There were his eyes," she said, "and after a while his hair was all mussed up. 'Gee, I like you,' he said. '*I like you*.' Then he kissed me and loved me up. '*I like you!*' He was walking back and forth. 'I don't know if we ought to. Should we or shouldn't we? Should we or shouldn't we?' He was all excited and kissed me and loved me up some more. 'Well, seeing this is the first time you've come here, we'll let it go at that. I like you!'"

He gave her an envelope, in which she later found ten dollars, and told her he would give her "*some* present" if she would go away for a while with him. "I was just wondering where he would take me," she said, "and would his chauffeur drive us?" He asked her about me, and when she protested that I was "*one nice boy*," he said *he* wouldn't let a chance like that slip by him.

My father did a good deal of work for the company, although it was nothing in which he could take any great pride because, as he told me later, the company's mines were running out and the officers were keeping them open mainly to pay their own salaries. The company had not paid dividends for years. I do not think there was ever a stockholders' suit, but my father dealt with lesser claims against the management. It was not the kind of thing to restore his faith in himself. It was not the kind of triumph that would ever be memorialized in the *American Magazine*, a publication of the time devoted entirely to success stories. But it was something to do, and it meant an income he could count on.

My year was not quite the intellectual desert that might be inferred from my publications and my diversions. There were articles in the *Dial*, that remarkable magazine of arts and letters published during the twenties, which excited me, and I did some other serious reading. But there was no one with whom I could talk or even correspond seriously. I was confined to the autistic, not to say auto-erotic, satisfactions to be found in a notebook. I talked with and wrote letters to myself. What I said shows all too clearly that I needed someone to ask for definitions, explanations, and proofs. My notes also show idiosyncratic usages and turns of phrase which suggest the auto-didact.

One of the first serious books I began to read in that Dark Year was Bergson's *Creative Evolution*. Here is an example of my comments:

> . . . philosophy, fortified, reinforced by science, comes to an impasse. This desire to know everything (helplessly on the wrong track until Darwin and Huxley) has burned brightly in recent years as the Universal Secret has apparently begun to crack, but it has suddenly grown dim again. The oil of self-exaltation has run out; for man is discovering his place in the world, but he has discovered that it is a mean place. Above all else, perhaps, but not far above. Finalist or mechanist, which gives the greater place to man? Which exalts him?
>
> Bergson's *tertium quid* may prove interesting. I have read a little over 120 pages so far. It is filled with unconvincing analogies, but the central theme seems valid. The idea of the original push suggests the potentiality of the fertilized human ovum, but this does not simplify matters for me. It is difficult enough to conceive the latent power in a fertilized egg which can produce a mature organism, but to conceive, as Bergson apparently does, of a potentiality which produces a material whole which is only one of many possible wholes since this existing one is the single result of overcome resistance, is too much.
>
> I shall read the rest of Bergson with as open a mind as possible, but I have little hope of finding any acceptable view of life in him.

Another stimulus to serious thinking was E. A. Burtt's just published *Metaphysical Foundations of Modern Physical Science*, which I borrowed by mail from the Hamilton library. Here are a few samples of my comments:

> Man can know only those things which with his senses he perceives.
>
> The present greater knowledge of life is no more than proportionate to the extension of man's sensory power; and there is no reason to believe that could we be sensitive to life in its entirety we could understand it. True we should eliminate a great many superstitions and fears

which are born of ignorance; but above and apart from pure sense knowledge we should probably know no more of the secret than a child who has finally explored the innermost stuffings of his doll. . . .

We think beyond words. The artist, since he strives to present meaning by creating a similar meaning, comes nearer actuality than the philosopher who strives to give words to meaning. Meaning cannot be expressed by words because that would necessitate as many words as there are meanings, which are countless. An approximation of a meaning can be reached by a piling up of words describing it, but this in turn defeats the . . . end by a loss of spontaneity. Warning: my assertions must be understood to come from no authority but my own feeling. . . .

The extension of man's experience has led to comparison which is in itself only an extension. Evidence of the influence of comparison upon man's thought is clear in the present use of the word comparative. Comparative religion has extirpated superstition from the modern mind; comparative anatomy (together with paleontology) made likely the "discovery" of evolution.

The notebook provided no stimulating exchange, and that was a pity, but it encouraged self-observation—something I had up to that point rather carefully avoided. I justified keeping a notebook as a means of self-analysis in a preliminary note:

I want to check my mental progress, something which is difficult to do merely by day to day self-observation; I want the discipline in thinking that comes with writing one's thoughts; I want to know how much *mood* plays a part in my thinking; do my attitudes toward problems vary in intensity and even in substance according to my mental (and physical) condition?; and finally I want the record simply for a record.

I began to look at myself as a person:

WHAT I ACHIEVE I DESPISE

A few examples first. High marks at college, for instance, seemed to me at one time to be an indication of a kind of greatness. Had I never gone to college I would no doubt have continued all my life to admire the man who could be elected to Phi Beta Kappa. Now that I have been there, with, I hope, as few culpable tactics as possible, the illusion fades, and I see Phi Beta Kappa as a sort of reward for unimaginative plugging and large sacrifices on the side of freedom of mind.

At one time I admired the clever man, the man who could turn a brilliant remark now and then. I set out to achieve such a reputation. But though I never became a Christopher Morley or a Michael Arlen, I got far enough along to find that cleverness is the reward for a good deal of sacrifice on the side of sincerity and orderly thinking. And because I saw my way clear to achieving cleverness if I consented to the sacrifice, cleverness lost its glamour for me. Until at present nothing sets me against a man more than that he be clever. . . .

But why should I despise the things I attain? Is it because I am secretly conscious of my inferiority and feel that if I achieve a "great" thing I must have been mistaken as to its greatness? I think not. I think rather that I feel that greatness is merely the result of a happy combination of trivial influences, that the great man cannot help being great, the poor man cannot help being poor. My ability to trace my own development shows this to me again and again. My only satisfaction lies in discovering that I am wrong about my "inexorable evolution"—that perhaps I have imagined it.

I Ask of Life—

1. Pleasurable satisfaction of desire.

The cardinal necessity in obtaining this is restraint. We are creatures of desire, filled with hundreds of evolved cravings, and the satisfaction of all of these is neither possible nor would it be desirable. We must make use of our knowledge and intellect to choose those desires which will give us (in the sum total) the greatest pleasure. . . . Desire may move the world but intellect may mold desire. *But* intellect molds desire only when desire desires to be molded. . . .

The retreat was now a rout:

Nothing is worth doing. But we have the instinct to do, and we should be wise enough to do the thing which is most nearly worth doing.

The world considers me lazy because I do not earn bread. The world expects of me that I should measure up to its standard of strength, which means that if I "got a job" for eight hours of office work (minus the time spent in being friendly to the other employees, in arranging for a party for the evening, in arguing the merits of a baseball scandal, etc.), [if it] constituted a day and paid me respectable money, I should be a man. It's not so much my "being a man" that people desire, it is my being one of them.

I see clearly now that the only thing left for me to do in life is to justify myself for doing nothing.

BUT I COULD NOT GO ON doing nothing much longer. My year was drawing to a close, and I had not forgotten the terms of my contract. I had proved beyond any doubt that I could not make my way as a writer, and my father's recent experience had made the law still less attractive as a profession. What was I to do?

If I could have answered that question, I might have brought the Dark Year to a close much sooner. I did not make a break because I saw no alternative. It is true that I had never learned to protest or revolt. I never fought with my friends and only rarely quarreled with my family or teachers. I let the hazers at Hamilton College have their way without a struggle and I stayed a full week with my parents at the Essex and Sussex Hotel.

It is also no doubt significant that in my story Elsa's husband's name was Will. My mother called my father Will, but Elsa's story was mine, not hers. I lived it again and again during that year: no day seemed bad enough to justify the turmoil of an open break.

It would have made a great difference if there had been something I really wanted to do, but as the year now drew to an end I was no closer to anything that appealed to me. I had spent some time drawing floor plans of a country house—such a house as a writer might live in cheaply but comfortably with a lovely and sympathetic wife. It was not exactly the setting for a *vita monastica*, but it had some of its virtues. But how could I support myself? I had sent for some literature about chicken farms in California which showed how one could raise chickens and much of the food they needed on a single acre of land and make a living selling eggs and poultry. But it was a busy life and I was not sure that it would give me much time to think and write.

Better might be the physically disciplined life then being recommended by T. E. Lawrence. The army was his solution, but it was not mine. I considered getting a job simply as a chauffeur. Actually I settled for something even farther down the socio-economic ladder. A landscape gardener named Baumann took care of our lawn (and of the lawns and gardens of Scrantonians who were richer than we but not rich enough to have gardeners of their own). His nursery and headquarters were not far from our house, and I hired myself out as a laborer at thirty-five cents an hour.

I justified the move to my family, and they to our friends, by pointing out that I was in poor physical condition. I had not played golf, of course, during the winter, and had only occasionally walked around Lake Scranton. A job out-of-doors—temporary, naturally—was just what I needed to put me in the pink. To myself I gave my reasons in a sardonic sonnet:

HYMN TO LABOR, OR
ACTION AS THE SOLUTION OF DOUBT

(This the farewell to my discontent:)
Awake, my soul, from the dull seizure
Of the sweet hasheesh of Too-Much-Leisure
And of the sin of sorrow now repent!
(This, the farewell to my Love of Sorrow:
This the God-be-with-you to my doubt
Which henceforth I must learn to do without.)
Now rings the wild alarm! It is tomorrow!
Gird on, O Soul, your most assuring armor,
Finding in labor strangely occult meaning!
Forget not yet the glory of the farmer,
And at the Angelus, rest you from your gleaning!
O Man of Labor, lean upon your hoe:
Christ died for you, O Volga boatman, Yo!

Since I had no skills in gardening, I was put to rolling lawns (as I had rolled Annetta Kane's tennis court) and digging up and transplanting shrubs. I left our house early every morning with my dinner pail and went to Baumann's garage, where with perhaps a dozen other laborers I climbed into the back of a truck. We were dropped off in twos and threes with our equipment at various properties throughout the city. I spent many hours practically harnessed to another employee. The weather was unseasonably warm and I soon learned what it was like to work all day under a hot sun. One man I worked with was an old, uneducated Irishman whose verbal responses proved to be completely predictable. We would push the roller across a lawn, then swing the handle over to the other side and push it back, moving slightly off the previous track. If, as we reversed our course, I made a slight hopping step, as if my toe were close to the roller, he would inevitably say, "Watch it." A younger man with whom I rolled more difficult lawns with steep terraces showed greater variety. He would point to every passing girl and ask, "Would you, for a dollar?" and he told me how he wrestled with his wife and laughed as he recounted the damage they did to each other. Some of the other workmen were the kinds of people I had known in Susquehanna. One day in the nursery the foreman staged a race between two skilled Italians as they dug trenches in the deep soil with their spades. It was not railroad work, but it had a nostalgic ring.

I began to look into the possibility of landscape architecture as a career. Simply to be in touch with it was enough to arouse my interest because there was nothing else in sight. I consulted Baumann, and he told me with great pride that graduate study in the field took six years. I was saved the trouble of making a decision. I spent a day transplanting barberry bushes, carrying great armfuls from one part of a nursery to another. At home that evening I discovered that my chest was a brilliant red. I had unwittingly pricked myself thousands of times with the sharp spines of the barberry plants. At that season the air was full of grass pollen, and I had apparently given myself thousands of minute injections, for within a week I developed a severe grass allergy. It put an end to any outdoor activity when grasses were in flower. When I went to see Baumann to tell him that I was quitting, he told me that I was just on the point of getting a raise, but my career as a landscape architect was over. And once again there was nothing for me to do.

AND ONCE AGAIN I was spared the need to make a decision. My father came home one day and asked if I would be interested in writing a digest of decisions of the Anthracite Board of Conciliation. In 1904 there had been a bloody coal strike in the anthracite region, and President Theodore Roosevelt had set up a Board of Conciliation to settle grievances brought by unions or companies. Since then, hundreds of decisions had been handed down, and they were increasingly cited as precedents in new cases. The company lawyers could work more effectively if these decisions were digested for quick reference. It was hackwork, but it was a kind of writing, and I readily agreed to take the job. I had never been in a coal mine, of course, but that did not seem to matter. Within a month or two, without leaving my desk, I became a kind of authority on jackhammers, airways, blackhead, bottom men, check weighmen, gobshutes, docking systems, hoisting engineers, monkey headings, nozzlemen, peat rock, thin veins, and square topping.

I began work in the outer office of my father's old suite at the Hudson Coal Company. It was dull and monotonous. I made frequent trips to the water cooler and struggled to avoid dozing off. An eight-hour day was much too long for that kind of work. Since I was still suffering from hay fever, I suggested that I take the work with me to Bread Loaf, where in the pure air of the Battell Forest I would be more comfortable. I found that I could get a room in one of the annexes of the Inn without being a student at the school. Unfortunately, there was a field of alfalfa in full bloom just outside my room, and I found myself spending the morning working on the digest, sneezing, blowing my nose, and spreading wet handkerchiefs around the room to dry. It was the worst possible place, but my romantic experience at Bread Loaf two years before kept me there for more than a month. Then I went back to Scranton and finished the book by the end of the year.

It was privately printed under the title *A Digest of Decisions of the Anthracite Board of Conciliation*. My father was listed as co-author but for prestige only, and it was copyrighted in my name. It was no doubt intended to give the coal companies an advantage, but the union lawyer who prepared all the cases for the miners had a copy within the year, and some kind of balance was thus restored.

Writing the book was not a total loss. I read 1148 grievances and summarized the umpire's decision in each in a short paragraph. About 700 were classified according to the eleven awards and agreements of the original commission, but I had to work out a system of classification for the rest in terms of grievance committees, rates, relations between employer and employee, and a number of miscellaneous topics. It was not far from a Baconian classification of scientific facts.

The money I made on the *Digest* opened fresh prospects for a career. I began to consider graduate study. My life at Hamilton, as I looked back on it during that Dark Year, had been good, and I began to wonder whether I might not return for an M.A. in English. The college had no graduate program, but it had occasionally taken on a student for further work. I have forgotten whether I abandoned this effort to remain a fledgling for still another year or was rejected. It does not matter because I was beginning to consider an entirely different field.

PART V

I HAD APPARENTLY FAILED as a writer but was it not possible that literature had failed me as a method? One might enjoy Proust's reminiscences and share the emotional torment of Dostoevski's characters, but did Proust or Dostoevski really *understand?* Annetta Kane, my intellectual Catholic friend, had once quoted something of Chesterton's which came back to me with great force. The passage occurs in a preface to Dickens's *Old Curiosity Shop.*

> There is an odd literary question which I wonder is not put more often in literature. How far can an author tell a truth without seeing it himself? Perhaps an actual example will express my meaning. I was once talking to a highly intelligent lady about Thackeray's *Newcomes.* We were speaking of the character of Mrs. Mackenzie, the Campaigner, and in the middle of the conversation the lady leaned across to me and said in a low, hoarse, but emphatic voice, "She drank. Thackeray didn't know it; but she drank." And it is really astonishing what a shaft of white light this sheds on the Campaigner, on her terrible temperament, on her agonised abusiveness and her almost more agonised urbanity, on her clamour which is nevertheless not open or explicable, on her temper which is not so much bad temper as insatiable, bloodthirsty, man-eating temper. How far can a writer thus indicate by accident a truth of which he is himself ignorant?

That was my cue. I was interested in human behavior, but I had been investigating it in the wrong way. Alf Evers had said to me, "Science is the art of the twentieth century," and I believed him. Literature as an art form was dead; I would turn to science.

It was too big a change to come about all at once, and for a long time I was clearly ambivalent. At times I was quite violent: literature must be demolished. I wrote a note called "The Polemic Against Liter-

ature." But I continued to read poetry and fiction (the last volume of
À la Recherche . . . had not yet appeared). I could justify that as
pleasure; to get down to business I would turn to science.

THE SCIENCE that concerned itself with behavior (animals or human)
was said to be psychology, about which I knew very little. "Phil. 1–2"
with its brief demonstration of the two-point limen had not been in-
formative, but the subject matter was not unfamiliar. As a child I had
had many opportunities to observe animals in the wild, and I had a
few glimpses of what might be done with them in captivity. I once
overheard Jack Palmer explain that the bronco buster in the rodeo
stopped short of "breaking the will" of a horse so that it could be
ridden again in the next show. A friend and I once tried to get pigeons
drunk by soaking corn in whiskey. Napier, the Scottish mathematician,
is said to have succeeded in doing so, but we failed. Nor was I successful as a trapper. Advertisements in magazines like *Popular Mechanics*
told of the money to be made from furs, and I bought two or three
Victor jump-traps (the patent of which was originally held by the
Oneida Community, which would later interest me for a different
reason), and I set them in what were said to be the right places, but
I never caught anything. One of Ernest Thompson Seton's wily animals not only avoided all traps but showed his contempt for the
trapper by defecating on them, and I sensed a similar battle of wits.

I once saw some performing pigeons at a county fair in New
York State. The scene was the façade of a three-story building. Smoke
appeared from the roof, and a presumably female pigeon poked her
head out of a window on the top floor. A fire engine moved in from
the wings, smoke pouring from its boiler. It was pulled by a team
of pigeons appropriately harnessed, and other pigeons with red fire
hats rode on the engine, one of them pulling a string which rang a bell.
Somehow a ladder was put up against the building, and one of the
fire-pigeons climbed it and came back down, followed by the pigeon
from the upper window.

Shortly after we moved to Scranton, I wrote a note about something that happened one day in our driveway.

LIFE AND DEATH

I did not see the beginning, but doubtless the Black Bug was the aggressor, for when I came upon the battle it had fixed its teeth in the side of the Earthworm and was letting itself be flung about as the Worm fought. Most of the action of the Worm was lost, but it had one play which occasionally took effect. It made a loop of itself beginning at the head and gradually worked it backwards, at the same time tossing about wildly. The loop stroked one side of the worm for its entire length, and one time in about four it succeeded in brushing the Bug away. Unfortunately, the Bug almost immediately fastened itself again and it would be some time before the Worm had the luck to get rid of it with its loop. At each wound . . . a drop of blood would appear, mingled with the mucus which the Worm secreted at each point of attack; so that each effort of the Worm to rid itself of the Bug resulted in a fresh opening and no doubt considerably hastened death. Its movements became spasmodic and feeble; it grew slightly purple in color as if poisoned. The Bug was now satisfied to proceed from wound to wound, drinking the blood which had come out. Then, apparently satiated, it crawled three or four times about the dead body and then amused itself by crawling back and forth underneath.

My father, possibly because he never quite understood how to get on with people, was always watching them, and he frequently called my attention to their behavior. From his office window he could watch Wright Glidden park his Packard near the First National Bank, and he once commented on the great precision with which he did so. At a baseball game he pointed out how our catcher fooled the umpire, who stood behind the pitcher, by bringing his glove into a strike position after catching the ball. As a practiced orator he was alert to verbal foibles, and once told me with a smile that a friend's wife, trying her hand at public speaking for the first time, had called for action "at once, immediately, and now!" And he once reported that a well-known figure in Scranton often ended a sentence with "and things and things and things." My research into the digressions of Professor Bowles may have been inspired by some such remark. He never showed me his set of Havelock Ellis, but those sectional bookcases in Susquehanna had contained six or eight volumes on applied psychology, published by an "institute." They were attractively bound, with white spines and great white embossed seals on their blue covers, and in one of them, I remember, it was argued that an advertisement for chocolates showing a worker shoveling cocoa beans into a roasting oven was "bad psychology." And almost every day I read the essays of Dr. Frank Crane in the Binghamton paper.

Any unusual behavior puzzled me. A classmate of my father's became totally paralyzed and spent his life in bed, attended by his wife. When he died, however, it was said that his body immediately lost its rigidity. How was that possible? At some kind of outdoor church fair there was a booth in which you threw balls at dolls mounted on a rack. The dolls were restored to their place by pulling a rope from the front of the booth. Once, when the woman who ran the concession was picking up the balls under the dolls, some wag pulled the rope, and the woman dropped to the ground in alarm. I wondered why she had confused the sound of the rack with the sound of a ball being thrown.

When I was in third grade, our teacher was talking to the fourth-grade class at the other end of the room. I was reading, and suddenly I put up my hand and waved it to attract her attention. She asked me what I wanted, and I said that I had been reading a certain word just as she had said it. Both classes laughed, and perhaps I deserved to be laughed at, but I had noted an important and rather curious effect of coincidental verbal stimuli.

Once in a rather noisy street I was trying to talk to a friend in a store window. I shouted to him and then strained to hear his reply, but I could not make out what he was saying—until I discovered that there was no glass in the window. His voice was reaching me loud and clear, but I had dismissed it as part of the ambient noise and was listening for a fainter signal. On our canoe trip, too, I had been impressed by that "conscious phenomenon" and I tested physical reality with some care.

Ward Palmer was curious about human behavior. He told me that his father (as a specialist in automobiles) had once been called to the phone in the middle of the night about an accident. Half asleep, Ward had listened to the conversation without really hearing it until his father said, "Dead?" whereupon he was instantly wide awake.

In high school I began to write a treatise entitled *Nova Principia*

Orbis Terrarum. The project itself—nothing less than a new principle of the universe—was expansive enough without the Latin title, but that was, I suppose, my tribute to Francis Bacon. The first two pages of this work survive. They begin: "Our soul consists of our mind, our power of reasoning, thinking, imagining, weighing, our power to receive impressions, and stimulate actions of our body; and our conscience, our inner knowledge of write [sic]." This was not a generalization based on my own observations, and it is perhaps just as well that the manuscript soon breaks off.

I gained some important fringe benefits from my advanced courses with Bugsy Morrill. I dissected a cat preserved in formaldehyde, and I made quite acceptable slides of a chick and a pig embryo, but more important, as it turned out, was the fact that Bugsy called my attention to the writing of Jacques Loeb. I read *Physiology of the Brain and Comparative Psychology* and *The Organism as a Whole,* and I was impressed by the concept of tropism or forced movement— for example, by those creatures that "loved the light" but swam resolutely into the dark end of a tank when the light was coming in the right direction.

At Bread Loaf, of course, I had written that play about "the glands that change personality," and in my senior year I wrote a term paper for Chubby Ristine on Hamlet's madness. I discussed the original reason why Amleth, in the chronicle by Saxo Grammaticus, had put on his "antic disposition" and cited other historical examples of feigning insanity to escape revenge. I argued that the type of madness assumed by Hamlet (somewhere I had picked up the term "involution melancholia," and I badly overworked it) was responsible for much of the controversy about whether Hamlet was really mad.

The stories I had sent to Frost, as well as "Elsa," were all psychological, and so was much of my serious reading during that year in Scranton—from Dostoevski to Proust. There was even a bit of animal behavior, because the only episode I remember from *The Peasants* is one in which a girl takes a cow to be serviced by the parish bull, and the priest keeps the excited bull away for a time "to make a better calf."

Those books Dr. Fulton had lent me which traced the behavior of famous people to medical problems touched on psychology, and when the doctor took out my appendix, I was particularly interested in how I should lose consciousness when going under ether. I convinced myself that the last thing I sensed was the bending of my right elbow as someone presumably moved my arm.

Proust was practicing a kind of psychology when he sought to explain strange recollections, and I myself began to analyze a few instances of Proustian recall in my own experience. Here is an example:

> I see my mother writing a note to Mrs. John DeWitt, and the next day, while writing some notes on packing, the picture of a bedroom flashes into my mind. I am unable to identify it, even to orient myself in it; and I am ready to conclude that it is one of the few scenes I have dreamed of but never remember actually seeing. Suddenly it comes to me that the room is that of John DeWitt, the son of the woman my mother was writing to; and I further remember that the only time I ever saw it was while waiting for him to *pack* some clothes in a knapsack.

A diagram below the note shows two intersecting lines with an arrow pointing to the intersection, and the words "Cf. James." Introspection also seemed important quite apart from its literary uses. Here are two relevant notes:

> In a railroad car I watch a heavy black smoke blow against my window. It is not until I smell a very faint odor of coal gas that I revolt at this *suffocating sight*.

> A half-cloudy afternoon takes on the meaning of a rainy one when a few drops of water are spilled on my hand, although I know it is not rain.

I was also intrigued by the after-image of movement. I often rode on the rear platforms of trains and was familiar with the fact that the track seemed to move toward the train after the train stopped. It occurred to me that in riding on a straight track there must be some point in the distance where the after-image of movement just overcomes the physical recession of the tracks so that a point would appear to be standing still, but it was nevertheless a point that was always changing.

During the year I wrote a long note about my synaesthesia, recording the colors I associated with numbers. I thought I could trace the effect to the colored alphabet book printed on cloth that I had as a child. "If this is true a useless meaningless association has persisted for years."

I began to take psychology seriously as a field. The Hamilton College library lent me a book on the emotions by MacCurdy, and somewhere I picked up a book on perception by Parsons.

THERE WAS TO BE one curious digression. In the Susquehanna library I had been intrigued by books of arcana, and at Bread Loaf a professor from Boston University had taken rather seriously a number of supernatural phenomena, including some photographs that children were said to have taken of fairies. I read Ouspensky and Claude Bragdon, and began to play with their versions of space, time, and the fourth dimension. Here is a sample from my notebook, showing how far I could stray from the path of science.

> *Meaning* is relation; depending upon, and changing with, time, space, and space time. It derives from time, space, and space time and from nothing else. At a given point in time a thing is; and it is, and has meaning, not because of its component parts but because of their place in space time. The buttercup I am looking at is composed of cells, the cells of molecules, the molecules of atoms, the atoms of electrons and protons, and they, for all we know, are of such stuff as life is made of. The buttercup is and has meaning because of the arrangement in space time of its parts.

A note would begin with a reasonably interesting observation: "I sit in a train at a station and coincidentally with the slow motion of my head from left to right I hear the slow creak of wheels. Immediately I perceive that we are moving, and it is a shock to find that we are not." But I would then quickly muddy the waters: "The apparent movement of matter which is derived from our third dimension is realized as non-movement because we have learned the meaning of move. . . . The accumulation of facts created a meaning which was in effect retrogressive, i.e. . . . , with a two dimensional understanding I should have taken the meaning of 'moving' without the correlated facts." (In my analysis of Proust's style I noted at one point that he "hints at my retrogressive theory.")

I WAS FLOUNDERING in a stormy sea and perilously close to drowning, but help was on the way. The *Dial* published some articles by Bertrand Russell which led me to his book *Philosophy*, published in 1927, in which he devoted a good deal of time to John B. Watson's behaviorism and its epistemological implications. Here was a different approach to meaning and a theory of knowledge. I liked what Russell said of Kant: He "has the reputation of being the greatest of modern philosophers, but to my mind he was a mere misfortune." So much for Bill Squires! As for behaviorism—

> This philosophy, of which the chief protagonist is Dr. John B. Watson, holds that everything that can be known about man is discoverable by the method of external observation, i.e., that none of our knowledge depends, essentially and necessarily, upon data in which the observer and the observed are in the same person. I do not fundamentally agree with this view, but I think it contains much more truth than most people suppose, and I regard it as desirable to develop the behaviourist method to the fullest possible extent.

The refreshing thing was how quickly Russell, following Watson, got around to facts:

> The scientific study of learning in animals is a very recent growth; it may almost be regarded as beginning with Thorndike's *Animal Intelligence*, which was published in 1911. [It began with his "Animal Intelligence: An experimental study of the associative processes in animals," a monograph published in 1898.] Thorndike invented the method which was adopted by practically all subsequent American investigators. In his method an animal is separated from food, which

he can see or smell, by an obstacle which he may overcome by chance. A cat, say, is put in a cage having a door with a handle which he may by chance push open with his nose. . . .

In my copy I underlined the phrase "which he can see or smell" and on the following page when Russell refers to the maze "with food outside where the rat could smell it," I underlined "where the rat could smell it." Russell, again following Watson, was trying to interpret the Law of Effect as an example of the substitution of stimuli. Russell stated the principle in this way:

> *When the body of an animal or human being has been exposed sufficiently often to two roughly simultaneous stimuli, the earlier of them alone tends to call out the response previously called out by the other.*
>
> Although I do not agree with Dr. Watson in thinking this principle alone sufficient, I do agree that it is a principle of very great importance.

It was, of course, Pavlov's principle of the conditioned reflex. It would be a long time before I saw the mistake which Russell and Watson were making and in which I concurred when I underlined those phrases, because the course of psychology as a science of behavior was to follow the unproductive path of stimulus-response psychology for many years.

Inspired by Russell, I bought Watson's *Behaviorism*. I lost interest in epistemology and turned to scientific issues. I was back with Jacques Loeb and forced movements, and I began to glimpse the possibility of technological applications.

When a book by Louis Berman, an endocrinologist, appeared under the title *The Religion Called Behaviorism*, I took up the cudgels and wrote a review which I sent to the *Saturday Review of Literature*. They did not publish it, but in writing it I was more or less defining myself for the first time as a behaviorist.

As I read further in Russell and Watson, I moved from "philosophy" toward an empirical analysis. I was still using terms like "forethought" and "intelligence" and talking about experiments with mazes, but I was looking at behavior. For example, I wrote a note on the process of learning to pack a suitcase, essentially according to the Law of Effect. At first one throws things into a suitcase in no order whatsoever and with the immediate consequence of not having enough room for everything and the deferred consequence of wrinkled clothing or a burst tube of toothpaste. Later on, one "tries another route" (I was still lost in the maze) and puts the suit in the bottom of the case carefully folded and packs the tube in soft clothing. I had still a long way to go, but I was on my way.

And in November 1927 an article by H. G. Wells in the *New York Times Magazine* confirmed my decision to abandon literature and turn to psychology. The article was given a headline rather than a title:

MR. WELLS APPRAISES MR. SHAW

He Contrasts the Contribution of the Playwright
With That of Pavloff, Russian Scientist, and
to Whom Does the Future Belong: the Man of
Science or the Expressive Man?

I have before me as I write a very momentous book. It is entitled "Conditioned Reflexes," and it is by Professor Pavloff of Leningrad. It is not an easy book to read, but it is not an impossible one, and when one has read, marked, and learned one finds—I find—that one has at least attained the broad beginnings of a clear conception of the working of that riddle within us which is perpetually asking us riddles, the convoluted gray matter of the brain.

As Wells read, he was reminded of another great man for whom, he said, "I have an admiration and affection as least as strong as I have for Professor Pavloff, though my admiration is of an entireiy different character, George Bernard Shaw. I recall that Professor Pavloff is one of the greatest of vivisectors—'those scoundrels,' Shaw called them— and that, according to Shaw, it is his habit to boil babies alive and see what happens."

Vivisection aside, Wells was intrigued by "the remarkable contrast of these two eminent figures," with both of whom he himself had something in common:

I come somewhere between them, in my humbler measure I partake a little of both. I do not know what Pavloff thinks of Shaw, probably about as much as he thinks of the "proletarian science" of Moscow. But we have Shaw's ringing "scoundrel" for Pavloff properly on record. I have been amusing myself for some minutes with that amusing game of the "one life belt." Probably you know and play that game. You put it in as a problem rather after the fashion of "The Doctor's Dilemma"; if "A" is drowning on one side of a pier and "B" is equally drowning on the other, and you have one life belt and cannot otherwise help, to which of the two would you throw it? Which would I save, Pavloff or Shaw? I do not think it would interest the reader to give my private answer. But while I was considering it I was manifestly obliged to ask myself, "What is the good of Shaw?" And what is the good of Pavloff? Pavloff is a star which lights the world, shining above a vista hitherto unexplored. Why should I hesitate with my life belt for one moment?

And why should *I* hesitate? There was no reason at all. It was to be graduate study in *psychology*. But where should I go? I knew nothing about departments of psychology. John B. Watson was no longer teaching. He had been dismissed from Johns Hopkins because of a divorce which had become one of the newspaper scandals of the twenties. My professor of "Phil. 1–2" was not likely to be of help, but I went back to Hamilton to talk things over with Bugsy Morrill and Stink.

I went first to see the President, and he had no trouble in giving me advice. He reached into the bottom drawer of his desk and pulled out a yellowing mimeographed folder designed to answer just such a question as I had brought to him. He looked up psychology and found that the two outstanding departments in psychology were at Columbia and Harvard. I would discover later that neither department was then outstanding. Evidently the ratings had been made many years before when Münsterberg and James were at Harvard and James McKeen Cattell at Columbia.

Bugsy had been successful in getting many of his pre-medic students into the Harvard Medical School and recommended Harvard on the strength of that. (And he had something to show me—a large black volume called *Conditioned Reflexes* by the Russian physiologist Pavlov!) When I got back to Scranton, Dr. Fulton strongly supported Harvard because he had done a bit of post-graduate work there himself. And so I applied to the Department of Psychology at Harvard for admission as a graduate student in the fall of 1928 and was accepted the following spring. It is possible that I could have entered in February if I had known enough to ask, but, so far as I knew, academic years began in the fall.

My DECISION WAS, of course, a tremendous relief for my father and mother, and in a conciliatory and affectionate mood my father suggested that we go to Europe the following summer. I had had my fill of vacationing with my parents, but Europe might be different, and I agreed, with the proviso that I should leave early and spend a month or two on my own before joining them. Even so, four or five months remained before I would leave.

I spent them in Greenwich Village. I had seen the Village with Alf Evers, but the chance to spend a few months there came through other friends. Early in the fall of '27 a young woman spoke to the audience at the end of a lecture at the Century Club. She was promoting a series of concerts and lectures and she made her point by reciting a little poem, each stanza of which ended with the line: "It isn't your town, it's you."

I talked with her afterward and made some condescending remark about the poem. She admitted that it was not to her taste either, and when we had talked a little more she introduced herself—she was Emily White—and suggested that I come down that evening to meet her husband, who had come with her to Scranton. After dinner I drove down to a boardinghouse in the center of the city, where they were staying.

Norman White was a charming man who was then editor of a house organ called the *Glass Container* ("See what you buy. Buy in glass"). He had an ironic sense of humor about life in general, and liked Max Stirner's *The Ego and His Own*. They were both liberal and seemed to know all about contemporary literature. They invited me to visit them in New York, though they would not be able to put me up in their small basement apartment.

I went down on a Saturday morning and checked into a nearby hotel, and that evening I attended my first Village party. There were eight or ten of us, and we had Prohibition gin highballs. The talk was intellectual, with a touch of local politics. I told them I was going to study psychology, and someone brought up hypnosis. Could I hypnotize people? I had read something about hypnotism but had never tried it, but that did not stop me, and I offered to hypnotize a young woman who had particularly caught my eye. Her name was Stella, and she was dark, with flashing eyes and a pleasant musical laugh, and rather resembled Ellen at Bread Loaf. She volunteered to be my subject. She must have been extremely susceptible because when I went through some of the standard paces she responded beautifully. As a post-hypnotic suggestion, I told her that after she had awakened I would adjust my necktie and she would then come over and kiss me, and, rather embarrassed, I turned to the others and said, "She'll hate to do that!" When I later tested this suggestion by adjusting my tie, she did indeed come over and kiss me, but she had evidently taken my comment as part of the instructions and wept and protested.

I talked with her and discovered that she was married. Her husband was in the army and stationed at a fort in New Jersey. She was living in an apartment on Barrow Street. I asked her if I could come to New York and see her, and she said yes, and we set a date.

After my disastrous year in Scranton that party was terribly exciting. Prohibition liquor was expensive, and we did not get very high, but the company was delightful, and my first appearance in public as a psychologist had been a dramatic success. The next morning I went back for breakfast with Norman and Emily White, and they suggested that I come to New York and get a job until it was time to go to Europe in the spring. I went back to Scranton and talked it over with my parents, and they were only too happy to agree. I had a little more work to do on the *Digest*, but then I could leave Scranton for good.

As IT HAPPENED, two girls I knew were driving, or rather being driven by their chauffeur, to New York for the weekend of my date with Stella, and they offered me a ride. I checked into a hotel and turned up at the apartment on Barrow Street precisely on time, carrying a large gardenia, a flower which Stella, who had spent some time in Hawaii, had said she particularly liked. She was waiting for me and we kissed almost at once. I went into the bedroom with her as she put on some finishing touches. Possibly because of the tour of duty in Hawaii, there was a slightly Oriental touch to the apartment. She loved horses, and the ashtrays were cloisonné Chinese stirrups. We kissed a bit more, and then, as I had carefully planned, I recalled a passage in Remy de Gourmont's *Nuit au Luxembourg* in which the author speaks highly of "desire without anxiety," and I asked whether, as we ate dinner, I could enjoy that emotion. She said I could, and I was unable to resist trying to take some immediate advantage of this concession, but she insisted that we go on to dinner.

We walked over to Marta's, a speakeasy and restaurant just a few steps from Washington Square. Stella was known there, and when they saw her through the little opening in the door, they let us in. Marta herself sat behind the cash register, and at Stella's request issued a card which I might use to gain admission. It was a business card, and on the back Marta scrawled a description of me, "*Faccia magra*," to be used by the doorman.

Marta's was the meeting place for the Silent Birdmen, an organization of aviators who had been in the war, and there was a large propeller on the wall of the main dining room. We dined in the back, however, which was open to the evening sky. Our waiter had seen Stella before and gave us excellent attention, and we had cocktails and wine with our dinner. Desire without anxiety was all very well, but I was anxious to get back to Barrow Street, and we eventually left.

I spent the night with Stella. It meant a great deal to me, and it was a long time before I realized that it meant much less to her. I was still unskilled in the art of love. I could offer quantity but not quality, and Stella was too nice to complain. Perhaps she hoped for progress. In any case she suggested that when I came to New York I should room with her. Another girl was actually sharing the apartment, and I could have a cot in a small alcove. Everything would look all right to her husband on his occasional visits.

We had a leisurely breakfast, and I went back to my hotel and picked up my things, and my friends met me, and we drove back to Scranton. I was too proud of my night with Stella not to make it pretty clear that I had spent the night with a girl. I told my father and mother that I had arranged to room with a "family" in New York, and I could give them an actual mailing address.

I MOVED TO NEW YORK and began life in that strange ménage. The other girl, Doris, had a nine-to-five job and was up first in the morning and soon out of the apartment. I would then hop into bed with Stella, who, as a model in a fashionable clothing store, had a more leisurely schedule. Eventually she would shower and take contraceptive precautions, the nature of which I never fully understood, and dress, and we would then have fruit, coffee, and toast, and she would be on her way. Alone in the apartment, I played the phonograph. I particularly liked Paul Whiteman's version of *Rhapsody in Blue* and someone singing "The Man I Love." Later in the day I would go out to wander about Manhattan. I rode double-decker buses from Washington Square to Riverside Drive and Grant's Tomb (Gulden's mustard was advertised on the backs of all the seats). I took the subway from Sheridan Square to Pennsylvania Station or Times Square (the risers of all the stairs carried red-and-blue advertisements for Iodent Toothpaste Numbers 1 and 2).

Occasionally I would answer an advertisement or call at an employment office. One advertisement looked promising: A writer was wanted for a weekly paper. It turned out to be a vanity racket. The paper published short paragraphs about likely prospects: so-and-so was holding a twenty-fifth-anniversary sale in his hardware store on such-and-such a street; he was well known, one of the community's most substantial citizens, and so on, and so on. Hundreds of such paragraphs were indeed printed, but in a weekly with no subscribers. Each item was clipped and sent to its subject, who was told that he could buy copies in quantities at a fairly high price. The editor quite frankly explained the racket and also quite honestly told me he did not think I would be happy in the job.

I found all the big employment agencies almost deserted. I was given forms to fill out and told that I would be contacted if a suitable job arose. I got only one call—from a small agency run by a sympathetic woman. Something had turned up in which she thought I might be interested, and I went to see her. A rich man had acquired a fairly large private library, and he wanted it catalogued. She thought my Hamilton experience would fit me for the job. I was strongly tempted. Atavistically, I could picture myself working—perhaps living —in the home of a wealthy family, with plenty of time to write. There might even be a pretty daughter whom I would get to know. But it was not clear how long the job would last, and my friends advised me against it.

I continued to see Norman and Emily White and met other friends of theirs. Among them were John and Marion Woodburn. *Harper's* magazine had run a short-story contest to which I had submitted "Elsa," and the winner was a Princeton student whom John and Marion knew and of whom they said I reminded them. The parties at their apartment were "literary" and lots of fun. Since I was the only one who had not worked all day, I could contribute a full share. A kind of shorthand called Speedwriting had just been developed, and I invented Speedtalking, plagiarizing much of it from the stereotyped speech of a drunk.

An occasional Saturday-night party would last all night, and we would go for breakfast to Alice McAlister's on Eighth Street. At one such party I met a young Scandinavian whose wife had ambitions as an actress and had been advised by her agent that *au naturel* was the secret of her beauty and that she should use absolutely no make-up. He and I got to discussing geometry, and we tried to reconstruct Pythagoras's theorem. I suddenly realized the relevance of a problem in my Sam Lloyd puzzle book. You are to arrange two squares, make two straight cuts, and fit the pieces together to form one square. Obviously the one square is the square on the hypotenuse. From this we worked out the proof.

By this time I had my own copy of Pavlov's *Conditioned Reflexes*, and I read it while being stimulated in all these pleasant ways. In doing so I demonstrated the validity of Pavlov's thesis, because the book took on much of the glamour of *la vie bohémienne*. The following September John Dos Passos would be writing to e. e. cummings from Russia: "Saw Pavlov's dogs in Leningrad. . . . Most of his work on the physiology of the brain has been via the salivary glands of a dog where he can measure the secretions. The whole thing is coming out in an English translation this year. . . . Everybody says it'll annihilate Dr. Watson [John] and make Freud look like thirty cents." But I should not have been bothered if I had heard him that spring, because Watson had already used Pavlov to strengthen his position, and I still had no interest in Freud.

I saw something of John Hutchens, who was living on Morton Street. Hutch and I sometimes had dinner at Jimmy's, a speakeasy on Barrow Street, where you could get a hot rum punchino served in a coffee cup for one dollar, but we went most often to Julius's, a famous speakeasy several doors of which had been padlocked by the authorities. It had sawdust on the floor, a stuffed alligator over the mirror, and a coeducational toilet. Spiked beer was a dollar a glass.

One evening Hutch asked me to go to a violin concert. He was reviewing plays for his paper, but the music critic was ill or out of town and had asked Hutch to take over. He knew I played the piano, and thought I could suggest some useful phrases. We went to the concert and then to a Western Union office, where Hutch got a typewriter, and as I talked, he typed out some kind of review, which went downtown by wire to his paper for publication the following morning—to be read, I suppose, by that poor devil of a violinist who had nothing but my incompetent analysis to paste in his scrapbook.

I continued to see Alf Evers, who was still at the Art Students League. I spent some time at the Metropolitan Museum. At that time Sir Thomas Lawrence's *Calmady Children*—a beautifully painted but sentimental picture of two small sisters—was prominently displayed, and I spent a lot of time just sitting and looking at it, wholly under the control of the subject matter. Alf was tolerant, but he was able to get me interested in the Impressionists, and I bought a reproduction of a self-portrait of Cézanne. At the Whitney Museum I saw a gauzy nude by John Carroll, one of the painters Edward Root collected, and I priced it, but it was $5000 and that was rather beyond me at the time. Alf and I went to a performance of *Die Walküre*. Ward Palmer had had almost no Wagner, and I was not ready for it, and I found the stagecraft of the fire scene rather ridiculous.

*   *   *

THE AFFAIR WITH STELLA was not made to last. For one thing, the ménage was not stable. Doris resented my being there, and problems arose about sharing provisions. We bought our supplies at a grocery store around the corner and sometimes dined together. One day Doris came in when we were having a small party and went to the kitchen to get herself something to eat. I told her that I had just put some eggs in the refrigerator and asked her to help herself. "Oh, no," she said, "those are your eggs," and she poured herself a glass of milk and walked into the other room, where she started talking to our guests. I was disturbed. Her remark was certainly not in the spirit of community, and I thought it implied that I was not making a reasonable contribution to the household. I took an egg from the refrigerator, walked in and held it up to her, and said, "I give you this egg." She flew into a rage. She took the egg and threw it across the room, followed it with the glass of milk, and dashed into the bedroom crying.

I moved out of the apartment the next day. My affair with Stella continued, but under much less propitious circumstances. I had met her husband when he came to a party or two but never quite understood their relationship. I saw it in a better light one afternoon when I was at the apartment. Stella was in bed, but I was sitting fully clothed on a chaise-longue reading to her. Suddenly the front door opened and her husband dashed into the bedroom. He looked us over, then explained that he had burst in because he had had to go to the toilet, which he then proceeded to do. After he had left the room, Stella looked at me and shrugged her shoulders.

Eventually she told me our affair was over, and when I tried to argue with her, she became quite blunt. She said that she had never enjoyed sex with me. When I reported this to Hutch, he said, "But she obviously had," and I said, "Yes," but his comment puzzled me. I was still strangely naïve. There had been no foreplay in our affair and, in fact, little affection. It is hard to understand why Stella did not teach me a few things, simply to improve her own pleasure, but it was evidently not yet the thing a young woman could do.

*   *   *

308

FROM STELLA'S I moved into a roominghouse on Morton Street near Hutch's apartment. The quarters were pleasant enough until one evening I went out and left the gas heater burning by mistake. When I came back the room was very hot, and shortly after I went to bed I began to be bitten. The heat had brought the bedbugs out of the walls. This was a new glimpse of life in Greenwich Village, and it frightened me. I dressed and packed all my clothing in my trunk, and since all the chairs in the room were upholstered, I sat on the trunk, where I thought I should be reasonably free of contamination, for the rest of the night. When I complained the next morning to the landlady, she admitted that bedbugs were a problem but said, "The bed is clean." I found another room, again on Barrow Street, but far to the west near Ninth Avenue, a small room with a bare minimum of furniture, and there I stayed until I left the Village.

I had not yet received the money for the *Digest* and was living on an advance from my father, and when this began to run out, I started to look for a job in earnest. I discovered that I had been making a great mistake. Those employment agencies so nearly deserted in the afternoon were full of feverish activity at nine o'clock in the morning. I began to fight for attention with a lot of rather desperate people. One agency sent me to the Shubert Theatre Company, where I was interviewed by a man who, strangely enough, knew that Hamilton College specialized in public speaking and who thought I might therefore be prepared for just the job he had in mind. He wanted someone to go out and sell blocks of theatre tickets to companies that might give their employees an evening at the theatre as an incentive or bonus. I had none of the instincts of a salesman, however, and I am not sure which one of us decided that the job was not for me.

Hutch tried to help by taking me to see Cleveland Chase, Jack's older brother, who might have some ideas. I said I had thought of writing book reviews, and Cleve typed out several letters of introduction to the editors of book departments of newspapers. I took them around without much success. I think it was Harry Hansen who tried to find out why I should want to write book reviews and then got rid of me by giving me a second-rate volume by a second-rate writer. I took it home, read it carefully, and wrote a review with the right number of words and sent it in. I heard nothing further about it.

Fortunately, one of my friends had learned that a small bookstore run by the Doubleday, Doran company in McCreery's department store on Fifth Avenue needed a part-time salesman, and I applied for and got the job. I was paid $15 a week. On the days I worked I was on my feet steadily from nine to five, except for a short luncheon break, and I got to know the agony of clock-watching toward the end of the afternoon. It was a small shop and not very busy, and I did not make many sales. My biggest single sale, in fact, was to a woman who bought perhaps a dozen books but who, alas, turned out to be a "shopper," a person who went from department to department in the store to check on the skills of the salespeople. I was called in for an interview and told how I might improve my salesmanship, and the books were promptly put back on the shelves.

The manager of the store was a Miss Stahler, who knew very little about books and less about running a store. Representatives of the company dropped by from time to time to check up on the quantities of new books she was stocking. On the strength of *South Wind* she had invested heavily in another book by Norman Douglas, and most of the copies had to be sent around to other Doubleday, Doran stores. She once used my sales drawer in the cash register for a $2.50 sale while I was out to lunch and actually rang up $52, and I was called to account for a shortage of $49.50.

I got something out of the job, because there was a copy of Watson's *Psychological Care of Infant and Child* on the shelves, and I read it bit by bit between customers. I was also invited to an evening meeting to hear about the company's new books. John Farrar was there and showed off in his boyish fashion. I told him I had met him at Bread Loaf, and he looked at me very closely. The company gave us free copies of books in the hope that we would read them and promote them, and among them was Aldous Huxley's *Proper Studies*, a collection of essays on psychological and educational problems which seemed to indicate that he too was turning from literature to science.

I had become a vegetarian, and I found that a restaurant across the street from the bookstore served a vegetable-plate luncheon, which became my daily fare. I started having evening meals at a small dining room called, I believe, the Open Gate. It was run by two women who looked very much like Gertrude Stein and Alice B. Toklas. Gertrude served in the dining room and Alice cooked in the kitchen, and they also served a vegetable plate. I had discovered Chumley's, where customers still played chess and Go, but vegetable plates were not on Chumley's menu, and I deserted the restaurant with regret.

The job made a big difference in my social life. I was now tired in the evening and no longer contributed much to the life of a party. Moreover, my circle of friends was disintegrating. A girl named Lucille, whose husband was an army officer stationed in Ohio, had an attractive apartment, and I spent the night there after my blow-up with Doris. There was nothing between us—she was just offering me an available divan—but, as it turned out, I barely escaped being beaten up. The following weekend we were having a party at Lucille's, and her husband walked in unannounced. He was a burly military type, and the party immediately evaporated. Everyone knew that Lucille had given me a place to sleep the week before, and I was roundly congratulated on my luck. Trouble began when Norman White fell in love with Lucille. Emily left Norman but pulled a diplomatic coup by moving in with Lucille. My Scandinavian friend had also left his *au naturel* wife, and the Woodburns were soon to separate.

I began to see girls who were not in the group. One was an artist who actually made a good living as such. She sketched people who were appearing in plays, and the *New York Times* ran one of her sketches almost every Sunday. She had an old upright piano in her studio, and I had a chance to play again after a period of drought. It was not a very Bohemian setting but it was friendly and relaxing. I persuaded a pretty customer to have dinner with me and then, on a second date, to go to my room, although when she saw the grimy building in which I lived, she hesitated and finally consented to go in only after warning me, "My father knows where I am." I went boating in Central Park with another attractive girl whom I met in the store. But spring had come, and I was soon to return to Scranton and then leave for Europe.

*   *   *

I SAILED FROM NEW YORK on the S.S. *Colombo* of the Italian line, bound for Naples with intermediate stops in the Mediterranean. The tourist-class quarters were cramped and the food greasy and uninteresting, but most of the passengers were students and there were a social director and a small orchestra and a slightly aging dancer who wore various exotic costumes and shared a cabin with an older man whose personal possession she seemed to be. In First Class I discovered a fellow Scrantonian—a Mrs. Daniel, who was the Jewish wife of the Scottish organist in the cathedral. She was very bright and witty and I wished I could have known her during the Dark Year. Unfortunately, I had limited access to First Class and did not see much of her or of the daughter who was with her on the trip.

My cabinmate was a blustering young Texan named Frank. He boasted of his sexual prowess with the girls back home, and was particularly proud of the fact that he refused to wear a condom. He suggested that we shoot craps. I had never played for money but did not know how to refuse. The stakes were not very large, but I had the most extraordinary luck, and won rather a lot of money. The next day he said he would like a chance to win some of it back. We played again, and again it seemed impossible for me to lose, and he never asked me to play again.

He was a hard drinker, and I had not yet learned how to enjoy my freedom. One night he challenged me to drink champagne glass for glass and see who went under the table first. I don't know whether I went under the table, but I did find myself hanging on the outside of the railing of a loading bay on a lower deck watching the foamy waves slip by a few feet beneath me. Somehow or other I managed to climb back and go to bed.

Frank's sexual prowess remained verbal; he made no effort to meet girls, although there were many on the ship. I met a graduate student in psychology at the University of Iowa; she knew much more about psychology than I, but she was not a behaviorist, and that was that. There was a makeshift costume party, and I danced with a girl from Boston who had borrowed a shirt and trousers and was dressed as an *apache*. I was rather startled when she said that we must look like homosexuals, and almost immediately I proposed that we look for some quiet spot among the lifeboats, but she was not interested.

I was aware of being an American tourist and of what Sinclair Lewis, H. L. Mencken, or Ezra Pound would say about me, and I did my best to act like someone who had crossed the Atlantic many times. At the costume party I went as a tourist with binoculars slung on one side and a camera on the other and a Baedeker in my hand, and I talked about the Eeful Tower and must have been thoroughly obnoxious. My French was useless, but I had studied a little Italian in anticipation of the trip and, since the crew spoke no English, a few words proved to be useful and gave me a certain international tone.

We stopped at Gibraltar and Frank and I were shown around the battlements by a young soldier whom we obviously did not tip enough. In Algiers there were young men on the dock who were ostensibly selling postcards which they pressed against visitors' chests but were actually slipping them under the clips of fountain pens, which they removed from breast pockets. We were taken to a rug factory, where we saw very small girls weaving Oriental rugs, tying and clipping colored yarns on huge vertical looms, and we sat on terraces and had drinks while rug vendors at our feet refused to take no for an answer. And, of course, we visited the Casbah. I went into a small store and said, "*Avez-vous de chocolat?*" and to my amazement the woman handed me a chocolate bar. I had used my French on someone who did not speak English! In a bookstore I bought *Le Temps retrouvé*, the last volume of Proust's *À la Recherche du temps perdu*. (Tucked into the volume was an advertisement for *Un Souvenir d'enfance de Léonard de Vinci* by Professor Sigmund Freud.)

We went on to Palermo, and I went up to Monreale, where I first saw the art of the past *in situ*. The great golden Byzantine mosaics were unlike anything in books or museums, and when I stepped out into the beautiful cloister, I gasped.

We went on to Naples, where I said goodbye to my shipmates and signed up for standard tours to Capri and Pompeii. I was rowed into the Blue Grotto by an Italian in fisherman's costume singing "*O sole mio*," and at Pompeii I was taken, with the other male members of the party, into a small room to see a beautiful white marble statue of a boy with an erect penis piped for use as a fountain. I went on to Rome by train and saw the Forum and the Sistine Chapel and was taken around the city by drivers who whipped their horses unmercifully. It was very hot, and Rome was full of Americans, and I could not pretend that I was not one of them. I escaped by taking the train across the Campagna to Tivoli. I asked a driver for a hotel where there were no Americans, and he took me to the Albergo del Plebiscito, on one side of a square with a church on the other. My room was small and rather cramped and I ate my meals alone at a table set up in front of the hotel. The waiter had once followed his profession in America and he pointed to my knife, spoon, and salt cellar, and gave recognizable versions of their English names. I spent my days in the gardens of the Villa d'Este trying to read Descartes in Italian. I had not quite escaped from America because one evening in the square a band played "Over There," a vestige of the World War that we were not yet calling the First.

The train from Naples to Rome had been hot and dirty, and I decided to go on to Venice by air. Commercial aviation was still primitive, but the plane I flew in was an advanced model and the fuselage was covered with corrugated aluminum rather than canvas. There was space for four passengers. We did not fly very high, and the shore of the Adriatic, which we followed during the last part of the flight, was beautiful.

In Venice I stayed in a *pensione* just behind those two bronze men who strike the hour with their hammers. I was running out of time because my father and mother would soon reach Paris, and I saw little of the city. I flew on to Vienna and saw even less of that.

To get to Paris it was necessary to fly to Basel in Switzerland, and then to Brussels. For some reason I missed my plane to Basel, but the airline put me on another plane which went by way of Munich. Unfortunately, I had no German visa, and this was discovered at the Munich airport, where we were forced to leave the plane for an hour or so. I was having a beer when several German soldiers entered the restaurant shouting, "Herr Skeenair!" They took me before an official, where I explained that I was en route to Switzerland and had not even intended to land in Germany. Nevertheless, I had committed a grave offense. Fortunately, I was able to get a visa then and there with the payment of an appropriate sum of money.

At Basel I had lunch with the Dutch pilot who was to fly me to

Brussels. His plane was a single-engine Fokker left over from the war. It had an open cockpit and space for a few passengers in the fuselage. The pilot spoke a bit of English, and when they brought him the weather report, he looked at it, turned to me, and said, "Bumps." I asked if I could ride in the cockpit, and he agreed, but I would have to get into the cabin first. There I joined four fat German businessmen and we taxied out to the end of the airstrip. The pilot motioned to me to come up through a small door and I strapped myself into the other seat. We took off, and the weather prediction was soon confirmed. Rain came into the cockpit, and I was soon wet through. Our route was almost due north, but the wind was from the west and very strong, and the plane was pointing directly northwest during most of the journey. We stayed close to the ground so that the pilot could gauge his drift. The Germans, made uneasy by the "bumps," occasionally knocked on the little door and made inquiring gestures. Before we reached Brussels the weather cleared a bit and, to my relief, the pilot picked up a small microphone and began to talk with the airport.

I completed my journey that afternoon as the only passenger from Brussels to Paris. The two-engine plane had been a bomber in the war, and wicker chairs had been installed in the area occupied by the bombardier in the front of the plane, reached by passing through the cockpit. The two engines went in and out of phase, grinding rhythmically, and we stayed so close to the ground that I could see horses, sheep, and even geese and chickens scurrying in all directions as we passed. We landed at Le Bourget—a year later than Lindbergh, and after a considerably shorter flight.

I JOINED MY FATHER and mother at the Hôtel des Saints Pères, a small hotel on the Left Bank then much favored by Americans, with a charming *maître d'hôtel*, Monsieur Jean, who spoke English. And there, whether I liked it or not, I became a typical American tourist. We did the Champs-Elysées from the Arc de Triomphe to the Place de la Concorde. We went up the Eiffel Tower. My father placed a wreath on the grave of the Unknown French Soldier in memory of two Susquehanna boys who were buried in France. We went to the

Folies Bergère to see naked girls and to the Louvre to see the Mona Lisa and the Venus de Milo. (In the Louvre I broke the routine by trying a small psychological experiment. As you went up the stairs toward the Winged Victory of Samothrace and turned to the right, there stood in those days a primitive bronze statue of a charioteer, interesting to specialists but not to the general public. People were streaming up the stairs and on into the galleries, paying no attention to the charioteer. I began to study the statue in a conspicuous way, moving around it, ducking down to look up at it, and so on, and other visitors were soon curious to see what I found so interesting. After I had accumulated four or five people and seen that they in turn were attracting others, I walked a few yards away to see how long the Adoration of the Charioteer would last. It was a matter of minutes before a short supply of newcomers failed to hold the critical mass, and the charioteer returned to his solitary vigil.)

We went to American Express and hired a chauffeur and limousine to drive us to Château-Thierry, where American boys, some of them from Susquehanna, had fought, and to Fontainebleau and Versailles, where the peace treaty had been signed. The limousine was luxurious. My father and mother sat in back and I had a comfortable jump seat. There was a glass plate between us and the driver with a speaking tube for communication, but either the tube did not work or the driver preferred not to hear, for after two or three embarrassing attempts, my father and I abandoned the tube and took to rapping on the glass.

Paris was not entirely given over to tourism. Mrs. Daniel and her daughter were there, and I went with them to the Musée de Cluny. Mrs. Daniel thoughtfully took me aside and pointed out the chastity belt. One of the girls I had known well in Scranton was staying at the Hôtel des Saints Pères with her mother, and she and I had an evening or two together. One night after dinner we were all having coffee in the hotel lounge, and I mentioned that at the Sistine Chapel I had bought two large tinted photographs, one of the Delphic Sibyl and one of Adam and Eve being driven from the Garden. My friend wanted to see them, so I brought them down from my room. My mother had had a glass of wine at dinner and may have been a little tipsy—and if so, for the first time in her life—and when she saw

Adam's nudity, she rather inadequately suppressed a giggle and made some comment about young people these days. Later, as we drove off for an evening together, my friend said, "Fred, you are awfully nice to your father and mother." She herself had been no great rebel, but my efforts to adjust to my parents' style had surprised her.

One evening when my father and mother and I were walking in the Rue des Saints Pères, we ran into Jack Chase and his mother. Jack was living in Paris at the time, translating a novel of Dumas *père*. His brother, Cleve, had published a rather successful translation of *Twenty Years After*, the sequel to *The Three Musketeers*, and Jack was working on another of Dumas's books. He and I arranged to spend an evening together, and he took me to some of the popular bars—among them Le Brasserie du Dôme and the Jungle. He introduced me to a girl who, he said, posed for and slept with some of the best artists. (His French was not fluent; I was surprised at how often he fell back on expressions like "*C'est la vérité.*") Neither Prohibition gin in Greenwich Village nor that champagne on the S.S. *Colombo* had prepared me for Paris, and I drank too much.

Another evening I took a girl who was staying at the Hôtel des Saints Pères to the Dôme. We sat on the *terrasse* and I heard two young men at a table behind us trying to decide whether I was American or English. I turned around, craning my neck to look at them, and as I turned back, they burst into laughter and exclaimed, "American!" Someone was making a movie, and the street was floodlighted, and when the girl and I hailed a taxi and got in, someone shouted "*Bonne nuit*" and there was a great laugh. We ran into Jack Chase and went with him to a less fashionable dive where there was some kind of floor show. I noticed an attractive girl sitting at the bar, and Jack, who often took pleasure in getting people into small troubles, asked me why I didn't speak to her. After two or three more drinks, I saw that she was still there and went up to her, and the following conversation ensued:

"*Combien?*"

"*Trois cent francs.*"

"*Deux cent.*"

"*Bon.*"

She took me around the corner to a very small hotel where I paid a man a few francs, and he gave her a key, and we went upstairs. She held out her hand, and I gave her two hundred-franc notes, and she tucked them in her stocking. I am not sure how long we were there. I remember lying in bed muttering, *"J'en suis désolé. Trop de whiskey. Trop de whiskey. Désolé. Trop de whiskey."* After a while she got up, squatted on the bidet and washed herself, and got dressed. She waited to make sure that I was going to get dressed and not occupy the room all night, and then left. For my two hundred francs I had at least learned how one used a bidet. Jack had taken my girl home, and I went back to the hotel alone. I scraped up enough for my taxi fare but had almost nothing left for a tip. There were many coins of very little value in circulation at the time, and I gave the driver eight or ten of them. He looked at them with disgust, scattered them across the sidewalk, and drove off.

I PERSUADED MY FATHER and mother to fly to London rather than take the Channel boat. They were not happy about the prospect, but the company's brochure was encouraging: "Every Imperial Airways Aeroplane has enclosed and ventilated cabin, two or three engines, lavatory accommodation, and drinking water." There was a single row of seats on each side of the cabin, and a steward was in charge. We took box lunches to be eaten en route, but my father and mother were not hungry and I had my choice of the contents of all three. (Our flight was duly reported in the *Transcript* when the news reached America.)

In London I became a standard tourist again, and this time there was no one to save me. We joined the English Speaking Union and hired a chauffeur and a limousine and went to Salisbury to see the Cathedral, and on into Devonshire, where my father tried to find someone who remembered his father's family, without much success. We visited a quaint resort town on the southern coast and bought souvenirs. Back in London, we went to Westminster, the Tower, the changing of the guard, and the British Museum. We also went to the studio of an artist whom my father and mother had met on the boat coming over. He had given them his address, although I cannot believe they seemed like prospective patrons. My father may have been pleased to have me see him in an unconventional setting. But it was not like artists' studios in the movies, and we simply had tea in badly chipped cups. Afterward we went for a walk in Hyde Park, and my father was rather shocked by some of the more amorous couples. "I shouldn't think they'd allow that," he said. Eventually we took the train to Southampton and boarded the S.S. *President Harding*.

It would not have done for my father and mother to travel in anything less than First Class, and I had carried my tuxedo all over Europe so that I could return in First Class with them. It was not much fun. We met a family from Pittsburgh with a daughter about my age, and for the inevitable costume party she and I swapped clothing. I borrowed an umbrella and went as Sadie Thompson, with all the gestures I could remember from Jeanne Eagels in the Broadway production of *Rain*. Afterward I danced with girls, but no one mentioned any lesbian significance.

In Paris I had bought three books by Henri Bergson: *L'Evolution créatrice*, *Matière et mémoire*, and *Sur les Données immédiates de la conscience*, and late one afternoon, sitting on deck, I was reading one of them. Suddenly I was startled by a very loud blast of a bugle. A member of the crew had come up behind me and had taken this customary way of announcing that dinner was served. After dinner I came back and began to read again. I went down the same page, and as I approached the point at which I had heard the blare of the bugle, I could feel perceptual and emotional responses slowly building up. The very thing Pavlov would have predicted! The summer was over and serious business lay ahead.

We returned to Scranton, and once again I filled that wardrobe trunk with clothes, books, and a portable typewriter. I would have a friend in the Boston area because Raphael Miller would be in his second year at the Harvard Medical School, but I had only the vaguest notion of what I should find in the Department of Psychology. I knew only that I was entering a new world. Susquehanna, Hamilton College, the Dark Year in Scranton, and Greenwich Village had been "precisely my necessity," but they were behind me. They had left their mark on that "new arrival born to Attorney William A. Skinner and his wife Grace" twenty-four years earlier, but a very different environment was now to take over.

ACKNOWLEDGMENTS

I am grateful to Mrs. Jeanette Brownell for help concerning the history of Susquehanna and its environs. Mr. Eugene Graves and Miss Isabel Graves have kindly given me the notebooks and papers of their aunt, Miss Mary Graves. Miss Annelise Katz of the library of the Department of Psychology and Social Relations at Harvard and Mr. Frank K. Lorenz of the Hamilton College Library have given much-appreciated help. I thank Mrs. Alexandra Huebner for her part in the preparation of the manuscript. I am also grateful to the following for having read and commented on an earlier version of the text: my wife, Eve, my daughters and their husbands (Julie and Ernest Vargas and Deborah and Barry Buzan), Harry and Elena Levin, Fred S. Keller, Barbara Ross, Wanda Minge-Baucus, and Sister St. Francis Kane.

A NOTE ON THE TYPE

The text of this book was set in Electra, a Linotype face designed by W. A. Dwiggins (1880–1956), who was responsible for so much that is good in contemporary book design. Although much of his early work was in advertising and he was the author of the standard volume *Layout in Advertising*, Mr. Dwiggins later devoted his prolific talents to book typography and type design and worked with great distinction in both fields. In addition to his designs for Electra, he created the Metro, Caledonia, and Eldorado series of type faces, as well as a number of experimental cuttings that have never been issued commercially.

Electra cannot be classified as either modern or old-style. It is not based on any historical model, nor does it echo a particular period or style. It avoids the extreme contrast between thick and thin elements that marks most modern faces and attempts to give a feeling of fluidity, power, and speed.

This book was composed, printed, and bound
by The Haddon Craftsmen, Scranton, Pennsylvania.
Typography and binding design
by Christine Aulicino